Marketing Identities through Language

Marketing Identities through Language

English and Global Imagery in French Advertising

Elizabeth Martin

First published 2006 by
PALGRAVE MACMILLAN
Houndmills, Basingstoke, Hampshire RG21 6XS and
175 Fifth Avenue, New York, N.Y. 10010
Companies and representatives throughout the world

PALGRAVE MACMILLAN is the global academic imprint of the Palgrave Macmillan division of St. Martin's Press, LLC and of Palgrave Macmillan Ltd. Macmillan® is a registered trademark in the United States, United Kingdom and other countries. Palgrave is a registered trademark in the European Union and other countries.

ISBN-13: 978–1–4039–4984–4
ISBN-10: 1–4039–4984–0

This book is printed on paper suitable for recycling and made from fully managed and sustained forest sources.

A catalogue record for this book is available from the British Library.

Library of Congress Cataloging-in-Publication Data
Marketing identities through language: English and global imagery in French advertising / Elizabeth Martin.
        p.   cm.
    Includes bibliographical references and index.
    ISBN 1–4039–4984–0
    1. Advertising – France.   2. Advertising – Language.
3. Multilingualism.   4. Multiculturalism.
5. Intercultural – communication.   6. Globalization.
HF5813.F8M37 2005
659.1'0944 – dc22   2005049995

10   9   8   7   6   5   4   3   2   1
15   14   13   12   11   10   09   08   07   06

Printed and bound in Great Britain by
Antony Rowe Ltd, Chippenham and Eastbourne

In loving memory of Ann, whose friendship meant the world to me, and whose beautiful artwork continues to lift my spirits

Contents

List of Tables and Figures

Tables

Figures

Preface

This book explores the ways in which advertisers address consumers in France with English and global imagery through a blending of text, music, and imagery. Advertising discourse is a rich source of data for linguistic analysis, whether it be the bilingual puns exhibited in slogans (for example, Hépar, Givenchy, Lavazza, Coca Cola), the imitation *verlan* used by the SNCF to address younger audiences, or the invented 'pot pourri' language combining French, English, German, Spanish, and Italian slang spoken by chimpanzees to sell OMO laundry detergent, all of which, and more, are described in detail in these pages. Advertising is also a visual means of communication where images play an important role in conveying information about the product and creating a positive emotional response. Much of this book, therefore, is devoted to advertising discourse as a multimodal experience, where brand names and slogans are reinforced by movement and illustrations, and music soundtracks create an atmosphere that contributes to the overall message of the campaign. Indeed, creative teams working on advertising have myriad techniques at their disposal to attract attention to their creations and entice the consumer. They push the envelope at every turn, producing linguistic combinations that one simply does not encounter in any other context. Working within the confines of language legislation in France (the 1994 Toubon Law most specifically), these individuals are all the more daring and innovative in the multilingual discourse they are able to produce: full of puns, symbolism and humor.

Audiences in France are also being treated to a collage of imagery from around the world in their advertising, where cultures are blended into an idealized universe, and landscapes are presented in such a way as to evoke certain emotional reactions and concepts in relation to the product. It is a world where a photograph of a highway leading into Beijing can assure the readers of a magazine ad that Bouygues provides its cell phone services anywhere on the planet, where Toyota sells its Yaris to the French by positioning it, through dialogue, imagery and music, as *la French voiture*, and where 'Nessie' the Loch Ness monster makes a rare appearance to associate the brand (Ballantine's Scotch Whisky) with its country of origin.

As a linguist I am intrigued by the mixing of languages and multiple layers of symbolic and cultural meaning that these examples of French

advertising exhibit, and I cannot help but admire those who constructed these advertisements, some of which are extremely artistic and entertaining. There are certainly manipulation and ideological processes at work, but there is also humor, beauty, and intrigue produced by unexpected combinations of music, text, and imagery that spark our imagination. I feel privileged to be able to view these examples from a multilingual, multicultural perspective and I hope to instill in my readers an appreciation for advertising as an art form, as well as a playground for multilingual creativity. And if I am able to dispel certain myths regarding our respective languages and cultures along the way, that will be icing on the cake.

ELIZABETH MARTIN

Acknowledgments

This book could not have been written without the assistance of individuals on both sides of the Atlantic. I would like to begin by thanking all of the many advertising professionals working in the following advertising agencies in Paris who gave their time to be interviewed for this project: Action d'Eclat-Archipel, BDDP, Euro RSCG, J. Walter Thompson, McCann-Erickson, Ogilvy & Mather, Optima Media, Publicis Conseil, Saatchi & Saatchi, and Young & Rubicam. I am also very grateful to a journalist from the advertising trade magazine *Stratégies* who graciously consented to be interviewed and whose insights were extremely helpful. I owe a special thanks to Luc Decroix, International Advertising and Consumer Marketing Manager at TAG Heuer headquarters in Switzerland, who sent me an advertisement featuring Steve McQueen when he learned about my project, and to Chérie FM who provided additional information via e-mail regarding one of their print advertisements discussed in these pages. I am also very grateful to the Tetley commercial team who supplied an English translation for a slogan appearing in one of the illustrations in this book. Renault also sent me some information regarding one of their advertising campaigns that I found very helpful and have included in a footnote. A special thanks as well to Danielle Candel from Université Paris 7 for clarifying some information about the terminology commissions in France as my manuscript went to press. I am also extremely grateful to the editing, design, production, and marketing staff at Palgrave Macmillan for their expert work and assistance. Jill Lake, Melanie Blair, and Keith Povey deserve special thanks for guiding me through the copyright permissions, editing, and production processes.

I would also like to extend my appreciation to the following companies who generously granted copyright permission to use their advertisements as illustrations: Allied Domecq PLC (for Ballantine's Scotch Whisky), BMW Group, Carlsberg Breweries, Ford Motor Company, Marnier-Lapostolle, Luigi Lavazza SPA, L'Oréal (for Gemey-Maybelline), Mandarin Oriental Hotel Group, Nicolas Feuillatte, TAG Heuer, The Tetley Group Limited, and Volkswagen France. I am particularly grateful to Getty Images for allowing the use of their visual for the cover illustration. I would also like to acknowledge Carmen Vega-Carney, Editor of *The Journal of Language for International Business* (JOLIB), for granting

me permission to use various examples printed in my 2005 article. Every effort has been made to obtain permission to reproduce copyright material. If any proper acknowledgment has not been made, or permission not received, we would invite copyright-holders to inform us of the oversight.

For their cultural insights, tireless energy, and enthusiasm, I am particularly indebted to my lofty team of multilingual research assistants at the University of Illinois at Urbana–Champaign who painstakingly catalogued and transcribed a good portion of the data featured in this book, including Michelle Bishop, Marie Chatelier, Leila Ennaili, Marc-Igal Haddad, Cédric Louyot, Emmanuelle Olivier, Virginie Reali, David Vidal, and Jérémie Vilain. I could never have written this book without their dedicated and cheerful assistance. This project was supported by funds from the University of Illinois Research Board, the University of Illinois Humanities Released Time Program, and the Department of French at the University of Illinois at Urbana-Champaign to whom I am very grateful. I also owe a debt of gratitude to the following individuals who graciously volunteered to read chapters in their early stages and whose comments have been immensely helpful, including Tej Bhatia, Zsuzsanna Fagyal, Andrea Golato, Alice Hadley, Suzanne Hilgendorf, Douglas Kibbee, and Fabien Wecker. Thank you so much for taking time out of your busy schedules to review my work and for your many precious pearls of wisdom. I am particularly grateful to Zsuzsanna Faygal, Andrea Golato, Suzanne Hilgendorf, and Douglas Kibbee who carefully read the very first draft of my manuscript cover to cover and helped me to improve it in ways I never dreamed possible. Peter Golato also provided very helpful information, along with some much needed technical support as I was sending off the manuscript. All errors that remain are entirely mine.

I owe much to Eyamba Bokamba who introduced me to the field of sociolinguistics and who continues to share with me his insights on language-mixing and gentle philosophy on life. I am particularly indebted to Braj Kachru for welcoming me into his circle of World Englishes and helping me appreciate the multilingual environment in which we live. I want to thank both you and Yamuna for your vision, your kindness, your humor and, most of all, for encouraging me as you do. I also want to express my gratitude to the many other friends and colleagues who cheered me on from beginning to end and whose moral support has made all the difference, including Jariya Charoenwattana, Zsuzsanna Faygal, Monique Fecteau, Brian Fields, Alain Fresco, Karen Fresco, Andrea Golato, Pete Golato, Alice Hadley, Henry Hadley, Samira

Hassa, Suzanne Hilgendorf, Richard Hoffman, Doug Kibbee, Francine Kirschner, Michel Kirschner, Michèle Koven, Scott Locke, Geneviève Maheux-Pelletier, Laurence Mall, Tracy McCabe, Patricia McClelland, Mylène Priam, Denise Prulière, Eva Ridenour, Viviane Ruellot, June Taylor, and Fabien Wecker. I truly am blessed. Scottie, you are my soul partner, my rock, and my inspiration. Your beautiful friendship, words of encouragement, and insatiable humor are more precious to me than I can express with words. How lucky I am to have you in my life. Michel and Francine, thank-you for your many years of loving friendship, for sharing your culture with me, your wonderful cuisine, and for making me laugh. Pete and Andrea, your friendship is so precious to me. Thank-you for cheering me on to the final line, for your incredible support, and for providing lots of chocolate to fuel my imagination. I don't know what I would ever do without you. Alice, thank-you for your many kind words of encouragement and pearls of wisdom. You are a special friend and a wonderful colleague. Michèle and Brian, you are such loyal friends, and you were there when I needed you most. Thank-you for believing in me. You're the best. Last but not least, I want to thank my family for their steadfast generosity, love and patience.

Introduction

This book examines advertising in France from different media to determine the extent to which globalization and the spread of English have affected advertisers' choice of visual and textual components when targeting French consumers. Emerging from this analysis is a consumer for whom both local and global identities are continually reinforced through advertising discourse. Through language and imagery, advertisers create a panoply of border-crossing experiences, specifically tailored to the campaign strategy at hand, while encouraging their audiences to view these messages from their own cultural perspective. Through their exposure to this tapestry of foreign cultural imagery and discourse, French consumers are continuously experiencing the world as global citizens while maintaining their own cultural identity.

To place the advertising samples presented throughout this book in their sociocultural context, an overview of globalization is provided with specific attention to international marketing, consumer perceptions of global brands (for example, Starbucks, McDonald's), and American cultural influences on French consumer behavior. Included in this discussion will be a description of French–American relations following the terrorist attacks of September 11, 2001. Anti-globalist and anti-advertising activist groups will also be addressed. This section will lead into a discussion of global imagery in French advertising across media and will examine the use of multiracial casting *à la Benetton* and the mixing of images from different parts of the globe in French advertising to reflect a 'global village' philosophy. Exotic foreign imagery is also used for mood enhancement purposes, as an attention-getter, and/or to reinforce the brand image. This analysis across media reveals, however, that the visual treatment of Anglophone countries in French advertising continues to be highly stereotypical, featuring images such as kangaroos and alligators to represent Australia, Native Americans and the desert South-

1

west for the United States, and the Lochness monster for Scotland, just to cite a few examples. As American-inspired images are particularly prevalent in the corpus, we will examine their use in French advertising in more detail as well as French perceptions of America from an historical perspective.

Throughout this discussion, we notice how global images can convey a wide range of meaning, reshaping the French consumer's identity from both a global and local perspective. While venturing into exotic landscapes and viewing the world's cultures through the carefully crafted discourse of advertising, media audiences are also encouraged to remain on the surface, so to speak, interpreting these images through their own cultural lens. Due to their 'foreignness', however, such images are a very effective way of attracting attention and entertaining audiences while creating certain positive associations for the product.

Selecting imagery that is exotic, entertaining or otherwise appealing, however, is only one of many strategies used when tailoring international campaigns to multiple markets. Adaptations for the French market may include, for instance, the metric system depicted in visuals (Ford), references to soccer (Coca Cola), French cuisine (Toyota), popular media (comic strip character *Astérix* in advertising for McDonald's) and local business practices (IBM). They may also take into account the French consumer's appreciation for natural ingredients (Dove deodorant) and environmental protection (Audi automobiles) or appeal to their sense of logic and intelligence (Nestlé chocolate syrup). In order to highlight the cultural specificity of these campaigns, a section outlining various concepts that appeal to the French, as well as creative strategies commonly used in French advertising (such as symbolism, humor and sexual appeals) will begin this discussion.

The blending of global and local identities is also evident in the manipulation of language. Given the global spread of English, another main objective of this study, therefore, is to explore in detail the bilingual creativity exhibited in product names, slogans, signature lines, dialogue, and music soundtracks (or jingles) with specific attention to lexico-grammatical features, phonology, semantics, and issues related to translation. English emerges from this study as a primary element in advertising for certain products and consumers along with varieties of French designed to mirror language as it is used in society. While certain English borrowings appeal to very specific consumer groups (teenagers, women, corporate executives, and so on), the French are coining new terms with rather unorthodox spellings to replace established borrowings for use in advertising copy (for instance, *pschittt* for 'spray'). English

in French advertising is functioning simultaneously as both a global and local language where a locally brewed variety co-exists with monolingual English product names, labels, and slogans distributed in global markets. Through hybridization, puns, pronunciation cues, and other forms of linguistic creativity, the advertising industry is using a 'Frenglish' blend in their messages for the French market that specifically appeals to this audience, tapping into the appropriation of English borrowings into French as experienced in everyday communication. These examples will also illustrate how the mixing of languages in advertising operates very much like visual images, associating particular values and concepts with the product, evoking emotions and contributing to the overall 'look and feel' of the advertisement.

As the influence of English on the French language has been a topic of considerable debate in France, however, this book also explores the efforts of the French government to control the use of English in the media (for example, the 1994 Toubon Law) and will feature members of the advertising industry in France voicing their opinions regarding this legislation. Also included in this discussion are additional analyses of advertising copy distributed in France demonstrating precisely how advertisers are circumventing the legislation in their quest to continue to use English as a persuasive and provocative tool of communication.

Although this book is presented from a sociolinguistic perspective, it is my hope that the examples and discussion contained within these pages will speak to several groups of scholars and practitioners, including linguists interested in language-mixing in advertising discourse and the role of English in a global context, cultural anthropologists interested in the representation of language and culture in the media, practitioners of advertising and marketing in both international advertising agencies and multinational companies with an interest in French consumers and/or other Europeans, and researchers in international marketing and advertising.

This exploration of English and global imagery in French advertising will proceed as follows:

Chapter 1 opens with a section describing the theoretical framework of the book, an interdisciplinary approach that draws from anthropological and 'socially realistic' approaches to linguistic analysis (Firth, 1935; Hymes, 1972; Halliday, 1973, 1978), social semiotics (for example, Voloshinov, 1929; Bakhtin, 1981, 1984, 1986; Barthes, 1972, 1977), and the World Englishes paradigm (Kachru, 1982, 1986a and b, 1996). The second half of this chapter will summarize the work of other linguists and communication scholars who have analyzed advertising discourse

(for example, Williamson, 1978; Geis, 1982; Vestergaard and Schrøder, 1985; Cook, 1992; Myers, 1994, 1999; Tanaka, 1994; Goddard, 2002). Previous studies that examine images of the 'Other' in advertising (for instance, O'Barr, 1994; Maynard, 2003) and language-mixing involving English in various countries (for example, Bhatia, 1987, 1992, 2000; Piller, 2001, 2003; Kelly-Holmes, 2005) are also included in this discussion.

Chapter 2 provides an overview of 'globalization' as it is defined by the advertising industry with a primary focus on global images commonly used in advertising in France today and the manner in which textual elements in French advertising copy mirror the social and linguistic behavior of today's global consumer. Included in this discussion will be the impact of technologies for global communication (e-mail, chat, text messaging, and so on) on the language of advertising as seen in France, the use of multiracial casting and images from around the globe, and the representation of cultural identity, stereotypes, and foreign languages in French advertising copy. This chapter also describes protest movements on both sides of the Atlantic, including anti-globalization and anti-advertising activists in France, the boycotting of French products in the US, and the 'freedom fries' linguistic phenomenon in the US in reaction to France's refusal to participate in the American-led coalition in Iraq.

Chapter 3 examines French perceptions of Americans and the United States and the role that American imagery plays in French advertising. Through a content analysis of images used in billboard, television and magazine ads in France, American-inspired themes most commonly used to seduce the French consumer are presented and described in terms of their cultural authenticity and likely appeal to French audiences. The images discussed include American landscapes, celebrities, lifestyles and cultures (for instance, Native Americans, corporate executives, basketball players), fictional television and movie characters, references to American television programs and Hollywood musicals, American symbols (such as Uncle Sam, stars and stripes), and other American cultural artifacts (recipes, use of inches and miles, and so on).

Chapter 4 discusses the adaptation of international advertising campaigns for French audiences. Issues that may arise include the appropriateness of verbal and visual elements of advertising copy, differences in humor, local attitudes towards nudity and sexuality, brand name selection, packaging and labeling, and, most importantly, understanding the local consumer's sensibilities and world view. Through an in-depth

analysis of numerous advertising examples across media, this chapter illustrates how multinational companies are now adapting their campaigns to the European market (and the French in particular) as well as the role of English in these local adaptations of global advertising.

Chapter 5 explores in more detail the use of English in various contexts (such as product names, signature lines, slogans, dialogue, and jingles) and media. The main focus of this chapter is linguistic creativity involving both English and French with detailed descriptions of lexicogrammatical features, phonology, and semantics. Also included in this chapter are various issues related to the translation of English elements in advertising copy and the motivations for using English in advertising that targets consumers in France.

Chapter 6 provides a brief historical overview of language planning in France and highlights French government intervention in advertising aimed at 'protecting' the French language from the influence of English. Legislation limiting the use of foreign languages in the media (for example, the 1994 Toubon Law) and agencies that regulate the advertising industry, such as the BVP (*Bureau de vérification de la publicité*) and the CSA (*Conseil supérieur de l'audiovisuel*), are included in this discussion. Specific areas of the Toubon legislation that pertain to advertising are discussed in detail (such as the required 'equally legible, audible and intelligible' French translations for foreign languages used in slogans and dialogue) along with reactions of members of the French advertising industry to the Toubon Law as reported during ad agency interviews in Paris.

Methodology and data

The advertising and interview data for this book were collected in March, April, May, and June of 2002. Data collection involved (i) recording television commercials appearing on major networks in France during prime time; (ii) purchasing bestselling magazines targeting a representative sample of the French population; (iii) photographing billboard advertisements; and (iv) conducting audiotaped interviews with members of the advertising industry working in Paris. The corpus includes 2,930 TV commercials, 3,695 magazine advertisements, a much smaller sample of billboard ads (52) and postcard ads (7) included primarily to show advertising directed at tourists, and approximately 20 hours of taped interviews.

The selection of magazines for this analysis (Table 1.1) was made based on criteria such as circulation figures, male/female readership and

Table 1.1   Magazines included in the study

Title	Category	Circulation figures (2003–2004)
Art & Deco	Home interest	413,491*
Ça m'intéresse	General interest	230,310
Capital	Business/Finance	361,450
Chasseur français	Hunting/Fishing	511,303
Femme Actuelle	Women's magazine	1,346,850
France Dimanche	News/People	537,011*
GEO	Travel/Culture	382,604
L'Equipe Magazine	Sports	378,275*
L'Expansion	Business/Finance	163,355
L'Express	News	548,195
Le Figaro Magazine	News	497,585
Management	Business/Finance	87,294
Marie Claire	Fashion	467,485
Modes & Travaux	Women's magazine (needlecraft)	505,563
Notre Temps	Seniors/Retirement	1,029,927
Paris Match	News/People	712,575*
Prima	Women's magazine	692,633
Santé Magazine	Women/Health	393,063
Science & Vie	Popular Science	361,273*
Star Club	People/Entertainment (magazine for teenagers)	305,543*
Top Santé	Women/Health	503,815
TV Magazine	TV guide	4,891,437*

*2004 only
Source: www.diffusion-controle.com/fr.

topical focus (for example, travel, health, women's issues, science, economics, business, home improvement, retirement, entertainment, and so forth) in order to obtain a representative sample of advertisements from popular magazines read by consumers from different socio-demographic and socio-economic backgrounds.[1]

In order to ensure equal representation for both weekly and monthly magazines, one issue per month was randomly selected for analysis. This selection process resulted in a total of 3,695 magazine advertisements, of which 58 per cent (2,153 advertisements) contained either English or global imagery.

The 2,930 television commercials included in the study were recorded from major networks during prime time. Due to their larger audience figures and relatively high concentration of advertising, TF1, France 2,

France 3, and M6 were selected as TV channels to be recorded for this analysis. Recordings were conducted on a daily basis during peak viewing periods (prior to and following the noon news broadcasts, the evening news, and immediately prior to the evening movie). Of the 2,930 commercials recorded in this manner, 50.4 per cent (1,478 TV spots) contained either English elements in the product name, copy, dialogue, or jingle, or imagery from locations other than France (Asia, Africa, the Americas, Australia, other parts of Europe, and so forth), examples of which will be discussed in detail throughout the book.

To supplement these data, audiotaped interviews were conducted in some of the leading advertising agencies in Paris. Several excerpts from earlier interviews (Martin, 1998a) that are particularly relevant to this study are also included in this discussion. Ad agencies participating in these interviews included Action d'Eclat-Archipel (an agency specializing in pharmaceutical products), BDDP, Euro RSCG, J. Walter Thompson, McCann-Erickson, Ogilvy & Mather, Optima Media, Publicis, Saatchi & Saatchi, and Young & Rubicam.[2] The focus of these interviews was 'globalization' as it is viewed by the advertising industry and the use of English in advertising distributed in France. Specifically, respondents were asked to comment on the role that globalization has played in the design of ad campaigns in recent years, the impact it has had on French consumers in terms of their product choices and reactions to global brands, and the strategies used by multinational corporations when communicating with French consumers, including American brands such as McDonald's and Coca Cola which are commonly cited in the literature on globalization (for instance, Barber, 1996; Ariès, 1997; Klein, 2000).[3] As regards the use of English in French advertising, the respondents were asked to describe the motivations for inserting English in various types of ad campaigns and comment on French consumers' (perceived) reactions to English used in this context.

A content analysis of these advertising and interview data illustrates how English has become one of the most popular strategies used to place a product or service in an international context and create other positive associations for consumers. It also clearly highlights the 'global' nature of much imagery found in French advertising today and the importance of tailoring an advertising message to local audiences.

1
Linguistic Analyses of Advertising

Linguistic theoretical framework

Context of situation

This study of English and global imagery in French advertising draws on the work of those who have defined and described in detail the contextual use of language. It therefore takes into account the sociocultural setting in which the communication occurs, the interlocutors involved, the intended message of the communication, the genre of discourse, and other sociolinguistic parameters. Indeed, a creative team's decisions regarding the verbal and visual elements of advertising copy will depend on a host of contextual considerations, including the intended audience (country or region, specific segment of the population), the product or service, the main selling point or advertising message, media, budgetary constraints, and so on. The incorporation of English and global imagery in the design of an advertising campaign also entails a contextual analysis on an entirely different level, where certain choices of music, text, and images are required to attract attention, enhance recall, convey information about the product, evoke certain connotations, and entice the consumer.

In this regard, the present study fits firmly within the realm of 'socially-realistic linguistics' in the tradition of J.R. Firth (1935), whose notion of 'context of situation' was based on 'a *social person* interacting as a *social being* within the network of social rules determined by the social and cultural context in which the person functions' (Kachru, 1982:65). This general framework for linguistic study was further developed by Hymes (1972) who described 'context of situation' in terms of: (i) the form and context of the message, (ii) the setting, (iii) the participants, (iv) the intent and effect of the communication, (v) the key, (vi) the medium, (vii) the genre, and (viii) the norms of interaction.

A student of Firth's, Michael A.K. Halliday (1973, 1978), later added a new dimension to the notion of 'context of situation' by describing communication in terms of predictions. Essentially, this interpretation of communication is based on the idea that interlocutors generally anticipate what others are going to say next, based on the situation in which the talk occurs. Halliday and Hasan (1985: 10) describe this ability to predict as being a vital key to human communication:

> The situation in which linguistic interaction takes place gives the participants a great deal of information about the meanings that are being exchanged, and the meanings that are likely to be exchanged.

According to M.A.K. Halliday's conceptualization of 'context of situation', discourse is comprised of three essential components: *field* (that which is happening), *tenor* (participants, statuses and role relationships), and *mode* (communicative goals of the participants, function of the text, channel, rhetorical mode, and so on). Using his child's use of language and the process of socialization experienced in childhood as an illustration, Halliday also describes language in terms of context-specific behavioral alternatives (or 'meaning potential'), emphasizing what the speaker can actually *do* with the language.

Applying this conceptualization of meaning in human communication to advertising texts, one notices how advertisers have become very adept (informed by audience research and other measures) at predicting audience interpretations of certain types of appeals and styles of discourse. The importance of anticipating audience reactions to certain styles of advertising becomes particularly evident when one examines the research on cross-cultural differences in messages directed at different markets, a topic that is described in detail in Chapter 4.

In more recent years Halliday (2003) has applied this conceptualization of language to the global spread of English, which contributes to our understanding of language-mixing with English in advertising used in non-Anglophone countries. He observes, for instance, that the efforts of language-planning agencies to compile lists of new words to replace borrowings (a situation that exists in France, as will be discussed in Chapter 6) are short-sighted as they ignore the functionality and 'systemic processes' by which a language evolves. Referring to the formation of new words, he identifies the following criteria that drive this gradual transformation (*ibid.*: 408):

1. *not just new words, but new word-making principles;*
2. *not just new words, but new word clusters* (lexical sets);
3. *not just new words, but new meanings;*
4. *not just new words, but new registers* (functional varieties).

His emphasis on meaning resurfaces in his summary of the model (*ibid.*: 409): 'Taken together, then, these are strategies for making meaning, for expanding the effective meaning potential of a language.'

When examining English embedded in French advertising discourse, we find similar 'semogenic strategies' (*ibid.*: 416). In regards to the first category, 'new word-making principles', we notice, for instance, that English words or expressions borrowed into French sometimes switch grammatical categories. Thus, when used in French discourse, English verbs may become adjectives (for instance, *villes relax*, 'laid-back cities') or nouns (for instance, un *smoking*, 'tuxedo') or vice versa (for instance, *Free shoesez-vous*, 'Buy yourself some Free Shoes'). The possessive marker in English ['s] also contributes to new word formation in French where it is commonly adopted along with other English borrowings to denote either a singular or plural noun (for instance, *un pin's, 16 extra's*), abandoning its possessive quality altogether. As for 'lexical sets', the second category, the influence of English is very noticeable in computer terminology in French (*surfer le net, internautes, cédérom, e-mail*) and other domains, often producing lexical items that are closely related (*e-mail, e-business, e-marketing*, and so on).

'New meanings', the third category, also arise when English is borrowed into French, some of which are a direct result of advertising, such as the term 'light' used to denote 'sugar free' beverages (for example, *Coca- Cola Light, Schweppes Indian Tonic Light*). Finally, the formation of new words resulting from the global spread of English has created entirely new modes of discourse or 'functional varieties' (the fourth category), one of which is certainly code-mixed advertising. Indeed, English has permeated advertising discourse across cultures creating a separate genre in its own right. Experienced in this context, the very presence of English (in the form of a product name, slogan, jingle, and so on) associates the product with such concepts as elitism, quality engineering, and modernity. Due to the flexibility afforded copywriters in their construction of advertising discourse, the bilingual creativity found in advertising also surpasses that of more conventional forms of communication. Thus, Halliday's observations regarding the English language provide valuable insight for the analysis of code-mixed advertising in France. This analysis will expand on Halliday's model, however,

by combining language with imagery, examining them from a marketing perspective.

In his discussion of global language, Halliday (2003: 416) also points out several fundamental differences between 'International English' and 'Global English', noting, for instance, that the former has evolved 'to adapt to the meanings of other cultures' whereas the latter 'has expanded – has become "global" – by taking over, or being taken over by, the new information technology'. Applied to the present study, we notice how the French are continually being addressed visually and linguistically as both global and local consumers, and that both 'varieties' of English (International and Global, according to Halliday's conceptualization) appear to be operating simultaneously. If one considers the verbal elements of French advertising across media, for instance, one notices that English experienced by French consumers in this context may, in some cases, be directed at international audiences in multiple markets, as is the case with many product names (Foster's – Australia's Famous Beer™), slogans (Nike's *Just do it*™), signature lines (Nokia. Connecting People™), and jingles (Kodak. Share Moments. Share Life™). To save production costs and reinforce the identity of the brand, English presented in this manner remains the same in advertising distributed in countries around the world. Close examination of French advertising copy also reveals, however, that the English aimed at French audiences may also be a locally brewed variety where English is mixed with French using some of the 'semogenic strategies' (*ibid.*: 416) outlined above. This use of English in French advertising is strikingly different from the 'global campaign' variety in that it has been created (or chosen) by the French for their own communicative purposes, conveying meanings that speak directly to this audience (for example, *French tops* to denote hit singles played by French radio stations, and so). To explore the many intersections of meaning between global and local communication, the present analysis further develops Halliday's description of 'International' and 'Global English' by presenting the multiple faces of English in juxtaposition with imagery and overall advertising strategy, interpreting this English presence from a French perspective.

Social semiotics

Any analysis of text, music, and images in advertising from a sociolinguistic and socio-psychological perspective, however, also requires an understanding of the symbolism behind these multimodal elements and their perception by media audiences. Certain constructs associated with the field of social semiotics are useful in this regard.

Wray (1981: 4) provides the following definition of this approach to linguistic analysis (see also Scollon and Scollon, 2003; and van Leeuwen, 2005):

> Semiotics is the study of signs . . . Specifically it is the study of semiosis, or communication – that is, the way any sign, whether it is a traffic signal, a thermometer reading of 98.6 degrees F, poetic imagery, musical notation, a prose passage, or a wink of the eye, functions in the mind of an interpreter to convey a specific meaning in a given situation.[4]

The notion of 'sign' commonly used by semioticians was first introduced by Swiss linguist Ferdinand de Saussure (1857–1913).[5] Leeds-Hurwitz (1993: 23) writes:

> As outlined originally by Saussure, each sign comprises a duality, such that it can be understood to have two parts; these he termed the *signifier* and the *signified*. The signifier is visible or in some way present (such as a flag); the signified is invisible but referred to (the country to which the flag belongs and which it represents). In other words, the signifier is the explicit aspect of a sign, present during the interaction, a material presence of some sort; the signified is the tacit element of a sign, what might be termed an 'immaterial' presence, something literally absent yet functionally present because it has been invoked.

In the French cultural theorist Barthes' analysis of signs, which he interprets within the broader framework of *mythology*, we find a tri-dimensional pattern which includes the *signifier*, the *signified* and the *sign* itself. Barthes considers the third component in this triad as 'the associative total of a concept and an image' (Barthes, 1972: 114) and describes myth as a socially determined 'system of communication' (ibid: 109) whereby 'any material can arbitrarily be endowed with meaning' (*ibid.*: 110). Barthes refers to this process more specifically as 'mythical inversion':

> myth consists in overturning culture into nature or, at least, the social, the cultural, the ideological, the historical into the 'natural'. What is nothing but a product of class division and its moral, cultural and aesthetic consequences is presented (stated) as being a 'matter of course'. (Barthes, 1977: 165)

Therefore, as will be demonstrated in many of the examples discussed in this book, the presentation of objects (such as sofas, automobiles, deodorant), people (such as movie stars, athletes, children), foreign languages, and other 'signs' found in advertising evoke certain associations and meanings carefully constructed by advertisers in their effort to seduce consumers. Indeed, according to Barthes (1972: 109), essentially everything within our realm of existence can become a form of myth as 'every object in the world [is] open to appropriation by society' and 'the universe is infinitely fertile in suggestions'.

In his own analyses of advertising discourse and imagery, Barthes introduces a number of other concepts to illustrate the various levels of interpretation (or 'readings') that visual and verbal elements may produce in the mind of the consumer. Using a French print advertisement for Panzani (an Italian brand of pasta) as an example, he notes that the product name itself, Panzani, for instance, has a meaning which is both *denotational* (literally indicating the name of the company) and *connotational* (symbolically evoking the idea of 'Italianicity'). The illustration used in the advertisement, on the other hand, depicts a string, fish-net grocery bag (typically used when shopping at farmers' markets in France) containing the Panzani brand pasta, tomato sauce, and parmesan cheese, along with a fresh tomato, pepper, onion, and so on. From this image, a 'floating chain of signifieds' emerges, implying a recent trip to an open-air market, fresh produce, the idea of Panzani providing all the necessary ingredients for a wholesome meal, and so forth. Thus, to borrow Barthes' terminology, the advertisement in question offers a *linguistic* (textual) message, a *coded iconic* (cultural or symbolic) message, and a *non-coded iconic* (literal) message. Although the signifieds in this latter category are quite simply the identifiable objects one notices on the page, Barthes reminds us that 'the viewer of the image receives *at one and the same time* the perceptual message and the cultural message', a situation which is obviously very calculated from the ad maker's point of view (Barthes, 1977: 36).

Barthes' notion of *anchorage* as a primary function of the linguistic message in advertising (and other genres) is another useful construct. Barthes introduced this term to refer to the process by which linguistic elements (such as a slogan or caption) encourage (or 'anchor') preferred readings of an image:

> the text *directs* the reader through the signifieds of the image, causing him to avoid some and receive others . . . it remote-controls him towards a meaning chosen in advance. (Barthes, 1977: 40)

Thus (to cite one of Barthes' examples), an advertisement for d'Arcy fruit preserves uses the caption *'as if from your own garden'* to describe the few pieces of fruit lying on the ground next to a ladder depicted in the photograph. The very attractive idea of gathering fruit from one's own private garden is thus planted like a seed in the consumer's imagination while any less desirable interpretations of the product shown in the illustration (such as artificial ingredients) are all but eliminated (*ibid.*: 39–40). This is a particularly useful model for describing how images relate to text in advertising (producing literal and symbolic meaning) and how both combined can direct audiences to a specific set of interpretations. Applying these concepts to the present corpus, one observes that a product name or slogan may draw attention to the illustration or that, conversely, the visual elements can direct the reader to the text, as in a BaByliss advertisement for a men's razor where the close-up of a man's unusual haircut (featuring the word 'TOP' shaved on the top of his head) serves as an attention-getter followed by the slogan: *Au top de la technologie.* This 'anchoring' strategy is used consistently in the construction of advertising discourse and is therefore directly applicable to this study.

Barthes' analyses of advertising also provide valuable insight for anyone seeking a better understanding of the French psyche. In *Mythologies*, for instance, Barthes (1972: 58–61) provides a multifaceted analysis of wine in French society. He very aptly describes the act of drinking wine in France as 'a kind of conformism' or 'coercive collective act' (*ibid.*: 59), noting that 'a Frenchmen who kept this myth at arm's length would expose himself to minor but definite problems of integration . . .'. In French society, he observes, 'knowing *how* to drink is a national technique which serves to qualify the Frenchmen' (*ibid.*: 59). A drink of wine symbolizes 'the spinning out of a pleasure' regardless of the context (*ibid.*: 60):

> It exalts all climates, of whatever kind: in cold weather, it is associated with all the myths of becoming warm, and at the height of summer, with all the images of shade, with all things cool and sparkling. There is no situation involving some physical constraint (temperature, hunger, boredom, compulsion, disorientation) which does not give rise to dreams of wine.

Observations such as these enable us to explore the French mentality in more depth and are therefore very useful when analyzing the verbal and visual elements of advertising copy designed specifically for the

French. As my analysis will reveal, however, consumers in France are also being addressed, through global imagery and English, as global consumers. Thus, any culture-specific meanings such as those described by Barthes are more directly applicable to campaigns aimed at French audiences only (as opposed to global campaigns distributed internationally with few or no modifications).

The multiplicity of meaning

In the writings of Marxist theorist Valentin Voloshinov (1929), we find some of the most basic elements of social semiotics as it is practiced today.[6] Focusing on the utterance (or 'speech act') as a social phenomenon, Voloshinov observed the fundamental *multiplicity of meanings* of any given text and its diversity of interpretation (or *multiaccentuality*) depending on its situation of use. According to this philosophy, every utterance is shaped by the value judgments of speakers as determined by the social situation in which the communication occurs (Voloshinov, 1929: 104). A word's 'multiaccentuality' (or 'multiplicity of meaning') stems from the notion that it is endowed with an *evaluative accent* which changes according to situations of use. Although Voloshinov was referring to daily communicative interactions (that is, speech), the following observation rings very true for advertising across media where words take on different meanings and associations depending on the audience, perceptions of the brand, the product, and elements displayed in the visual, the text, and (in cinema, television, and radio advertising) the music soundtrack:

> The meaning of a word is determined entirely by its context. In fact, there are as many meanings of a word as there are contexts of its usage. (Voloshinov, 1929: 79)

Simply put, 'it is precisely a word's multiaccentuality that makes it a living thing' (*ibid.*, 1929: 81).

Applied to the present study, however, the notion of 'multiplicity of meaning' takes on an entirely new dimension. Not only are we dealing with language in several different modalities simultaneously (written, spoken, sung), but we are also examining the use of English as (a) a foreign language (in France) and (b) as a persuasive element in non-conventional discourse (advertising). Thus, an English borrowing such as 'body' may have one set of meanings in its native context ('human body', 'legislative body', 'body of water', 'richness of flavor', to cite just a few), another meaning in France (where *'body'* is used to refer, for

instance, to a certain type of women's lingerie), and yet another meaning in French advertising, where *'body'* may also be used in product names to underscore the firming properties of a cellulite cream (for example, Lierac Body Lift, Phytomer Body Déclic, and so on). A single word or phrase therefore produces multiple interpretations depending on the context in which it is used. In advertising, as in the conversational discourse described by Voloshinov, one also notices that within a single context as well, an utterance can produce several different layers of meaning. In a print advertisement for Versace sunglasses, for instance, the English term 'EYEWEAR' presented in bold lettering as an attention-getter indicates the use of the product (to improve one's vision) but also, through the mere presence of English, creates positive associations with the brand, such as modernity, sophistication, and international appeal.

Voloshinov's Russian colleague Mikhail Bakhtin (1986: 91) further emphasizes the 'dialogic' construction of meaning, claiming that no elements of communication exist in isolation:

> Utterances are not indifferent to one another, and are not self-sufficient; they are aware of and mutually reflect one another . . . Each utterance is filled with echoes and reverberations of other utterances to which it is related by the communality of the sphere of speech communication.

One of the most basic notions introduced by Bakhtin is that of *addressivity*, whereby 'an essential (constitutive) marker of the utterance is its quality of being directed to someone [and] each speech genre in each area of speech communication has its own typical conception of the addressee' (Bakhtin, 1986: 95). According to this model, all forms of communication are shaped by the immediate or delayed reaction of the listener/addressee whose 'actively responsive understanding' is anticipated by the person who initiates the communicative interaction (*ibid.*: 97). Bakhtin (*ibid.*: 68–9) argues that 'when the listener perceives and understands the meaning . . . of speech, he simultaneously takes an active, responsive attitude toward it [and that] the speaker himself is oriented precisely toward such an actively responsive understanding'. In the context of advertising, this has certain implications. In the 'dialogue' between the designers of an advertisement and the audience, a cognitive, affective, and behavioral reaction on the part of the consumer becomes the primary objective of the ad.

Bakhtin's notion of 'hidden dialogicality' is particularly relevant to advertising where a message is carefully designed to produce a calcu-

lated response from consumers. His description of a 'one-person' conversation captures the personalized discourse so often exhibited in advertising texts:

> Imagine a dialogue of two persons in which the statements of the second speaker are omitted . . . We sense that this is a conversation, although only one person is speaking, and it is a conversation of the most intense kind, for each present, uttered word responds and reacts with its every fiber to the invisible speaker, points to something outside itself, beyond its own limits, to the unspoken words of another person. (Bakhtin, 1984: 197)

Central to this model of 'dialogicality' is the idea that the meanings of words stretch well beyond common dictionary definitions to reflect individual and contextual differences (note the *'body'* example cited earlier). Referring to that which the speaker wishes to say as his or her 'speech plan', Bakhtin (1986: 88) characterizes this notion in the following manner:

> one can say that any word exists for the speaker in three aspects: as a neutral word of a language, belonging to nobody; as an *other's* word, which belongs to another person and is filled with echoes of the other's utterance; and, finally, as *my* word, for, since I am dealing with it in a particular situation, with a particular speech plan, it is already imbued with my expression.

A word, therefore, does not specifically 'belong' to any one individual, nor any one culture. This 'multivoicedness of meaning' (Bakhtin, 1981) is a particularly useful construct in examining the variety of ways in which English has been appropriated by certain native speakers of French and the different 'readings' one can associate with an advertisement, or a single element thereof (such as the product name, slogan, illustration, and so forth).

The World Englishes paradigm

To explore the appropriation of English by French consumers and the diverse interpretations it can produce in the context of advertising, another model, the World Englishes paradigm introduced by Braj Kachru (1982; 1986b), provides a powerful and elegant theoretical framework. With its focus on language contact and change, borrowing processes and hybridization, bilingual creativity, language attitudes,

and other issues related to the use of English in countries all around the planet, this particular approach has greatly inspired this analysis on code-mixed advertising within the context of France. In contrast to those who have referred to English as a language of control, and the spread of English as a form of linguistic imperialism (Phillipson, 1992; Tsuda, 1994), scholars who have drawn from the World Englishes paradigm describe English in terms of its wide range of functions in different sociocultural contexts and the various linguistic processes by which local communities have transformed it to fit their own cultural contexts of use.

Using a 'Three Concentric Circles of English' model to emphasize the functional roles of English, certain historical considerations, and different types of language contact, Kachru (1986b) describes countries as belonging to either the 'Inner Circle', 'Outer Circle' or 'Expanding Circle'. Whereas the 'Inner Circle' reflects 'native-speakers' of English (in countries such as the USA, UK, Canada, Australia or New Zealand), the 'Outer Circle' contains countries in which English is essentially used as an additional language (such as for administrative purposes in Asia and Africa). The 'Expanding Circle', on the other hand, includes areas of the world where English is learned and used as a foreign language (for example, China, Egypt, Indonesia, Israel, Japan, and so on). This 'Expanding Circle' also includes France and other European countries (Berns, 1988; Flaitz, 1988; Kahane and Kahane, 1992; Deneire and Goethals, 1997; Truchot, 1997; Taavitsainen and Pahta, 2003).[7] As Kachru (1986a: 122) notes: 'these three circles represent three distinct types of speech fellowships of English, phases of the spread of the language, and particular characteristics of the uses of the language, and of its acquisition and linguistic innovations.'

Central to this model of 'English across cultures' (Kachru, 1996) is the notion of *pluricentricity* whereby English has acquired new linguistic and cultural identities in a variety of intranational and international settings. The resulting localized/nativized varieties of English often feature lexical items and syntax that would seem odd to English speakers from the Inner Circle (many examples of which appear in this corpus). English also serves as a 'link language' enabling its users to communicate across geographical, linguistic, and cultural borders and is perceived as having 'material' value in terms of career advancement and gaining access to science, information, and technology. The use of English in certain contexts may also carry other positive – or negative – connotations as indicated in the following list of labels symbolizing the 'power' of English (*ibid.*: 142):

Positive	*Negative*
National identity	Anti-nationalism
Literary renaissance	Anti-native culture
Cultural mirror (for native cultures)	Materialism
Vehicle for Modernization	Vehicle for Westernization
Liberalism	Rootlessness
Universalism	Ethnocentricism
Secularism	Permissiveness
Technology	Divisiveness
Science	Alienation
Mobility	Colonialism
Access code	

These labels provide a useful framework for discussing the connotative value of English within the context of France. In advertising directed at multiple audiences worldwide as well, both positive and negative connotations apply depending on the country in which the product is being advertised, the consumer group addressed by the campaign, and the (visual, verbal, and musical) elements displayed within the advertisement itself. Thus, when audiences in Japan see the English text 'MADE IN FRENCH ALPS' (Mueller, 1996) displayed as a headline in a print advertisement for EVIAN (mineral water), English is operating as an access code (from the French company's perspective), a vehicle of expression for reaching consumers who do not necessarily understand French. English may also serve as a 'cultural mirror' for companies who want to accentuate the country origin of the brand, as seen, for instance, on product labels for alcohol beverages used as attention-getters in advertising distributed around the globe (for example, Foster's – Australia's Famous Beer).

If the main selling point of an advertisement is the superior technical performance of the product, however, English may symbolize technology, whether it is a man's razor (as in the BaByliss example earlier), a digital camera (Fujifilm FinePix 2600 Zoom) or computers (such as the expression *Ensemble, entrons dès aujourd'hui dans la dynamique 'POWERING THE INFORMATION AGE'* used in French advertising for Fujitsu Siemens Computers). In French advertisements for face and body creams, advertising executives interviewed in Paris (as discussed in Chapter 6) claim that English reassures the consumer that the product has been scientifically tested and is proven to be effective. Consider, for example, the *Lipodiet Process* of Christian Dior, *Bikini Anti-Cellulite Spray*,

or the *Intensive Renewing Beauty Treatment* of Clarins' *Huile 'Tonic'* (advertised as *'leur best-of de produits et méthodes pour un corps parfait'*). Products that are perceived as 'modern', 'chic' or 'glamorous' will also feature English in their advertising (Dolce & Gabbana *Light Blue* perfume, L'Oréal *Casting Color Source* hair color, and so on). As for the negative connotations of English in advertising, those interviewed in advertising agencies in Paris also noted that English would be much less appealing to French audiences if associated with traditional French products, such as French wine or cheese, an attitude reflected in the 'anti-native culture' label provided by Kachru. It is therefore not surprising that the English used in advertising for these products as they appear in the present corpus is inserted solely in the music soundtrack for mood enhancement purposes.

In light of the creative expression and expansion of meaning exhibited in code-mixed advertising directed at French consumers that will be featured in these pages, Halliday's advice regarding the appropriation of English (as opposed to its rejection) seems rather fitting:

> Rather than trying to fight off global English, which at present seems to be a rather quixotic venture, those who seek to resist its baleful impact might do better to concentrate on transforming it, reshaping its meanings, and its meaning potential, in the way that the communities in the outer circle have already shown it can be done. (Halliday, 2003: 417)

As they say, the proof of the pudding is in the eating. Indeed, despite legal restrictions on the use of English in French advertising copy (such as the 1994 Toubon Law, discussed in Chapter 6), copywriters continue to insert English in their texts aimed at the French market, reshaping its meanings in a very significant manner while imitating the French community's language practices. Thus, audiences in France are being exposed to several varieties of English used in both colloquial discourse and marketing. It will also be demonstrated that much of the English used in French advertising (particularly in slogans, dialogue, and descriptive copy) reflects the French grammatical system (for example, *Je dunkerai for you*), cultural identity and worldview, and that English is very often inserted to appeal to the French sense of humor (for instance, *Sleeping partner* slogan for Banque Populaire), logic and aesthetics. By appropriating English to suit their own communicative needs, speakers of English in the Outer and Expanding Circles have become, in the Hallidayan sense, 'creators of meanings' rather than 'consumers of the

meanings of others' (Halliday, 2003: 417), as the examples included in this book will clearly demonstrate.

Drawing inspiration from this interdisciplinary theoretical framework, I illustrate how English is used not only as a prestige language symbolizing certain concepts and myths associated with the product being advertised (and as a link language among members of the advertising industry), but also as a pair-language for bilingual puns and slogans specifically directed at French audiences. In this regard, English is simultaneously functioning as both a global language directed at multiple audiences worldwide and a local language which has been refashioned to reflect the French reality in terms of linguistic and cultural perceptions. Combined with this use of both global and international English (to borrow Halliday's terminology) is a tapestry of imagery carefully selected by advertisers to convey certain positive associations (quality engineering, glamor, sophistication, international appeal, and so on), evoke humor, or create a world of illusion where everything and everyone seems desirable. When addressing the French specifically (as in the case of local adaptations of global campaigns), however, the discourse and imagery of advertising must be packaged in such a way as to appeal to this particular consumer group.

I also argue that French legislation targeting English has had a limited effect on language use and attitudes in France within the context of advertising. Despite persistent warnings from those who would like to protect the French language and culture from what they view as a linguistic and cultural invasion from the United States, the use of English remains a ubiquitous element of advertising aimed at French consumers (including advertising distributed by French companies selling their products in France). By appropriating and reshaping English for their own communicative purposes, the French are expressing themselves through a newly formed variety that is uniquely their own. With its local adaptations and culture-specific meanings, this form of expression is much more a reflection of the French identity than that of any country belonging to the 'Inner Circle' of English as described by Kachru (1986b). Advertisers contribute to this ever-evolving linguistic construction of identity by continually pushing the envelope in terms of creative expression, producing imagery-enhanced multilingual messages that are seductive, meaningful, and entertaining. Indeed, with a repertoire of communicative strategies that reach far beyond those available in other forms of discourse, those who design advertising copy are keeping their finger on the pulse of society and have found ingenious ways of marketing identities through language.

Approaches to advertising

The aim of this section is to provide an overview of the research on advertising published by linguists and communication scholars who have approached this phenomenon from a variety of perspectives. Advertising has been described by some researchers, for instance, as a form of manipulation, a deliberate use of language, symbolism and imagery to lure audiences into a fantasy world where dreams and desires may become reality. Advertisements also perpetuate social myths and contribute to cultural self-image (female imagery being one example) and may be disguised as other forms of discourse as a way of concealing their main objective (to sell goods and services). To explore issues such as these, we will begin this literature review with an examination of the ideological processes in advertising (Williamson, 1978; Vestergaard and Schrøder, 1985; Fairclough, 1989) and will include in this discussion the representation of women (Tanaka, 1994; Kilbourne, 1999; Machin and Thornborrow, 2003).[8] Others who have analyzed advertising discourse have focused on word play in advertising copy, presenting advertisements more as a form of entertainment (for example, Grunig, 1990; Cook, 1992; Myers, 1994). Strategies used by ad makers to attract attention to their creations and stimulate the curiosity of their audiences include the use of foreign languages for special effect, and imitation varieties (Myers, 1994; Martin, 1998a), both of which are featured in the present corpus as well. To explore the use and perceptions of English in advertising distributed to international markets specifically, we will then turn our attention to marketing blunders involving poor lexical choices for brand names and slogans (for instance, Mueller, 1996; Zeff and Aronson, 1999; Goddard, 2002) as well as code-mixed advertising using English as a pair language in different countries (for example, Bhatia, 1987, 1992, 2000, 2001; Larson, 1990; Hilgendorf, 1996; Baumgardner, 1997, 2000, 2005; Martin, 1998a and b, 2002a and b; Piller, 2001; Jung, 2001; Hsu, 2002; Einbeck, 2004; Kelly-Holmes, 2005; Meurs *et al.*, 2004). The remainder of this section explores the relationship between language, culture and identity, examining how consumer identities are constructed through language contact and cultural imagery in advertising. Included in this discussion is a study on the representation of America in Japanese advertising (Maynard, 2003), cultural stereotypes (O'Barr, 1994), and country-of-origin appeals that associate product characteristics with a particular language or culture (Haarmann, 1984; Kelly-Holmes, 2000; Piller, 2001). We will also explore the 'linguistic capital' of certain languages (Kelly-Holmes, 2005), the reflection of

identity through different varieties of English (Myers, 1994; Gill, 2000), and audience reactions to language-mixing and other communicative devices used in this genre (Geis, 1982; Gerritsen *et al.*, 2000; Meurs *et al.*, 2004). This very broad description of approaches to advertising research from a sociocultural and linguistic perspective will demonstrate the many different aspects of advertising discourse across cultures and will lay the groundwork for the remainder of the book where the construction of French consumer identities through language and imagery will be the primary focus.

Ideology in advertising

The connections between language, power, and ideology in advertising have been examined by many scholars interested in critical discourse analysis. Fairclough (1989: 199–211; 1992: 113–17), for instance, outlines certain 'colonizing trends' evident in advertising texts. Drawing on Jürgen Habermas' (1984) analysis of modern capitalism and its 'colonization' of our everyday existence, Fairclough (1992: 214) emphasizes the fact that the *strategic discourse* of advertising is 'colonizing' more *communicative* discourse types.[9]

> Under the influence of advertising as a prestigious model, the blending of information and persuasion is becoming naturalized, divisions between them in orders of discourse are being fractured, and as a consequence the nature of 'information' is being radically changed.

Applying this notion to the discourse of public information, he illustrates how an advertisement for a specific product can disguise itself as a public service announcement.[10] He also notes the rather disturbing trend of voters making electoral decisions based on advertisements which have been carefully crafted by political campaign advisors:

> People's involvement in politics is less and less as citizens, and more and more as consumers; and their bases of participation are less and less the real communities they belong to, and more and more the political equivalents of consumption communities, which political leaders construct for them. (Fairclough, 1989: 211)

Fairclough (*ibid.*: 199) further describes the ideological processes in advertising in terms of 'the relationship it constructs between the producer/advertiser and the consumer, the way it builds an "image" for the product, and the way it constructs subject positions for consumers'. He

notes in particular that this relationship is largely constructed through 'synthetic personalization' (or the use of 'personalized' textual features such as various forms of direct address) whereby 'the addresser speaks to the audience members in her own voice, about a commodity which chimes with both' (*ibid.*: 205). The ideological frame evoked for the audience's interpretation of an advertisement:

> packages together social subjects in particular sorts of relationship, activities, settings, values, and so on, in a powerful prescription for how one should live, or at least what one should acknowledge to be the best way to live, in the modern world, together with the myth that this lifestyle is open to everyone. (*ibid.*: 206)

Fairclough also acknowledges the growing importance of images in today's society, noting that audiences are more susceptible to visual images in advertising because of the commonly held notion that 'the camera doesn't lie' (*ibid.*: 208).

Judith Williamson (1978: 175), who has written extensively on ideology in advertising, makes a similar observation:

> You may not really believe that some minor ingredient is going to transform your casserole into a cordon-bleu dish, but the *images* of the grateful, hungry, appreciative husband and son tucking into a hearty meal provided by the woman stay long after the actual claims made on behalf of the product have been forgotten. It is the images we see in ads which give them significance, which transfer their significance to the product. This is why advertising is so uncontrollable, because whatever restrictions are made in terms of their verbal content or 'false claims', there is no way of getting at their use of images and symbols.

Exploring images of nature, science, history, and magic found in advertising messages, she illustrates how various combinations of signs (or 'referent systems') in a given advertisement transfer symbolic meaning to the featured product. The ideological nature of these 'hollowed out systems of meaning' is evident in the fact that a symbol's original significance becomes irrelevant in the context of advertising as long as the connection between the image and the product is established in the consumer's imagination. Her description of an historical figure in a Holsten beer ad is one of many examples she uses to illustrate this process (Williamson, 1978: 168):

On every bottle of Holsten we will see a picture of the Black Knight, we are told. And this advertisement actually makes explicit the total lack of substance in its signification: 'Nobody knows for certain who he is but he's long been a symbol of the Holsten brewery in Hamburg' . . . So a completely hollow symbol is used to signify both history and the beer: and in connecting the two the beer becomes the '*historic beer*'. Clearly the material substance which has been knocked out of history has become transferred to the beer: the referent system may be empty, but the beer has a '*full*, distinctive taste'. What history has lost, the taste of beer has gained.

She makes a similar remark regarding scientific claims in advertising, noting for instance the magnified cross-section of skin diagrammed in an ad for Vichy skin care products, accompanied by a copy riddled with pseudo-scientific jargon with the photo caption 'to make skin care that works, you have to understand the skin'. Regarding this illustration, Williamson observes:

> While seeming to be an explanation, it is really a *symbol*: it denotes the skin, but connotes *science, facts, seriousness*; it represents the miraculous system of science but is empty of meaning in itself. (Williamson, 1978: 118)

As for references to magic in advertising, Williamson (*ibid*.: 150) points to the 'festishism' of commodities whereby, for instance, a bottle of Haig scotch whisky can have a 'magic carpet effect', transporting the consumer to an imaginary place for relaxation ('Haigland' in this case) without the hassle of passports or luggage. Similarly, certain products are presented as having 'alchemic properties' (*ibid*.: 145–6), such as sauces which magically transform all other ingredients of a dish, or a hair coloring solution which acts as a 'magic potion', turning an ordinary 'Cinderella' figure into someone for whom 'life will never be the same again' (*ibid*.: 147).

In her discussion of references to 'the natural' in advertising, on the other hand, Williamson illustrates how images borrowed from nature are culturally transformed or 'cooked' (Lévi-Strauss, 1969) to create symbolic meanings that can be transferred to products.[11] This industrial transformation of natural objects (potatoes transformed into McCain frozen french fries, fresh oranges into Birds Eye canned orange juice, and so on) is presented by ad makers as an improvement on nature, providing the convenience and socially desirable values sought after by

consumers. In an advertisement for Coty Sunshimmer tanning gel, for instance, the headline reads 'Even the sun can use a little help' (Williamson, 1978: 106). Williamson describes the 'cooking' process in this particular case as follows:

> Sunshimmer imitates the sun, in that it tans you, but it compensates for all the sun's inadequacies: it tans you evenly, unlike the sun, moisturises your skin, unlike the sun, and above all, is *available*, unlike the sun . . . We thus see that the natural thing, the sun, is used as a referent for what Coty has *improved*: it is the *difference* between Sunshimmer and the sun, that is the chief selling point of the ad. In a 'neat little tube' you can buy 'cooked' sunshine. (*ibid*.: 106)

Images and concepts associated with nature, history and so on are therefore culturally transformed into 'systems of meaning' connected to objects with which they normally have no relationship whatsoever. One of the reasons advertising is able to function ideologically and influence consumers' attitudes and purchasing behavior is the fact that it is a shared experience. As Williamson puts it (1978: 170):

> People's real experience may be very similar but it remains isolated while what *is* a universal experience is the impact of media and social images . . . We need a way of looking at ourselves . . . We need to make sense of the world: which ads make us feel we are doing in making sense of *them*.

Vestergaard and Schrøder (1985: 159–60) elaborate on this notion, demonstrating how advertising exploits the ideological mechanisms of nature and 'the natural' by claiming that (i) product ingredients are natural (for example, shampoo); (ii) the product improves on nature (for instance, cosmetics); (iii) the processes of nature can be reversed (such as hair loss); and/or that (iv) there is a connection between the product and nature where none actually exists (for example, automobiles). One of their more interesting observations is that some advertisements cleverly *sympathize* with audiences who react negatively to claims such as these, noting, for example, that 'natural wild ingredients' (such as tropical fruit essences used in shampoos) are nowhere to be found in their products (*ibid*.: 170).[12] The authors conclude that:

> advertising is no static ideological phenomenon: it flexibly accommodates its messages to suit the changing climate of opinion among

the consumers . . . [The ad makers] try to carve out for themselves a niche in the market where persuasion follows different lines from the rest of the market.

In their analysis, Vestergaard and Schrøder (1985: 141–74) provide numerous examples of how advertisements suggest simple 'common sense' solutions to 'obvious' problems, reinforcing accepted social norms and stereotypes in the process. One unfortunate byproduct of advertising underscored by these authors is the 'normalcy of behavior' perpetuated by advertising messages where 'the really insidious ideological processes are those which treat a phenomenon as so self-evident and natural as to exempt it completely from critical inspection and to render it inevitable' (Vestergaard and Schrøder, 1985: 145). They also address 'the ideological market consciousness' of advertising illustrating through their examples how 'production is pictured in hopelessly nostalgic or romanticized terms which bear little resemblance to production in advanced industrial society' (Vestergaard and Schrøder, 1985: 147).

Their most provocative observations, however, are those related to the portrayal of women in advertising from the 1970s. In comparing images of women to those of men in advertising from this period, they note, for instance, that:

> while the feminine ideal *rejects* the natural features of women's bodies – hair, eyes, skin, teeth, nails, lips, etc. – the beautification products offered to men (mainly clothes) are merely meant to *enhance* the natural features of men's bodies, not to transform them. (Vestergaard and Schrøder, 1985: 75)

Other works published more recently (for example, Tanaka, 1994; Kilbourne, 1999; Machin and Thornborrow, 2003) seem to confirm that little has changed in this regard in the last 25 years. In her analysis of female representation in Japanese magazine advertisements, Tanaka (1994), for instance, observes that negative stereotypes regarding woman are reinforced through both language and imagery, demonstrating how such notions as 'intelligence' and 'individualism' reflect gender biases in advertising aimed at young women. When the word 'intelligence' is used to address this consumer group, according to her analysis, it invariably refers to a woman's physical appearance and sense of elegance (as opposed to wit), as seen in the following example, translated from Japanese by the author (Tanaka, 1994: 110):

Intelligence. That is (the secret of) your beauty. Your intelligence is seen in your clothes. Even in the lipstick which you wear. (slogan for Kanebo, a leading manufacturer of cosmetics in Japan)

A woman's individuality, on the other hand, is often associated in this context with elitism, being able to afford expensive luxury items imported from countries such as France and Italy, and imitating Western culture, as in the following slogan (also translated from Japanese):

Let's design our own hair this summer.
As American girls do.
As European girls do. (example cited in Tanaka, 1994: 120)

In other cases, Tanaka describes 'individualism' in these advertisements as being equated with irrational or 'childish' behavior, such as a (female) secretary tossing her typewriter out an office window after having apparently lost her temper (Tanaka, 1994: 125).

The messages perpetuated by advertisements targeting girls and women in Western countries reflect a similar pattern. The following comment regarding adolescent girls made by Jean Kilbourne (1999: 132), who has written extensively on the impact that advertising has had on American women, will come as no surprise:

Primarily girls are told by advertisers that what is most important about them is their perfume, their clothing, their bodies, their beauty . . . Girls of all ages get the message that they must be flawlessly beautiful and, above all these days, they must be thin.

This idea is further underscored by Machin and Thornborrow (2003: 453) who argue that the women appearing in *Cosmopolitan* (otherwise known as *Cosmo*) seem to 'rely on acts of seduction and social manoeuvreing, rather than on intellect'. In comparing 44 versions of the magazine distributed around the world, the authors found that a woman's power in this context is consistently defined by her ability to please and manipulate others (particularly men) and that 'consumerism [has] become a discourse with which women can and do signify their roles and identities across the globe' (*ibid.*: 468).[13]

Word play

The overarching theme of the linguistics literature on advertising presented thus far has been the manipulation of audiences through various

ideological processes. Cook (1992: 217), however, reminds us that due to the ephemeral quality of advertising and multiple audience interpretations, any critical analysis of this discourse type has its limitations:

> In a sense, an ad ceases to be itself when it is scrutinized, and it is impossible to study an ad as it is usually perceived. To treat an ad as something at the centre of attention transforms it. This makes ads frustratingly resistant to dissection and criticism, which always seems to be taking ads more seriously than they were intended.

Comparing verbal strategies used in advertising to similar devices found in poetry (repetition, puns, rhythms, rhyme, and so on), Cook (*ibid.*: 226) suggests that advertising sometimes provides entertainment to audiences who may be naturally attracted to 'light-hearted code play'. In the minds of most consumers, however, the gulf between literature and advertising remains very much intact (*ibid.*: 229):

> In comparison with literature, ads accept and glorify the dominant ideology while literature often rejects and undermines it. The fact that ads must answer to the brief of their clients may also lead to a feeling that ads are typically vehicles of deceit, while art is a vehicle of honesty.

Cook provides a very detailed analysis of text, images, music and iconicity in advertising that has since been cited throughout the linguistics literature on advertising discourse. Included in this discussion is an examination of the 'narrative voices' (Bakhtin, 1981) of various participants in advertising as well as illustrations of how this persuasive medium exploits phonological patterns (prosody) and different forms of 'deviation' for special effect (Cook, 1992: 139–41). Some commonly seen examples of the latter would be clipping ('telecom'), affixation ('provodkative'), compounding ('oatgoodness') and functional conversion, with nouns functioning as verbs, verbs as adjectives, adjectives as nouns, and so on (*ibid.*: 140).

Similar analyses of 'word play' in French advertising can be found in Grunig (1990) who outlines a variety of techniques used in constructing advertising slogans (for example, alliteration, rhyme, rhythm, graphological and morpho-syntactic modifications, and so forth) in such a way as to make them as alluring and memorable as possible for French audiences. She notes that one of the most common devices exploited in French advertising copy is polysemy, as in the following examples:

(1) *C'est pas du vol* <SNCF>
(2) *Entre la pose-moquette et la pose-rideaux, vive la pause-fromage* <Emmental>

The word *'vol'* in the first slogan (Grunig, 1990: 14) for France's national railway company, the SNCF (*Société Nationale des Chemins de Fer*), can be interpreted in one of two ways: either 'theft' or 'flight'. Thus, the slogan (*C'est pas du vol*) offers a double 'literal' meaning: 'It is not theft', and 'it is not a flight'. Taken in this context, the connotation would be that train tickets with the SNCF are quite affordable, and allow you to avoid the delays and inconveniences of air travel. In the second slogan (Grunig, 1990: 18), which alludes to redecorating a room, we find a play on words involving the homonyms *'pose'* ('installing', 'hanging', 'laying') and *'pause'* ('break') whose identical pronunciation in French produces the humor in the ad. A possible interpretation of this slogan might be the following: 'Between laying the carpet (*la pose-moquette*) and hanging the curtains (*la pose-rideaux*), isn't it wonderful to take a cheese break (*pause-fromage*).' Other parts of speech, including articles, can generate the same type of polysemy. In the following French slogan for Heineken (*ibid.*, 1990: 25), for instance, one notices that the team who designed this advertisement is playing with the specific vs. generic use of the definite article *'la'* whereby *'la'* may refer to both 'the' (as in 'the specific beer' or, in this case, Heineken) and 'in general' (as in 'beer as a general class of beverage') giving us the following interpretation:

> *La Bière qui fait aimer la bière* <Heineken>
> 'The Beer that makes you love all beer' <Heineken>

Hybridization (or *la technique du 'mot valise'*) is another common feature of Grunig's corpus. Consider the following slogan for a butter cookie (*ibid.*, 1990: 60):

> *Croustifondant* <Galettes Verkade>

This one-word slogan is actually the fusion of two separate lexical items in French: *croustillant* ('crunchy' or 'crisp') and *fondant* ('buttery', as in 'melts in your mouth'). With the final syllable (*'ant'*) being identical in both words, the copywriter was able to truncate *'croustillant'* (to form 'crousti') and attach the word *'fondant'* to it as a suffix. Given the 'buttery' and 'crunchy' connotations, the association with the product is unavoidable. Grunig also describes the use of alliteration whereby,

for instance, two or more stressed syllables of a word group begin (or end) with the same consonant sound or sound group. Included in Grunig's corpus were the following examples (both of which are classics):

> *Dubo . . . Dubon . . . Dubonnet*
> *Du pain . . . du vin . . . du Boursin*

Diagrammed and translated, the first slogan (*ibid.*, 1990: 194) for an *apéritif* could be interpreted as:

> Dubo → (C'est beau) → It's beautiful
> Dubon → (C'est bon) → It's tasty
> Dubonnet → (Dubonnet) → (the product name)

The second slogan (Grunig, 1990: 189) refers to a cheese spread which makes a lovely complement to bread and wine, an association which is not lost on any French consumer. Although the rhyme is lost in my translation, the image of wine and cheese is easy to appreciate in any language:

> *Du pain . . . du vin . . . du Boursin*
> 'Bread . . . wine . . . and Boursin'

Slogans may also attribute human characteristics to inanimate objects, as with the Carte Bleue Visa card that 'speaks every language' (*ibid.*, 1990: 158):

> *Carte Bleue Visa. Elle parle toutes les langues*

Or, they may attract attention by seeming to totally defy logic, as is the case with this slogan for Canderel artificial sweetener (Grunig, 1990: 95):

> *Ça ne change rien et c'est ça qui change tout* <Canderel>
> 'It doesn't change a thing, which changes everything'

A slogan for J & B Whiskey (*ibid.*, 1990: 105) uses a similar approach:

> *Debout le soleil se couche!* <J & B Whisky>
> 'Time to get out of bed, the sun is setting! <J & B Whisky>

Other strategies (*ibid.*, 1990: 47, 72, 158) include the use of antonyms (*la petite géante*, or 'the little giant', for Volkswagen), morphosyntactic modifications (*il n'y a que Maille qui m'aille*, or 'Maille is the only mustard for me') and mixing of the 'senses' (*Ecoutez comme c'est bon*, or 'Hear how good it tastes', for Krispi cereal, sold as Rice Krispies in the US). These many examples illustrate how practitioners in the advertising industry exploit a number of different verbal strategies to attract attention, create desire for the product, and enhance recall, resulting in a use of language that is unique to advertising.

Use of foreign languages

As for the use of foreign languages in advertising directed at native speakers of English, there has been very little research to date. Myers (1994), however, offers some very interesting examples, including a commercial for NIKE (aired during the All-Star baseball game) containing a Spanish voice-over that was rejected by one of the major American TV networks (CBS). Apparently, the use of Spanish (the language spoken by the largest minority group in the United States) to refer to the Dominican Republic as 'the Land of Shortstops' (*'La Tierra de Medio-campistas'*) was too intimidating for American audiences, despite the English subtitles and only 60-second exposure (Myers, 1994: 90). In another example (*ibid.*: 92), we find the use of French (with beautiful scenery and gourmet dining depicted in the visual) in a British campaign promoting vacation travel in the UK:

> *Say magnifique*
> *Say superbe*
> *C'est Jersey*

In this case, the French element *C'est* (meaning 'It is' or 'That is') is juxtaposed with the English verb ('Say') whose similar pronunciation produces the pun. The French cognates used elsewhere in this slogan (*'magnifique'* and *'superbe'*) ensure its comprehensibility while conjuring up images of French culture familiar to British tourists, or as Myers (*ibid.*: 93) puts it, 'the France of berets, bicycles, striped shirts, moustaches, baguettes, the Eiffel Tower, a glass of wine, an auberge'. This was a very clever way of shifting the joys of vacationing in France to the British countryside, enticing British tourists to explore Jersey rather than crossing the English channel. As Myers (*ibid.*: 92) notes, however, the use of languages other than English for special effect in advertising is typically limited to very few product categories and usually involves cultural

stereotypes. In this regard, foreign languages in advertising 'act more like pictures or music than like text' (*ibid.*: 96).

This is particularly true when one considers the insertion of foreign languages in print and television advertising that are likely to be completely unintelligible to the intended audience. Martin (1998a: 321–2) reports, for instance, that Carlsberg beer magazine advertisements distributed in France in the mid-1990s were using copious amounts of both Russian and Japanese text (Figure 1.1), providing no translation whatsoever for the reader. The slogan (in French), however, made the campaign's message crystal clear: 'Carlsberg. Probably everywhere on this planet' (*Carlsberg. Probablement partout dans le monde*). Knowing the meaning of the foreign language text was irrelevant as long as the consumer understood that the product being advertised had universal appeal, enjoyed by beer drinkers around the globe. More recent examples of 'exotic' languages used as attention-getters in French advertising are explored in Chapter 2.

Imitation varieties

The representation of foreign languages in advertising may also be purely suggestive, an imitation as it were, and may even be unintelligible to fluent speakers of the languages being inserted for special effect. In an ad for Oranjeboom beer distributed in the UK (Myers, 1994: 93), for instance, the slogan features Dutch words linked together in such a way as to sound like English when the slogan is read aloud (defying all rules of Dutch syntax). Adding to the slogan's appeal is the final tagline (offered as a reward to audience members who understand the pun):

De woord onder bus es Oranjeboom (*Not everyone will get it*)

While this is a clever way of highlighting the Dutch origins of the brand (using Dutch words ordered in an arbitrary fashion), Myers reminds us that anyone with knowledge of Dutch reading this out of context would consider it 'meaningless'.

The same principle applies to jingles which are often unintelligible when presented in a foreign language. Martin (1998a: 294–9) reports a heavy use of (unsubtitled) English language jingles in French television advertising for certain product categories (for instance, food and non-alcoholic beverages, automobiles, home appliances, toiletries), noting that intelligibility does not seem to be an important factor. More precisely, the English heard in French TV commercial jingles typically serves as a 'mood enhancer', with the actual meaning of the music

34

Figure 1.1   Carlsberg advertisement

日本経済新聞　1993年（平成5年）10月6日（水曜日）　12版（経済2）

CARLSBERG.

PROBABLEMENT PARTOUT DANS LE MONDE.

Carlsberg beer

Carlsberg au Japon.

九　かぐや姫の昇天

POUR LA SANTE. A CONSOMMER AVEC MODERATION.

soundtrack often being totally unrelated to the product or service featured in the ad. In some cases, the lyrics for French television advertising are even 'gibberish', written by individuals associated with the campaign in such a way as to simply 'imitate' English (*ibid.*: 313–14). Similar to the Dutch example cited earlier, this strategy, therefore, involves the creation of an 'imitation variety' constructed in such a way as to resemble English. In this case, however, the newly invented variety is used in the music soundtrack (as opposed to print) and is not meant to be intelligible to any audience (English-speaking or otherwise). It is simply inserted to create a certain atmosphere.

The use of 'invented' languages for advertising campaigns is especially noticeable, however, in the popular French television commercials for Omo laundry detergent. Taking language play to a whole new level, a creative team working for the Paris ad agency Lintas decided to design specifically for the campaign an entirely new language (which they called 'poldomoldave') comsisted of slang expressions from multiple sources (French mixed with English, Italian, Spanish, Arabic, and so on).[14] Delivered on-screen by a male/female couple of chimpanzees and their offspring, this 'pot pourri' of languages is easily understood by French audiences because of the careful selection of borrowed lexical items already familiar to the average consumer in France (for example, 'clean' from English, 'kif kif' from Arabic, etc.).[15] The expressions used are also short and catchy, which further enhances recall. In one commercial (aired in the mid-1990s) we see a series of play on words inspired by the product name *Omo Micro*, reflecting the fact that the detergent, although presented in its concentrated form in a very small (*micro*) box, is nonetheless quite powerful. The dialogue in this case features a quibble between a female chimpanzee and her husband who shows up in a filthy pair of overalls expecting her to wash them. The French text sprinkled throughout the copy ties the text together and clarifies the meaning for speakers of French, the intended audience.

Television Commercial for Omo Micro Laundry Detergent French Version

Female chimpanzee discussing dirty laundry with her husband

Female:	*Oh la la la la! [. . .] du boulot!*
Male:	*Daki Omo Micro et crapoto basta fuite!*
Female:	*Ah! Et c'est tout teeny weeny kiki?*
Male:	*Kif-kif, costaud!*

Female:	*Kif-kif, costaud. Ha! Qué sera sera!*
	(later . . .)
	Oh, ce bonhomme clean! Oh, ce doux doux lo coto!
	Bravo, mon Micro!
Voice-off	*Omo Micro*
	Omo Touti Rikiki
	Maousse Costo.

For readers whose French is fluent but perhaps not colloquial enough to grasp the code-mixed slang embedded throughout, a short glossary might be in order:

bonhomme	'guy, little fellow'
boulot	'work'
costaud	'strong'
costo	'strong', from 'costaud' (strong, sturdy)
crapoto	'filthy dirty', from 'crapaud' (toad)
doux doux	'very soft', from 'doux' (soft)
kif-kif	'but', from 'kif-kif' (It's all the same)
qué sera sera	'I'll believe that when I see it!' (Whatever will be will be)

The status of English as an international language becomes apparent in the international version which was distributed in countries other than France. Although some French remains in this exported version, the reliance on English for intelligibility (and universal appeal) in the adaptation is unmistakable, as is the continued use of slang for humor.

Television Commercial for Omo Micro Laundry Detergent (emphasis added)
International Version

Female:	Oh la la la la!
	Look at il lo **mess!**
	Oooh, **Not scrub the scrub, not more!**
Male:	**Take it easy, my** chérie.
	Voilà Omo Micro
	And go exit zie **muck!**
Female:	**My** pauvre **grubbie grubbie!**
	C'est **itsy bitsy teeny weeny?**

Male:	Mais mega **strong!**
Female:	Mega **strong?** Ha! Qué sera sera!
	(later . . .)
	Oh Mucho **clean!** Oh **so teddy cuddly!**
	Bravo mon Micro!
	What a big good guy!
Voice-off:	Omo Micro
	Tini Wini
	Mega **Rambo**

One particularly amusing element in this text is the reference to a Hollywood movie character (Rambo) played by the internationally recognized action film hero Sylvester Stallone. In carefully examining the copy of this international version, however, one notices a number of other phenomena that make the 'poldomoldave' variety created for this advertising campaign truly unique. In addition to the multilingual slang expressions (for example, *take it easy, my chérie*) sprinkled throughout the chimpanzees' dialogue, for instance, one finds elements of language used to address children (*itsy bitsy teeny weeny*), functional conversion (such as the English adjective '*grubbie*' used also as a noun in the expression '*ma pauvre grubbie grubbie*'), as well as various graphological (*tini wini*) and morpho-syntactic (*go exit zie muck*) innovations. Continually crossing the lines between child and adult language, colloquial and formal styles of speech, grammatical (*Voilà Omo Micro*) and ungrammatical (*What a big good guy*) sentence construction, and languages (French, English, Spanish, German, and so on), this invented variety could only occur in advertising where conventional wisdom regarding language use no longer applies.

Advertising bloopers

Native speakers of English who are surprised by the 'ungrammaticality' of such texts will be all the more perplexed by English-inspired product names being used in various parts of the world. In her textbook *The Language of Advertising*, Goddard (2002: 62) provides a sampling of product names that are commonplace in non-anglophone contexts but which many Anglophone consumers would find displeasing, to say the least. These include (in alphabetical order) *Bonka, Calpis Water, Charms Sour Balls, Colin, Crapsy fruit, Creap, Driply, Flirt, Gits, Japp, Kräpp, Naturot, Plopp, Plopsies, Pocari Sweat, SorBits,* and *Whatchamacallit.*[16] Additional advertising 'bloopers' involving English are available from multiple

sources (for example, Ricks, 1983, 1996; Cateora, 1990: 468; Terpestra, 1993; Axtell, 1994; Mueller, 1996: 154; Goddard, 2002: 61–4; Zeff and Aronson, 1999: 286–7). Zeff and Aronson (1999: 287) report, for instance, that Pepsi's Chinese translation for the slogan 'Come alive with the Pepsi Generation' was interpreted in China as 'Pepsi brings your ancestors back from the grave'. The product name *Coca- Cola* was equally perplexing for the Chinese consumer when first introduced, eventually forcing the company to slightly change their brand name for the Chinese market (ibid.: 287):[17]

> The Coca-Cola name in China was first read as 'Ke-kou-ke-la,' meaning 'bite the wax tadpole' or 'female horse stuffed with wax,' depending on the dialect. Coke then researched 40,000 characters to find a phonetic equivalent 'ko-kou-ko-le,' translating into 'happiness in the mouth'.

Similar advertising translation bloopers can be found in other parts of the world. Whereas the American Dairy Association's 'Got Milk' campaign translated as 'Are you lactating?' in Mexico, the slogan used by Coors ('Turn it loose') when translated into Spanish for Mexican consumers essentially told them that the beer would unleash a bout of diarrhea. Automobile manufacturers have also had their share of advertising blunders, having chosen product names that turned out to be somewhat undesirable in foreign markets (Mueller, 1996: 154). Ford's *Caliente*, used in Mexico, for instance, was actually a slang word for 'streetwalker' and therefore received mixed reviews. Another unfortunate product name distributed internationally was the Ford *Fiera* truck, meaning 'ugly old woman' in Spanish. When marketing their *MR2* in Canada, Toyota overlooked the dubious interpretation that their product name would produce in French-speaking Quebec. Perceived (and pronounced) as 'em-er-deux' by Quebecers, this automobile sounds very much like an expletive ('shit') in French, implying that the automobile in question is rather undesirable (as in 'shitty'). The Sunbeam curling iron marketed in Germany as *Mist Stick*, on the other hand, was interpreted by Germans as meaning 'Manure Wand'.[18] Indeed, brand naming is not to be taken lightly. As Goddard (2002: 60) notes:

> Because of the way we make connections between words and particular ideas, feelings and experiences, brand names are crucial for advertisers. They are very economic, acting as little concentrated capsules

of meaning. Where advertisers get it right, readers will do the work to generate all the intended connotations.

Companies translating their advertising slogans into English also fall into this trap, one memorable example being the slogan used in the US for a reputable Scandinavian vacuum cleaner: *Nothing sucks like an Electrolux* (Zeff and Aronson, 1999: 286).

Merely translating an advertisement can obviously lead to all sorts of culturally misleading innuendoes. To complicate matters, to be effective from a marketing perspective, advertising copy translations must also take into account the original campaign strategy, as noted by Mueller (1996: 154–5):

> The most effective approach in preparing copy for foreign markets is to begin from scratch and have all verbal communications entirely rewritten by a speaker of the foreign language who understands the complete marketing plan – including objectives, strategies, and tactics. (Mueller, 1996: 154–5)

Visuals and illustrations used in the campaign must also be scrutinized to avoid offending local consumers:

> Care should be taken in the selection of visual backgrounds and settings employed in both print and broadcast advertisements destined for foreign markets. These nonverbal communications should either reinforce the local culture in adapted campaigns or remain neutral enough to be accepted in all markets for those campaigns employing a standardized strategy. (Mueller, 1996: 157)

By heeding such advice, those who redesign global campaigns for local markets are much more likely to produce messages that are appealing and meaningful to their intended audiences.

English as a pair-language

Code-mixed advertising involving English borrowings aimed at non-native speakers of English began to spark the curiosity of linguists in the mid-1980s and continues to be a popular area of linguistic inquiry. Studies of this nature consistently report an overwhelming preference for English as a pair language in advertising, given its socio-psychological impact on consumers, whether it be in Europe, South America, Asia, or other parts of the world.[19] More often than not, English in this context

operates as an authoritative voice as seen, for example, in the use of English-language voice-overs reinforced by printed English text (Piller, 2001: 160), and the fact that English elements in advertising copy are typically displayed in a larger font as compared to local languages (Martin, 1998a: 255–9). Researchers working in this area have treated a number of topics including job advertisements (Larson, 1990; Hilgendorf, 1996; Hilgendorf and Martin, 2001; Meurs *et al.*, 2004), shop names (Thonus, 1991; Dumont, 1998; MacGregor, 2003; Schlick, 2003; Baumgardner, 2005), product naming (for example, Haarmann, 1984; Loveday, 1986; Baumgardner, 1997; Wilkerson, 1997; Friedrich, 2002), mixing of scripts (for instance, Bhatia, 2000; Jung, 2001), language legislation restricting English in the media (for example, Martin, 1998a), the functional roles of English in advertising for various products (for example, Bhatia, 1992), and different varieties of English in advertising (Gerritsen *et al.*, 2000; Martin, 2002a).

Despite the growing interest in language-mixing in advertising media discourse, however, most studies to date conducted by linguists have focused solely on print media, especially magazine advertising, with very few investigations of language contact in television commercials (for example, Martin, 1998a, 2002a; Gerritsen *et al.*, 2000), radio advertising (for example, Pavlou, 2002), or other broadcast media (such as cinema).[20] A very comprehensive analysis of language and script mixing in rural Indian advertising in both conventional and non-conventional media, however, can be found in Bhatia (2000). Basing his observations on a broad corpus of press, radio, and television advertising, as well as calendars, painted wall advertising, oral sales calls in rural markets, and advertising distributed to remote villages by video vans (locally known as 'video *raths*'), Bhatia observes that 'urban Indian elites do not hesitate to impose western forms and alien value systems on rural India through marketing, media, and advertising' (*ibid.*: 39) and that in India (as in other parts of the world) English has become the marker of globalization *par excellence*. This lack of sensitivity has led to a mistrust of mainstream advertising by rural populations in India (*ibid.*: 37):

> Alarmed at the invasion of their centuries-old lifestyle and value system and the total disregard for their sensitivities, the perception of villagers is turning overwhelmingly negative against urban media planners and advertisers.

Describing in exquisite detail less conventional media (which also incorporate various forms of folk media including poetry, drama, dance,

songs, opera, and puppet shows), Bhatia argues that multinational corporations targeting this market would be wise to incorporate themes that reflect rural Indian cultural traditions as well as multiple language and script mixing to maximize intelligibility (see also Mueller, 1996).

This growing body of research highlights the linguistic creativity exhibited in code-mixed advertising discourse and has contributed considerably to our understanding of the functioning of English in advertising around the world. Supported by the continuing global spread of English and today's mass media culture, code-mixed advertising involving English as a pair language is emerging as a genre in its own right, featuring stylistic patterns and communicative functions unlike that of any other form of discourse.

Language, culture and identity

In her critical review of the literature on language-mixing in advertising, Piller (2003) describes other recent studies as focusing on the ideological work of multilingual advertising and the construction of hybrid (consumer) identities through language contact. In an earlier publication, Piller (2001: 182) refers to advertising as 'the late modern discourse par excellence' and explores in detail the images associated with English in German advertising. Through this analysis, she observes that advertising in Germany presents English–German bilingualism as 'the "natural" option for successful middle-class Germans' (*ibid.*: 155). She has also noticed a shift in consumer attitudes regarding English in magazine advertising, although the images associated with Romance languages (such as French and Italian) have remained unchanged in televised media, as indicated by the following comment (*ibid.*: 169):

> In print advertisements, English has supplanted French, and Romance languages more generally, as the languages which traditionally connote *joie de vivre* for Germans. In TV commercials, on the other hand, French and Italian continue to be vested with these functions, mainly through the use of setting and accents. French is the language of love and carries erotic connotations whenever it occurs; Italian is the language of the good life as expressed through food.

In his analysis of linguistic and visual representations of Western culture in Japanese magazine advertisements, Maynard (2003) also explores identity formation, arguing that 'the Japanese anchor their self-identity within the multicultural spaces of advertising' (*ibid.*: 57)

and that 'ultimately Japanese cultural identity overrides and domesticates the West' (*ibid.*: 73). Having closely examined some 2000 print advertisements, he concludes that despite the daily consumption of American images in advertising in Japan, the local Japanese culture remains very much intact (*ibid.*: 73):

> In short, Japan appears to be in control of how it identifies with the West, through nostalgia and linguistic inventions that smack of modernity. Icons representing the West are part of the mosaic of cultural multiplicity pervasive in a globalized world. At least in the case of Japan, identity of self would appear to be firmly intact, and firmly in control.

Kelly-Holmes (2005), on the other hand, claims that code-mixed advertising discourse exemplifies a form of 'fake multilingualism' and that advertising strategies involving foreign words, dialects, accents, and so forth contribute to an ethnocentric view of languages and cultures, thereby reinforcing stereotypes of 'otherness'.[21] O'Barr (1994) also explores cultural stereotypes and the representation of 'Others' in advertising, using illustrations from around the world. Describing common portrayals of certain ethnic and racial groups in advertising, for instance, O'Barr focuses on the treatment (in visuals and text) of individuals who are considered outside the 'mainstream population', and most importantly, the 'social meaning' of ads in terms of image, ideology and power.

One of the ways in which cultural stereotypes are perpetuated through advertising is through the use of country-of-origin appeals, many of which are deceptive (Kelly-Holmes, 2005). The advertising campaigns for American automobiles, for example, often have a distinct American flavor, using patriotic imagery and lyrics sung by country recording artists, even though their products often contain Japanese or European components. Certain product characteristics are also associated with specific countries, such as reliability, quality engineering and precision with Germany, elegance, fashion, and gourmet cuisine with France, and so on (Haarmann, 1984; Mueller, 1996; Kelly-Holmes, 2000; Piller, 2001). In advertising, these associations result in various types of 'linguistic fetishes', such as French product names, slogans, and descriptive advertising copy used for cosmetics made in any number of countries, including Germany and the United States (Kelly-Holmes, 2005: 61). This intersection of meaning between global and local cultures will be examined in detail in Chapter 2.

Referring to the restricted number of languages displayed on the websites of many multinationals, Kelly-Holmes (2005: 83) notes that 'it seems impossible not to get the impression that the corporation sees certain languages as having linguistic capital and speakers of certain languages as "worthy" addressees, while others are deemed to be the opposite.' Her example of the Israeli website for Volvo avoiding Arabic is very provocative as is her description of McDonald's overall neglect of Spanish in their American advertising (*ibid.*: 84–5). Many would find it ironic that McDonald's does, however, provide 'scrupulously bilingual' advertising for the Canadian market in accordance with Canadian laws (*ibid.*: 84).

Examples of different varieties of English used as a pair language for special effect in advertising have also been reported in the literature. Myers (1994: 98), for instance, describes a South African ad for *Brooks* running shoes featuring a naked man with various pictures of the product covering his groin. Understood as a slang word for 'shorts' in one of the local languages (Afrikaans), the brand name *Brooks* produces a memorable pun when inserted in the accompanying slogan: 'I feel naked without my Brooks.' Myers (1994: 96) notes that foregrounding specific varieties of English, or 'accents' is a particularly popular strategy in advertising distributed in the UK. The following television commercial, featuring what is likely to be perceived in this market as a Manchester accent, clearly illustrates this technique (Myers, 1994: 96):

> The camera tracks across a marble floor, passing a bottle of perfume and a sunken bathtub. A woman wearing a black evening gown and high heels walks to a dressing table where she applies cream to her face, murmuring 'soft, rich'. A man in a dinner jacket enters from behind a curtain at the rear, and says:
>
> By 'eck petal, you smell gorgeous tonight
>
> . . . We then see that the cream she is applying is the foam off the top of a pint of beer. He takes a quick sip before helping her with her jacket, and wipes his lip with his sleeve. The ad is for Boddington's bitter; it's a pun on their slogan 'The Cream of Manchester'.

The humor here stems from the contrast between drinking beer (the 'common man's beverage') and the very elegant décor. The regional accent is also foregrounded by its posh surroundings. As Myers (1994: 96) notes: 'A Manchester (or exaggerated Northern) accent can convey

many things, but not continental sophistication.'[22] A former Texan now living in the UK, Myers (1994: 100) notes that for sociocultural reasons local varieties of English are much more prevalent in British ads than in ads found in the US:

> If American readers want to imagine British ads, they must think of a world in which the accent of Chicago is very different from that of Cleveland or Minneapolis, and is even different from that of Gary, and yet the upper class speaks the same accent around the country. And geographical accent is not tied to social class the way it is in the UK; a southerner or Bostonian does not abandon his or her accent at university. [Accents] are not useful in evoking a whole world of associations the way they are in UK ads.

It has also been documented that regional varieties of English in former British colonies are sometimes chosen over more 'standard English' in an effort to appeal to local consumers. Gill (2000), for instance, describes the preference for Malaysian English over British or American English in Malaysian radio advertising, noting that 'the English language and how it is employed in radio advertisements in Malaysia plays an integral role in reflecting Malaysian identity' (Gill, 2000: 89). As copywriters have a number of sub-varieties of Malaysian English to choose from, however, they must match the variety with the intended audience, brand image, and overall campaign strategy, hence the importance of hiring a local team with in-depth knowledge of the culture when adapting a global campaign for a specific foreign market.

Some attention has also been paid to audience reactions to advertising across media. Applying Grice's (1975) theory of conversational implicature to advertising discourse, Geis (1982) examines how viewers interpret television commercials and dissects the 'deceptive' communication techniques used in television advertising aimed at children. Research has also been conducted on consumer reactions to English in French and Taiwanese magazine advertisements (Checri, 1995; Hsu, 2002), magazine advertising in different European countries (Gerritsen, 1995), and Dutch television commercials (Gerritsen *et al.*, 2000; Meurs *et al.*, 2004). Several linguists and intercultural communication scholars have also conducted interviews in advertising agencies to determine their motivations for using English for specific markets (for example, Martin, 1998a; Bhatia, 2000; Gerritsen, *et al.*, 2000; Gill 2000; Ovesdotter Alm, 2003). Despite these efforts, audience interpretations

of code-mixed advertising text, visuals and jingles (particularly in terms of their cultural specificity) remain a largely untapped area for empirical research.

Whereas the linguistic analyses described herein explore a wide range of phenomena in advertising discourse including ideological metaphors, linguistic creativity, the use of foreign languages, and mixing with English specifically, very little attention has been paid to the intersection of meanings between global and local communication. The present study is an attempt to bridge the gap between research conducted by advertisers, intercultural communication scholars, and linguists by addressing both meaning(s) and verbal strategies featured in global and 'glocal' advertising discourse with specific attention to the sociocultural context in which the advertising communication occurs. To provide a comprehensive view of English and global imagery in French advertising across media, this discussion will include an examination of the use of American-inspired imagery and French perceptions of the US, French attitudes toward English, language legislation affecting the execution of advertising campaigns in France, and globalization as it is viewed by both those who produce and consume the discourse and images of advertising.

2
The Global Consumer

Globalization and advertising

The aim of this chapter is to provide an overview of globalization as it is experienced by both the advertising industry and the general public in France. To explore the advertising industry's response to globalization, we will begin this discussion with an examination of issues related to the standardization versus localization debate, cross-national research on advertising messages, and the 'hybrid identities' of today's global consumer as constructed through multicultural marketing and international campaigns.[1] Following this discussion, we will address globalization from the public's perspective, exploring, among other topics, consumer perceptions of global brands (for instance, Elliott, 2001) and the defacing of advertising by activist groups in France (Lichfield, 2003). To address the concerns of those who associate globalization with Americanization, this chapter will also include a discussion of the impact of American foreign policy on consumer preferences for global brands and French–American relations in recent years. Included in this section will be the post-9/11 'Freedom Fries' debate and efforts of advertising executives (and the US government) to improve America's image abroad (for example, Love, 2003; Melillo, 2003a and b).

Global images commonly used in advertising in France today mirror the social and linguistic behavior of today's global consumer.[2] Public debate over global brands differs from the representation of the global community in advertising, where audiences are drawn into a world of positive associations through imagery and discourse, a world of global interconnectivity, racial equality, and exotic landscapes, and where global cultures appear to be right at one's fingertips. At the same time, this portrayal of 'Otherness' reinforces the French cultural identity and

47

worldview through cultural and linguistic stereotypes which are used to convey specific information about the product and/or create a certain atmosphere. To contextualize this exploration of global discourses and imagery in French advertising, we will begin with an examination of the advertising industry's view of globalization.

Advertising industry's perspective

For the advertising industry, globalization involves shaping a product's campaign message for multinational audiences, and discussing whether or not such adaptation is desirable and feasible (Kanso and Nelson, 2002). The term 'globalization' was, in fact, first coined by Theodore Levitt, a well-known Harvard University professor and marketing guru, who supported the idea of advertising products in a standardized fashion for all markets across the globe (Levitt, 1983). Myers (1999: 222–3), a linguist whose work on advertising was cited earlier, sums up Levitt's argument as follows:

> The way forward, he said, was to make a good product, and make people adapt to it. Too expensive? They'll find the money. Too high-tech? They'll learn. Too British (or Japanese or German or American)? It will be seen as an advantage.

In today's global environment, however, the strategies used to reach consumers in different markets have come under increased scrunity. As Myers notes (1999: 56):

> Globalization seems all-powerful because it provides both a marketing strategy and a set of images. But it turns out that it is rather difficult to market most products at this level of generality. The iconography, typeface, and colours certainly remain the same around the world, but every global brand finally reaches the consumer at a particular time and place and a particular intersection of meanings, so there remains a need for all sorts of local knowledge in the agency and local modifications in the campaign.

In her book on international advertising practices, Turkish author Nükhet Vardar (1992) examines London-based ad agency executives' attitudes toward globalization and the pros and cons of adapting campaigns to specific markets. She concludes that 'in international marketing, agencies can only be as good as their [company] clients permit [and] globalisation will not work unless clients learn to centralise their own

strategy' (*ibid.*: 112). As has been discussed throughout the literature (for instance, Whitelock and Chung, 1989; Kanso, 1991; Terpestra and Sarathy, 2000), many advertising executives prefer to use a modified approach. Notes Vardar (1992: 26):

> In practice, neither an entirely standardised nor an entirely localised advertising approach is used. If international advertising is seen as a continuum between totally centralised and totally decentralised local campaigns, then most brands will fall between the two extremes. A combination of the two approaches is generally put into use in varying ratios, as the market conditions and corporate objectives dictate.

Furthermore, laws and regulations imposed on advertising messages differ among nations. Mueller (1996: 147) points out legal requirements for localization:

> Lu Biscuits had to develop twenty different versions of a TV spot to satisfy all the legal requirements necessary to market their cookies in Europe. In Italy children are not allowed to look at the camera while speaking of the product. In Austria and Germany children must always appear in the company of adults. In the Netherlands a child may eat chocolate on the screen – provided a toothbrush is also shown.

One must also take into account media availability and timeslot restrictions in different countries (Mueller, 1996: 147–8):

> the media that advertisers are permitted to employ can also vary widely. The media scene abroad does not resemble that in the United States. For instance, Sweden and Norway still do not permit radio or television advertising. Denmark finally began phasing in this type of advertising on a limited basis as recently as 1987. And in Germany, even though TV advertising is allowed, it is severely restricted – limited to twenty minutes per day and typically aired only in the evenings (5:00–8:00 P.M.) in blocks of five–seven minutes that do not interrupt programming.

In the case of France, television advertising on major (non-cable) networks is limited to a daily average of six minutes per hour and television commercials for cigarettes and alcohol are prohibited (Vernette, 2000:

126–8).[3] Nevertheless, when executed properly, a campaign adapted to local cultures can be very well received, as illustrated in the following example (Mueller, 1996: 150):

> An excellent example of this modified approach is a campaign developed by Coca-Cola. Several years ago, the firm's advertising agency, McCann–Erickson Worldwide, created an award-winning commercial showing Pittsburgh Steeler football star 'Mean' Joe Greene giving his jersey to a young boy who had offered him a bottle of Coke after a tough game. However, the advertisement could not be used outside the United States for two reasons. First, Joe Greene was unknown in foreign markets, and second, American football is not nearly so popular abroad as it is in the United States. Rather than abandon the concept, the agency adapted it to other countries by creating advertisements featuring stars of the more popular international sport of soccer. Advertisements in South America used the popular Argentinian player Diego Maradona, and those in Asia used Thai star Niwat as the heroes of the spots.

Indeed, the need to communicate with consumers of diverse cultural backgrounds and the recognition of the subtleties required in the adaptation process have led to a growing body of research on cross-cultural differences in advertising. To better understand audience preferences, international advertising scholars have compared the use of humor and sex role portrayal in advertising distributed in different markets (for example, Wiles and Tjernlund, 1991; Sengupta, 1995; Milner and Collins, 2000; Al-Olayan and Karande, 2000) and the informational content of advertising messages (for example, Noor Al-Deen, 1991; Zandpour, Chang and Catalano, 1992). The use of symbols, rhetorical styles and advertising appeals (for instance, Albers-Miller and Gelb, 1996; Caillat and Mueller, 1996; Cheng and Schweitzer, 1996) and the execution of creative strategies (for instance, Ramaprasad and Hasegawa, 1992) have also been well documented. Some additional studies have examined the manner in which music is used in television commercials in different countries (for example, Murray and Murray, 1996) as well as cross-national attitudes toward product placement in movies distributed around the world (for example, Gould, Gupta and Grabner-Kräuter, 2000). As this research provides specific recommendations regarding local adaptations of international campaigns, it is invaluable to advertising agencies who are directing their messages to different audiences worldwide.

French advertising, as compared to American advertisements, tends to be more sophisticated and aesthetically pleasing, making extensive use of symbols and metaphors (Cutler and Javalgi, 1992; Taylor, Hoy and Haley, 1996). Biswas, Olsen, and Carlet (1992) examined over 500 magazine advertisements from France and the United States and found that French advertising relies more heavily on sex, humor and emotional appeals, and that advertising aimed at American consumers is generally more informative in nature. A comparison of television commercials from France, the US, and Taiwan (Zandpour, Chang, and Catalano, 1992: 30) produced similar findings:

> US commercials, in contrast to their French and Taiwanese counterparts, often feature a celebrity or a credible source to provide testimonials or arguments in favor of the product. They keep the brand name before the audience, lecturing in a friendly, conversational tone with suggestions of loyalty and trustworthiness. US commercials are more likely to feature nutritional and safety aspects of products. French and Taiwanese commercials, by contrast, are more likely to make explicit promises that are beyond what the product can realistically deliver.

With information such as this at their fingertips, those who redesign global campaigns for different markets are much better equipped to seduce local audiences.

Cultural representation and identity

To communicate effectively with audiences around the world, one must also take into account the notion of cultural identity. Indeed, the representation of culture in advertising is a powerful strategy that can make or break a campaign. The use of Hollywood movie stars in advertising distributed internationally, for instance, has met with some resistance from those who feel that American faces and cultural values should not be used as a persuasive tool on consumers worldwide.[4] Referring to a television car commercial for the Toyota Altis starring Brad Pitt that was recently banned in Malaysia, Malaysia's Deputy Information Minister Zainuddin Maidin was quoted in the local press (*The Straits Times*, December 18, 2002, p. A1) as accusing advertising agencies of giving Asians an 'inferiority complex' by their frequent use of Western models: 'Why do we need to use their faces in our advertisements? Are our own people not handsome?' When asked by reporters why the commercial was banned by the government, he responded: 'We barred the advertisement as it appeared as a humiliation against Asians.'

One response to this influx of Western imagery has been advertising regulation. Frith (2003) notes, for instance, that all advertising distributed in Malaysia must be filmed locally. This 'made-in-Malaysia' (or 'MIM') stipulation has, as one might expect, made global campaigns more problematic for the advertising industry (Frith, 2003: 49–50):

> To conform to this requirement, multinational advertisers often film commercials in Malaysia and later run them in other parts of the region. So that the models did not appear to be country-specific, advertisers intending to run the spots around the region began using models that had a 'Pan Asian' look. These models were usually of mixed European and Asian ancestry. In the 1990s the Ministry of Information put a stop to this practice, pointing out that these models set an 'unattainable' beauty standard for the people of Malaysia. Today, models in ads must be identifiably from one of the main ethnic groups in the country: Chinese, Indian, or Malay.

Despite the advantages of globalized advertising campaigns touted by proponents of standardization (cost efficiency, simplified strategy planning, brand image consistency across markets, better quality control, and so on), Frith and Frith (1990: 181) argue that most advertising of this nature reveals 'an unexamined complex of Western values and practices and ignorance of the host culture'.

This being said, it is undeniable that many advertising agencies around the world are making a concerted effort to tailor their message to the cultural values and worldview of specific consumers, and they are using increasingly sophisticated methods. Atkinson (2003) reports in an article in *Advertising Age* that the ad agency Ogilvy & Mather Worldwide has created a 'global consumer-insights unit' whose mission it will be to 'track the emergence of tomorrow's trends'. One of their aims is to determine the cultural influence that certain cities have in this regard (Berlin and Buenos Aires being high on the list). Companies are also hiring smaller multicultural ad agencies specialized in the 'transcultural approach' to handle their campaigns directed at minority groups such as Latinos and African Americans in the United States (Dávila, 2001; Hunter, 2003). The chairman of one such agency (Claude Grunitsky from True, which handles campaigns for Nissan North America), describes the transcultural approach as 'based on cultural affinities rather than racial, ethnic or gender boundaries' and notes the more complex 'hybrid identities' of today's consumer (McMains, 2003: 12). Giuseppe D'Alessandro, Pepsi's director of multicultural marketing would agree:

'The multicultural mind-set is more about your interests, like music, than whether you're African American or Latino' (Wentz, 2003: S–4).

The representation of culture in advertising takes on a whole new meaning, however, in advertisements for Benetton (now known as United Colors of Benetton), whose provocative campaigns designed by Italian photographer Oliviero Toscani have caused considerable debate in France. In a book defending his motives for using extremely graphic images in his work (for example, man dying of AIDS, tattoo marking someone as HIV positive, blood-stained clothes of a dead soldier in Sarajevo, nun and priest kissing on the mouth, and so on), Toscani (1995) reveals that one of the first truly controversial Benetton ads of his creation was a 1989–1990 campaign featuring a black woman breast-feeding a white infant. According to Toscani (1995: 46–7), the campaign was well received in most countries, but was strongly criticized by Black minority groups in the United States who considered the ad a painful reminder of slaves caring for their white owners' children in antebellum America. Even more interesting was the reaction in South Africa during the time of Apartheid. There, surprisingly enough, the campaign was boycotted by the media on the grounds of being 'too anti-racist'. In his own defense, however, Toscani (1995: 46) describes his work as 'philosophical':

Je ne fais pas de publicité au sens classique avec cette affiche. Je ne vends pas de pulls. Ceux-ci, de bonne qualité, de toutes les couleurs, vendus dans sept mille boutiques à travers le monde, se suffisent à eux-mêmes. Je ne cherche pas à convaincre le public d'acheter – à l'hypnotiser – mais à entrer en résonance avec lui sur une idée philosophique, celle du brassage des races. La campagne s'appuie sur la devise de la marque, 'United Colors', qui devint bientôt le nouveau nom de Benetton . . . Elle 'colore' Benetton d'une attitude progressiste. Elle développe une image de marque, philos-ophique, au-delà de la seule consommation.

English translation (mine)

This poster ad is not advertising in the classical sense. I am not selling sweaters. Benetton's high quality products, sold in every color in seven thousand stores worldwide, speak for themselves. I'm not trying to convince the public to buy anything, nor do I want to mesmerize them. I simply want to communicate to them a philo-sophical idea, namely that of an intermingling, multiracial society. This campaign is based on Benetton's slogan 'United Colors', adopted as part of the company name soon thereafter . . . It shows Benetton

as having a more daring, progressive attitude, and develops a thought-provoking brand image that goes beyond mere consumerism.

Given their sheer shock value, and negative backlash from the viewing public, it is not surprising that Benetton's global campaigns have drawn commentary from scholars interested in media discourse (for instance, Giroux, 1994; Hoeschmann, 1997; Tinic, 1997). A recent study by Kraidy and Goeddertz (2003) examines the treatment of Benetton's 'We on Death Row' campaign in the American press (*Washington Post*, *New York Times*, *Los Angeles Times*, and *Chicago Tribune* specifically). Through an analysis of newspaper articles appearing before, during and immediately after the campaign, which was launched in January 2000, they conclude that the fundamental issue of capital punishment was 'obscured' by journalists in the US who, on the contrary, presented Benetton as a 'European entity' whose opinions on the matter were irrelevant. An excerpt from the *Washington Post* speaks volumes: 'It's unfashionable to kill our killers, as far as the rest of the world is concerned. But for now it's the way we're cut' (Stuever, 2000). Rather than noting the worldwide debate on capital punishment and human rights, 'the US press focuses on the suffering of the inmates' victims, presenting Benetton as insensitive to the victims' families because it is too busy glamorizing the murders for commercial reasons' (Kraidy and Goeddertz, 2003: 157). Although Benetton's approach to international advertising has been somewhat unusual, it does illustrate yet another strategy for communicating with a global audience (and one that is likely to remain imprinted on the minds of consumers for years to come).

Indeed, images speak louder than words and cultural imagery often evokes strong emotions as local audiences cling to their individual cultural identities and personal beliefs. Whether these emotional reactions are positive or negative, however, will depend on the ad maker's ability to tap into the cultural perceptions and worldview of their intended audiences. Through their analysis of current global trends and the multicultural perspective of today's consumer, however, advertising agencies are making every effort to address consumers in a language they understand.

Consumer reactions to globalization

The impact of globalization on various cultures has been the focus of intense debate among political scientists, linguists, anthropologists, sociologists, and communication scholars since the early 1990s, some of whom have studied this phenomenon within the context of advertising (for example, Myers, 1999; Bhatia, 2000; Elliott, 2001; Kraidy and

Goeddertz, 2003).[5] Indeed, the marketing discourse of global brands provides a treasure trove of data for examining how globalization is experienced at the local level.

Starbucks, for instance, with its worldwide reach and 'multicultural' themes prominently displayed in its brochures, coffee names, and packaging, is one of several corporate giants whose advertising has been 'decoded' in this manner. Elliot (2001) argues that as a marketing strategy Starbucks traces the beans in their trademarked blends to exotic locales (such as New Guinea, Kenya, Sumatra, and so on) to 'heighten coffee's consumer appeal' (p. 376) and that any sensitivity towards foreign cultures one might associate with this practice is 'wholly superficial' (p. 374). In a nutshell:

> while Starbucks' current marketing blends the exotic and familiar, and the local and global within its semantic coffeepot, the resulting brew is still poured from a Western perspective. An increased awareness of global culture displayed within Starbucks is wholly tempered by local and stereotyped representations. (p. 380)

Having recently opened several stores in Paris, Starbucks has received mixed reviews in the French press. The main fear, of course, is that the coffee chain will pose a threat to more traditional French cafés. Whether or not the brand will seduce French consumers, however, remains to be seen. As one French journalist (Evin, 2004) put it:

> *Pas sûr que les afficionados de la pause café acceptent de rejoindre un espace propret (tous les sites Starbucks sont non fumeurs) et aseptisé, quand bien même ceux-ci seraient dotés de bornes wi-fi et de fauteuils club recouverts de tissu. D'autant moins également que les prix, sans être prohibitifs, ne seront pas non plus ultra-compétitifs, avec un espresso vendu 1,6 euro.*

English translation (mine)
> There's no guarantee that coffee drinkers in France will embrace the clean and sterile atmosphere of Starbucks coffee shops (where smoking is prohibited), even if they provide high-speed wireless internet access and comfy arm chairs. Furthermore, their prices are not all that competitive, with an espresso selling for 1 euro and 60 cents.[6]

When considering consumer perceptions of global brands, one must also take into account certain economic, social and political conditions.

When the European Union refused to import hormone-injected beef from the United States, for instance, the White House retaliated by imposing high tariffs on a wide range of European products imported by the US, including Roquefort cheese, exported from France. Considering the latter action (which had serious economic repercussions for farmers in his region) as the last straw, a Frenchman by the name of José Bové organized various protests, the most notorious of which was the 'symbolic dismantling' of a McDonald's restaurant under construction in the southern French village of Millau (Bové and Dufour, 2002).[7] Highly suspicious of the use of hormones as growth stimulants in the American food industry, and associating McDonald's with the global reach of corporate America and the perceived Americanization of French culture, the French public largely applauded this initiative. Five of the protesters (all local farmers, including José Bové) were subsequently incarcerated, a situation which only increased Bové's popularity.[8] The following description of events that ensued after Bové's refusal to post bail speaks volumes (José Bové interview appearing in Bové and Dufour 2002: 34):

> *Quand j'ai refusé de payer la caution, je suis rentré en cellule sans que les détenus sachent si je sortais ou non. Ils ont appris par la télévision, au journal de 20 heures, que je restais en prison: ils étaient contents et se sont tous mis à taper sur les fenêtres. C'était vraiment émouvant . . . Les gars gueulaient par la fenêtre: 'C'est bien!' Le dimanche qui a suivi, les copains du Larzac et de la Confédération paysanne sont venus faire un pique-nique de soutien, avec de la musique, etc. Ils ont tourné autour de la prison en donnant un concert de klaxons. Les prisonniers qui étaient sur cette façade dominant la route d'accès au pont ont brûlé des trucs à la fenêtre et ont sorti des draps. Il se sont mis à gueuler des slogans 'Libérez José!', à taper sur les barreaux. Pour aussi être de la partie! Les gardiens étaient un peu tendus, mais ils m'ont gentiment conduit au troisième étage pour que je puisse voir les copains rassemblés devant la prison.*

English translation (mine)

When I refused to post bail, I was returned to my cell without the other prisoners actually knowing whether or not I was leaving. When they heard on the evening televised news that I was staying, they were ecstatic and started banging on the windows. It was really moving. Guys were yelling out their windows: 'Way to go, José!' The following Sunday, friends from Larzac and my farmers' union, the *Confédération Paysanne*, organized a picnic, with music, in front of the prison to show their support. They all circled the prison in their

cars honking their horns. The prisoners held on the side which over-looked the bridge leading to the prison, draped sheets out their window and lit things on fire. They started chanting 'Free José!' and banging on the bars of their windows as a form of participation. The guards were a little tense but they kindly led me to the 3rd floor so that I could see my friends gathering outside the prison.

This bold attempt by a private citizen to speak out against the impact of globalization on society has made José Bové into something of a folk hero in France, where he has been regularly interviewed on major radio and television networks and featured in the press (Viard, 2000). However, Bové himself is quick to point out that the primary aim of such activities (endorsed by his farmers' union organization, the *Confédération paysanne*) is to keep globalization in check and maintain an open dialogue rather than fuel any anti-American sentiment (José Bové interview appearing in Bové and Dufour, 2002: 29):

> *Nous ne voulions pas que McDo apparaisse comme la cible principale. C'était un symbole de l'impéralisme économique. D'ailleurs, nous n'avons jamais appelé au boycottage de McDo. Les journalistes ont vite compris et la plupart ont enchaîné sur les idées qu'il y avait derrière la symbolique anti-McDo. Nombre de responsables politiques, en revanche, ont plutôt appuyé le côté antiaméricain.*

English translation (mine):

> We weren't specifically targeting McDonald's. They were just a symbol of economic imperialism. Nor did we ever call for a boycott of McDonald's restaurants. The press caught on quickly, with most journalists reporting the ideas behind the anti-McDonald's symbolism. Many politicians, however, emphasized the anti-American aspect.

Indeed, the McDonald's Corporation has drawn much criticism in France over topics ranging from the nutritional value of their menu and marketing to children, to their hiring practices (Ariès, 1997; Gordon and Meunier, 2002).[9] Since launching a campaign centered on nutrition in February 2001, however, the corporation has also been defending its menu choices and trying to counteract widespread claims that McDonald's is partially responsible for the growing rates of obesity among children (Caussat, 2002). These efforts have included not only a full-length book manuscript outlining, for example, exactly how their

hamburgers are produced (see Delcayre, 2002), but also a series of editorial ads in magazines popular among French mothers (for example, *Santé, Marie Claire*). One such advertisement features the headline 'Does McDonald's make you fat?' (*McDo fabrique-t-il des obèses?*) and testimonials from nutrition experts claiming that McDonald's menu choices are exactly that: choices, and that McDonald's is not harmful to children if incorporated into a healthy, balanced diet.[10] According to one nutritionist quoted in the ad:

> *L'important, pour éviter un apport calorique excessif sur un seul repas, est d'instaurer un 'mode d'emploi' McDo et de penser, au repas suivant, à donner à votre enfant un repas plus léger en privilégiant les fruits et les legumes.*

English translation (mine)

> To avoid consuming too many calories in a single meal, it's important to adopt a McDonald's 'strategy', interspersing visits to McDonald's with lighter meals for your child, rich in fruits and vegetables.

Another states simply:

> *Il n'y a pas de mauvais produit, il n'y a que de mauvaises habitudes.*
>
> There is no such thing as a bad product. There are only bad habits.

In an effort to appeal to local consumers, McDonald's France also provides very detailed nutritional information regarding various menu items on its website (www.mcdonalds.fr).[11]

Nevertheless, both anti-globalization and anti-advertising activists in France continue to attract considerable attention in the media. No study of French advertising discourse would be complete, for instance, without a glance at the tactics of activist groups such as RAP. (*Résistance à l'agression publicitaire*) and *Casseurs de pub*, who routinely deface advertising in France as a means of protest.[12] Disseminating their information on the Web (www.antipub.net, www.casseursdepub.org) and organizing demonstrations via e-mail listserves and the Internet, individuals affiliated with these groups are occasionally hauled into court to face charges of vandalism. Lichfield (2003) describes the activities of one such group who invited 'flash mobs' armed with spray cans, markers, and paintbrushes to paint protest slogans on posters throughout the Paris Metro. The damages were estimated at 1 million euros.[13] These antics are commonly referred to as 'culture jamming' (Lasn, 2000) which

Naomi Klein, Canadian journalist and author of *No Logo*, a book that
has become the 'anti-globalization bible' in many countries around the
world, defines as 'the practice of parodying advertisements and hijack-
ing billboards in order to drastically alter their messages' (Klein, 2000:
280). Referring to such activities as a form of 'semiotic Robin Hoodism',
she describes the reason such actions are effective: (ibid.: 281)

> The most sophisticated culture jams are not stand-alone ad parodies
> but interceptions – counter-messages that hack into a corporation's
> own method of communication to send a message starkly at odds
> with the one that was intended. The process forces the company to
> foot the bill for its own subversion, either literally, because the
> company is the one that paid for the billboard, or figuratively, because
> anytime people mess with a logo, they are tapping into the vast
> resources spent to make that logo meaningful.

The anti-advertising movement began in Canada in the late 1980s in
the form of a Greenpeace-type organization known as the Media Foundation, whose bi-monthly magazine (*Adbusters*) is widely read by both
anti-advertising and anti-globalization activists. The magazine's website
(www.adbusters.org) is a leading source of information for the movement and internationally-sponsored events, such as 'Buy Nothing Day'
(scheduled the day after Thanksgiving, the busiest shopping day of the
year in the US), 'TV Turn-off Week' (scheduled in April), and the 'Unbrand
America Campaign'. Activists in France also participate in these events
(known in French as the *Journée sans achat*, *Semaine sans télévision*, and
Campagne de décroissance, respectively) following details provided, for
instance, on the previously mentioned RAP and *Casseurs de Pub* websites.
Certain members of the French advertising industry have also joined in
the movement. Through their own organization (*Comité des créatifs
contre la publicité*, or CCCP), the latter have tried to invite the general
population to participate in TV Turn-off Week by airing a spot describing
the event on French television. Their request for air time, however, was
refused by the agency (*Bureau de Vérification de la Publicité*, or BVP)
authorized to grant such approvals (Mariage, 2000).

These initiatives would certainly be applauded by *Adbusters* who suc-
ceeded in placing a full-page ad (costing $60,000) for their 'Unbrand
America Campaign' in the June 28, 2004 issue of the *New York Times*
(www.unbrandamerica.org). The ad featured a US flag in which the 50
stars had been replaced by 30 corporate logos for multinationals such
as IBM, Nike, McDonald's, Exxon, etc.[14] The copy read:

This July 4th
Because my country has sold its soul to corporate power
Because consumerism has become our new religion
Because a small group of neocons has hijacked our national agenda
And because we've forgotten the true meaning of freedom
I pledge to do my duty to take my country back.
Unbrandamerica.org
A flashpoint for civil disobedience.

The *Adbusters* website also features a variety of spoof ads for global brands, depicting everything from horses grazing in a cemetery, evoking the image of the ranchers on horseback seen in advertisements for Marlboro cigarettes, to Ronald McDonald silenced with a piece of tape over his mouth that reads 'Grease' (spoofing the McDonald's Corporation). In another spoof ad for McDonalds, we see a patient undergoing open heart surgery. In the foreground is a monitor labeled 'Big Mac Attack' incorporating the double arches of the McDonald's corporate logo in the visual representation of the patient's heart beat. Logos are also the main focal point of an anti-Bush/anti-globalization spoof ad sponsored by DemocracyMeansYou.com (retrieved from www. livejournal.com on July 6, 2004). The ad's message presents itself in the form of a parody of 'Bush syntax' ('Let me explainify the war against Iraq a little bit in Texas terminologragy') and a logo-ridden commentary alluding to a possible oil industry conspiracy:

> We *SHELL* not *EXXON*nerate Saddam Hussein for his actions. We will *MOBIL*ize to meet this threat in the Persian *GULF* until an *AMOCO*ble solution is reached. Our plan is to *BP*repared. Failing that, we *ARCO*ming to kick his ass.

Although this very creative discourse disseminated by activists is certainly thought-provoking (and, in some cases, entertaining), the bottom line in advertising remains effective communication and meeting the expectations of one's company clients. Whereas those who work in advertising have grown very adept at packaging global brands in such a way as to appeal to local consumers, there are still other factors that must be taken into account. These include the shift in consumers' preferences for certain brands that may occur as a result of current events reported in the media. American foreign policy, for instance, had a direct impact on the sale of American products in certain countries following President George W. Bush's decision to send

American troops into Iraq. This also had an adverse effect on French–American relations, as will be discussed in the following section on post-9/11 America.

Post 9/11 debates

Despite the advertising industry's efforts to address the cultural sensibilities of today's global consumers, there is a much darker side to globalization that cannot be ignored. In the wake of the September 11, 2001 terrorist attacks on the World Trade Center, for instance, the US government felt a pressing need to improve America's image abroad, particularly in Arab markets. Whereas the government originally considered collaborating with a team of advertising executives who were very keen on the idea (Love, 2003), Washington bureaucrats eventually decided to exclude their participation (Melillo, 2003b). Having been 'snubbed' by the State Department, the ad industry, however, is taking up the cause with its own task force led by Keith Reinhard, chairman of the advertising agency DDB Worldwide. One year prior to the 2004 US presidential elections, Melillo (2003b: 10) observed: 'Although [Reinhard] intends to make some of the task force's work available to the government, he said the private sector is better suited to addressing the issue of public diplomacy as Washington moves into another presidential-election cycle.' While it is true that presidential campaigns can bring projects such as this to a grinding halt as candidates struggle to present themselves in the best possible light to potential voters, the motivation behind this move on the part of the advertising industry has nothing to do with politics:

> What worries Reinhard, whose clients include Anheuser-Busch and McDonald's, are the results of a Roper–ASW study released July 1 [2003]. They show that for the first time since 1998, consumers in 30 countries signaled their disenchantment with America by being less likely to buy Nike products or eat at McDonald's. Worse, 11 of the top 12 US-based global companies, including McDonald's, Microsoft, Nike and Disney, saw their 'power brand' scores – a measure of how well they are known or liked abroad – drop or remain the same. At the same time, nine of the top 12 Asian and European firms, including Sony, BMW and Panasonic, saw their scores rise. (Melillo, 2003b: 10)

The Bush administration's decision to invade Iraq without a UN resolution supporting a military campaign did not improve the situation, and

France, of course, was one of the countries most vehemently opposed to this 'unilateral military action' on the part of the US (Abrate, 2005: 29). This, coupled with the fact that so many American soldiers died on French soil during WWII defending France from Nazi Germany, resulted in a wave of anti-French sentiment in the US.

The key mantra of Americans who support the war in Iraq has been 'freedom', a motivation perhaps for the renaming of French fries to 'Freedom fries' and French toast to 'Freedom toast' by Republican Representative from Ohio Bob Ney in March 2003.[15] The press, of course, had a heyday. Writes Timothy Noah in an article posted on slate.msn. com (March 11, 2003):

> No word yet on whether the House similarly plans to adopt the neologisms 'freedom horn,' 'freedom doors,' 'freedom kissing,' and 'freedom tickler'. (Noah, 2003)

Noah also reminds us that a similar 'propaganda frenzy' was launched against Germans during WWI:

> when Americans renamed sauerkraut 'liberty cabbage,' dachshunds 'liberty dogs,' hamburgers 'liberty steaks,' and German measles 'liberty measles'. Beethoven was banned outright. (Noah, 2003)

Serving on the Committee on House Administration, which oversees the House of Representatives' cafeterias, Ney described this initiative as 'a small but symbolic effort to show the strong displeasure of many on Capital Hill with the actions of our so-called ally, France' (*US Congress opts for 'freedom fries'*. http://news.bbc.co.uk, retrieved on July 13, 2004). This 'tit-for-tat' also extended into a boycott of French products sold in the US, fueled via the Internet by grassroots organizations such as Boycott Watch (www.boycottwatch.org) and Citizens United (citizensunited.org). Other reports in the media included a restaurant owner in Florida pouring his French wine in the gutter and French's Mustard publicizing the fact that their product was named after the company's founder, Robert T. French, and therefore had no connection whatsoever with France (Vannerson, 2004).[16]

There are many, however, who disapprove of these guerrilla tactics, including Miquelon, a watchdog group that has compiled an online list of 'French-bashing' activities in the US (www.miquelon.org/boycott. html). In an article published in the *Washington Times* (March 23, 2003), nationally syndicated columnist Alan Reynolds wrote:

I don't see how people manage to get angry at an entire nation, and particularly at only one of many nations opposing the Iraq war . . . Many Americans who are enormously fond of President Bush have, like the French, worried he may be jumping into a big, nasty tar pit.

Michael Moore's documentary *Fahrenheit 9/11*, contesting the 2000 US presidential election and denouncing George W. Bush's government policies, further fueled the debate. This American film maker won accolades in France, where he was awarded the coveted *Palmes d'or* for *Fahrenheit 9/11* at the 57th Cannes Festival in May 2004 (www.festival-cannes.fr). Describing the film as 'a jazzy reveille of facts and innuendos' designed 'to reach a drowsy electorate (p. 69)', *Time* magazine (Corliss, 2004) refers to Michael Moore as 'the outsider banging down the doors of the insiders' (p. 66). As would be expected, the film drew sharp criticism from the conservative right. Radio talk show host Rush Limbaugh, for instance, called it 'a pack of lies' according to Corliss (2004: 64). The White House, however, reserved comment, as did the Kerry campaign. The remark made by the White House Communications Director, Dan Barlett, during a press conference following the film's release in the US was clear but understated (Corliss, 2004: 69): 'If I wanted to see a good fiction movie, I might go see *Shrek* or something, but I doubt I'll be seeing *Fahrenheit 9/11*.' Specifically targeting globalization is another film, *The Corporation*, co-produced by Mark Achbar, Jennifer Abbott and Joel Bakan (www.zeitgeistfilms.com/corporation). Notes Tommy Nguyen, staff writer for the *Washington Post* (July 4, 2004):

The film examines corporate power – from the patenting of living organisms to market research into how children can nag their parents for candy and toys more effectively – with a startling array of facts and figures.

This film has also won several international awards (for example, People's Choice, Sundance, Best Canadian documentary).

As these examples illustrate, globalization and advertising have generated a lot of debate and creative dissent in recent years. Having examined this phenomenon from a variety of perspectives – from that of the advertising industry, the press, and media scholars, to the anti-advertising rhetoric of activist groups on both sides of the Atlantic – let us now explore the multitude of advertising copy decisions that are gradually transforming French media audiences into 'global consumers'. The following discussion is not presented as a form of anti-globalization protest

by any stretch of the imagination, but rather as an acknowledgment of the efforts on the part of copywriters, art directors, creative directors, and others who carefully craft these messages to address French consumers as the world citizens they have become.

Advertising with global discourse and imagery

A content analysis of several thousand television, magazine, and billboard advertisements recently collected in France reveals a number of visual and textual components being used in French advertising that appear to be by-products of globalization. These include (i) the use of discourse elements associated with the latest communication technologies, such as cell-phone text messaging, Internet 'chat', and emoticons ('smileys') used in e-mail; (ii) television programs imported and refashioned for French audiences; (iii) multiracial casting to reflect a 'global village' philosophy; (iv) exotic global imagery; and (v) the use of 'exotic' foreign languages as attention getters. Also present in the data, as will be discussed in detail, are various stereotypical references to countries perceived as 'Anglosaxon'. We will begin this section with an exploration of communication technologies featured in French television and print advertising.

Global media and communication technologies

With the advent of global communication networks, discourse elements associated with the latest technologies have also begun to appear in advertising copy. The Internet, for instance, is becoming a recurrent theme in French advertising, including references to e-mail, online purchasing, and other forms of computer-mediated communication. Consider, for example, several recent magazine ads for the SNCF, France's main railway company, directed at the younger, under 30 crowd.[17] Each ad in the campaign utilizes a different combination of computer keyboard symbols to relay a message related to the model depicted in the visual. One ad, for instance, uses two inverted computer keys – the colon: and the right parentheses) – to produce a smile matching that of the young woman in the visual, who is comfortably resting on her living room sofa, having removed her high heels after a long day at the office. The French copy uses phonetic repetition (the words *.com* and *comme*) for additional appeal:[18]

> *Voyages.sncf.com comme se faire livrer gratuitement son billet de train chez soi.*

(Voyages.sncf.com. Have your train ticket delivered free to your home.) my translation:

Reminiscent of emoticons used electronically to express emotions such as happiness, surprise, disappointment and so forth (otherwise known as 'smileys'), these pseudo slogans attract attention because of their uniqueness in the context of advertising, their simplicity, and their relevance to consumers' everyday lives (such as the use of computers to communicate via e-mail and the Internet).[19] The insertion of emoticons in the copy – being an artifact of computer-based communication – is also a clever way of drawing attention to the conveniences of online purchasing, via the SNCF website in this case, which is the main focus of the ad. A different keystroke combination, consisting of two dashes side-by-side (- -), is used in another SNCF advertisement to draw the reader's attention to the eyes of the Asian model in the illustration. The copy, in this instance, is directed towards airline travelers (urging them to make their airline reservations for international destinations using the SNCF website):

Voyages.sncf.com comme réserver son billet d'avion pour Tokyo.

(Voyages.sncf.com. Reserve your plane ticket for Tokyo.) (my translation)

Although by examining these ads one might be led to believe that references to communication technologies in French advertising are reserved for younger audiences, it should be noted that some effort has been made to include older citizens in this technology revolution. An article that recently appeared in *Notre Temps*, a French magazine aimed at older readers, combines step-by-step instructions for accessing information on the magazine's website (notretemps.com) with a breezy description of the site's user interface:[20]

Vous faîtes vos premiers pas. Tapez dans la barre d'appel http//www. notretemps.com et lancez la recherche. Vous voilà sur la page d'accueil. Vous reconnaissez, en bas à gauche, la couverture du magazine et l'annonce de quatre grands univers: Se rencontrer, un espace convivial d'expression et d'échanges; Apprendre, un monde de découvertes; Bouger, pour savoir ce qui se passe; Prévoir, savoir, pour ne négliger ni ses droits, ni sa santé. Cliquez, entrez, visitez.

English translation (mine)

So this is your first time on the web. Simply type our address (http://www.notretemps.com) into your browser and hit 'enter'. This will

bring you to our home page. In the bottom left-hand corner you will immediately recognize our magazine cover and discover four menu choices:

- Conversations: a friendly space for expression and interaction
- Learn More: a world of discovery
- Getting Involved: latest news and events
- Planning Ahead: how to protect your rights, and your health

Now all you do is click, enter, and explore.

Sprinkled throughout the text are invitations to explore the Web (*'Apprenez à maîtriser Internet, et découvrez comment envoyer des photos par e-mail'*) as well as topical references that would likely appeal to this age group, as in the following example:

> *Sur la page d'accueil vous remarquerez une ouverture Côté perso. Cet espace est hautement confidentiel, personne n'y peut accéder, à part vous. C'est là que vous pourrez ranger tous les renseignements précieux que vous désirez conserver dans différents domaines, santé, argent impôts, voyages, retraite, parents âgés, etc.*

English translation (mine)

> On the home page you will notice a *Personal Info* link. This space is strictly confidential. No one can access this section of the website except you. This is where you can store important information regarding your health, income taxes, trips, retirement, aging parents, and so forth.

The purpose of this discourse is to draw the older reader into the worldwide community of Internet users by reassuring them and speaking to them about issues that are highly relevant to this particular group of consumers.[21] As might be expected in Internet-related discourse, however, English borrowings also appear, including 'Internet', 'e-mail' (as seen above) and 'chats' (along with its French verb equivalent: '*chattez*').

Indeed, despite the French government's efforts to curb the use of English-language computer terminology in France, the general population continues to mix extensively with English in this domain, using terms such as *e-mail, Internet, surfer, CD Rom*, and so on in their daily interactions (Yaguello, 1998: 143–50). The influence of English is also

evident in the web addresses inserted in advertising copy distributed in France, regardless of the country origins of the brand, as seen in the following examples:

www.garnierbeautybar.com   (Garnier)
www.espressoandfun.com   (Lavazza)
www.volvocars.fr   (Volvo)

The abbreviated form of wireless communication known as text messaging, commonly used to send short typed messages via cell phone, is another interesting development in advertising discourse.[22] Referred to also as SMS (or 'texto' in French), this relatively new form of communication invented by cell phone users, mostly teenagers and upwardly mobile professionals, continues to evolve today. Given the necessity to shorten each word as much as possible, since the text is typed on numeric phone keypads, English-language messages such as 'I love you' and 'See you tonight', for instance, become 'I LUV U' or 'C U 2 NITE'. A few other English examples of this very extensively developed lingo include 'G2G' (got to go), 'LOL' (laugh out loud), 'SOL' (sooner or later), 'AFAIK' (as far as I know), 'WL' (will), 'W' (what?), and 'PXT' (please explain that) (see Trujillo, 2003). The French, of course, have their own version of SMS, some of which is surfacing in French advertising (for example, 'BJR' for (*Bonjour*), 'TOQP' for *'T'es occupé?*). However, much of the SMS found in French advertising is unmistakably borrowed from English.[23] The motivational factors for this type of borrowing include the desire to identify and reinforce the origins of the brand (as in the expression 'SOFT2YOU' appearing in a recent IBM ad) and to appear 'hip' or 'cool' to consumers by referencing British and American rap recording artists, American television shows, and other elements of imported 'pop culture'. Magazine ads for cell phone accessories and packages aimed at French teenagers, for instance, are riddled with abbreviated expressions (a likely result of text messaging but also indicative of youth slang), many of which depict English-sounding song titles for cell phone ring tones (for example, 4 my people, What's luv, U remind me).[24]

The term 'SMS' itself is also borrowed from English, referring to 'Short Message Service' (a term coined by the telephone company *Sprint*). It appears in a recent French ad for *France Télécom Orange*, one of several cell phone service providers in France. The copy alludes to the upcoming Paris Marathon and a microchip that runners can attach to their

shoelaces, allowing friends and family to watch their progress by peri-
odically receiving text messages:[25]

(Headline): *Pendant le Marathon de Paris envoyez des SMS avec les
pieds.*

(Copy): *A l'occasion du Marathon de Paris, vos proches pourront suivre vos
performances sur leur mobile. Grâce à la puce de chronométrage fixée sur
votre chaussure. Orange vous permettra de signaler par SMS, à trois person-
nes de votre choix, vos temps de passage aux 10e, 21e et 30e km ainsi
qu'à l'arrivée. Renseignez-vous sur www.orange.fr, www.parismarathon.
com et à Marathon expo (du 4 au 6 avril).* (Signature line): *Le futur, vous
l'aimez comment?*

English translation (mine)

(*Headline*) Send text messages with your feet during the Paris
Marathon

(*Copy*) During the Paris Marathon, your loved ones will be able to
follow your progress on their cell phones thanks to a motion-
detecting microchip attached to your shoe. With Orange, you can
automatically send text messages to three people of your choosing
as you reach the 10th kilometer marker, 21st kilometer marker, 30th
kilometer marker, and the finish line. More information is available
online at www.orange.fr, www.parismarathon.com or at the Marathon Exhibit (from April 4 to 6).

(*Signature line*) How do you envision your future?

Television programming exported to France from other countries is
making its way into French advertising campaigns as well. The absence
of this direct representation of television shows imported from abroad
in a similar corpus of French advertising collected in 1996 (Martin,
1998a) suggests that this use of popular TV shows as a form of global
media discourse in advertising aimed at French consumers is a new
strategy. The popular quiz show *Who wants to be a millionnaire?*, for
instance, was recently used in another France Télécom magazine advertisement.[26] Closely imitating the television program, the advertising
copy is presented in the form of a multiple-choice question, with the
quiz show title in French (*Qui Veut Gagner des Millions*) figuring prominently at the top of the page, alongside the France Télécom logo. The
correct answer to the question is highlighted using the color orange
to enhance audience recall of the product name (translation mine):

Where would you be more likely to win 10,000 euros every week?	
A: At the pin-ball machine in a bar on the beach?	B: At the greyhound races
C: On your Orange cell phone	D: In a boxing ring

Anyone reading the ad is invited to participate in a competition similar to that featured on the television program whereby they must use their cell phones to text message answers to seven questions of increasing difficulty to France Télécom in order to win a monetary prize. As in the Paris Marathon version described earlier, this ad also uses the English borrowing 'SMS' in the descriptive copy instead of its French equivalent ('texto'), along with several other anglicisms (*flipper, ring,* and so on.).[27]

Global imagery is also very frequently used in French advertising for computer products and services, emphasizing, for example, the possibility of instant communication in real time from any geographical location. With its famous slogan *Solutions for a small planet,* IBM was one of the first companies to feature global interconnectivity via Internet technology as the major theme in an advertising campaign. Conversations in real time typed in a chatroom by people on various continents (a staple in today's advertising landscape) were already appearing in IBM television commercials airing in France as early as the mid-1990s.[28] Microsoft, on the other hand, recently ran a two-page magazine advertising campaign in France (Martin, 2005) that featured night scenes of Paris (*Arc de Triomphe* and *Champs Elysées*) on one page and Tokyo (neon-lit downtown skyscrapers in the Geiza shopping district) on the other. The headline underscores the importance of both productivity and maintaining constant and instant communication with employees, business partners and clients in various locations around the world. This message is reinforced by essentially erasing the 12 to 13-hour time zone difference between Europe and Asia through an optical illusion and a simple phrase, *1 seconde entre soleil couchant et soleil levant* (one second between sunset and sunrise), thereby 'anchoring' (Barthes, 1977) a preferred reading of these paired images. Both the visual and the slogan also allude to the representation of Japan as the 'land of the rising sun', implying that (with software developed by Microsoft) those working in offices in Tokyo can continue working on a project when their associates in Paris log off for the evening (and vice versa). The image, slogan, and photo caption in combination direct the audience towards the follow-

ing desired interpretation: Microsoft can keep your company operating at full capacity 24/7. Thus, the literal message (that the sun is rising in Tokyo as it sets in Paris) denoted by the illustration and headline also offers at least one additional (symbolic) interpretation: In the business world, time is money. The images presented in this advertisement might also encourage yet another 'reading', namely that in these bustling nerve centers of the global business network (Paris and Tokyo), a company executive's work day often extends well into the evening (making efficiency even more of a priority). The traffic and nighttime illuminations in the visual reinforce this association while underscoring the notion that in today's global market 'time is of the essence'.

Multiracial casting

Although the ease of communication and global connectivity made possible by newer technologies can certainly be felt in French advertising across media, as these examples illustrate, the 'global consumer' concept is further reinforced in France through various types of carefully selected imagery. Consider, for example, the 'global village' paradigm which appears to be very popular in French advertising for certain product categories, such as, clothing, furniture, beauty products, and so forth. One of the most obvious manifestations of this has been multiracial casting. Indeed, the models used in French ads have moved far beyond the basic Western Caucasian or European variety and now include individuals of every imaginable race and ethnicity. A rather frequently used image in French advertising seems to be that of children of different races either working together to solve a problem or in playful interaction. A pharmaceutical company (Aventis), for instance, recently ran an ad in France featuring a young girl (Caucasian) and two boys (one Black, the other Asian) examining an object (not shown in the visual) with extreme curiosity. This theme of 'research and discovery' permeates the copy as well, describing how Aventis uses scientific findings to develop new medicines, vaccinations and other ways of treating disease. The signature line reflects a similar philosophy: *Notre challenge c'est la vie* (Life is our challenge). Another French ad, this one for the Volkswagen Sharan minivan (Figure 2.1), features six children of different races (two Caucasian, two Black, one Asian and one who appears to be North African) bouncing the planet Earth in the form of an inflated toy above their heads. The racial mix and Earth imagery used in this advertisement form a very positive image for French consumers, insinuating not only the brand's global presence but also a progressive, all-inclusive attitude towards every member of society

Figure 2.1 Volkswagen advertisement

regardless of their ethnic background. With its focus on children, this image is also very likely to appeal to parents with large families, the consumer group most interested in a product of this nature. The copy in this case reads:

> *Sachant que pour l'achat d'un Sharan TDI 115, Volkswagen vous offre 70 000 km de carburant, combien de fois pourrez-vous faire le tour de la terre?*

English translation (mine)

> If every time you buy a Sharan TDI 115 Volkswagen throws in 70,000 km of gas free of charge, how many times could you make it around the Earth?

Ads for Epson printers use a similar visual strategy. A recent campaign shows precisely what an Epson printer can produce for the ordinary user thanks to its *Print Image Matching* technology: a professional quality photograph depicting five children (again, of different races) playing on a sandy beach. Another ad, this one for Petit Bateau children's clothing, shows children of different ethnicity playing together in a city park. Clearly, the multiracial imagery increasingly found in advertising today reflects a 'global village' philosophy where people are seen as being much more racially mixed and internationally mobile than ever before.[29]

Obviously, one of the motivations behind multiracial casting is a desire to reach consumers of every race and ethnicity represented in the targeted population. Certain ethnic groups, however, are clearly under-represented in French advertising, such as North Africans, although indirect references to these cultures occasionally surface in campaigns directed towards younger audiences.[30] A print ad for Ray-Ban sunglasses, for instance, features three male college students playing American football on a beach (two of whom are wearing the product). Although the ad has a distinctively American feel, which is further reinforced by the English-language copy and 'Spring Break in Florida' atmosphere, the one model wearing the product in the illustration sports a highly visible multilingual tattoo (containing an Arabic expression meaning 'wisdom') on his upper arm. This single visual element operates as an attention-getter, is considered 'cool' in contemporary youth culture, and gives the campaign a more international and multiethnic flavor. The slogan appearing in English, however, remains totally narcissistic: My Ray-Ban and me* (subtitled as *Ma Ray-Ban et moi*). Arab faces, particularly those

of adults, on the other hand, are practically non-existent in advertising in France. Pan-Asian models, however, are becoming increasingly popular, even though Asians are far less visible than Arabs in the general population. The Asian model chosen to market a French cosmetic (Clarins *Paris Le Rouge* lipstick), for instance, exudes a certain exotic beauty and elegance, qualities that appeal to the average French consumer. Maps of various regions have also been recently featured in several campaigns in France as a means of placing the product in a global context. A little girl stepping across a world map, for instance, appears in an ad for a French bank (CCF), thus highlighting their worldwide customer service known as HSBC Premier, which is outlined in the copy:

Avec HSBC Premier, où que vous alliez dans le monde, vous n'êtes jamais très loin de votre agence.

English translation (mine)

With HSBC Premier, wherever you may end up in the world, your bank will never be too far away.

Mood imagery, illusion, and 'the best of both worlds'

Another way in which advertisers appeal to French consumers is to create a particular 'mood' in the campaign by making visual and/or verbal reference to distant locations considered 'exotic' by Europeans, such as India, China, Indonesia, and so on. This is particularly notice-able in advertising for home furnishing and decorative items. A French furniture ad for La Maison Coloniale, for example, mentions China and Tibet in the copy and has a distinctive Asian feel.[31] In another ad, table linens by Jose Houel are advertised to the French market using the Taj Mahal in the background visual, presumably as a sign of refined ele-gance. One of the most classic examples of this type of 'mood imagery' used to entice French consumers, however, can be found in French advertising for Roche Bobois furniture. A recent Roche Bobois campaign distributed in France features different *décors*, each of which reflects a certain lifestyle or culture. Included in this series of ads is a Japanese style living room, complete with lacquered bowls, floor-level seating, a rock garden, and bamboo trees, accompanied by a very 'zen' English-language slogan: 'Peaceful Time'.[32] It is interesting to note incidentally that Roche Bobois ads for the American market tend to rely heavily on French cultural references and French-language slogans as this 'look' is considered chic among American interior designers. Indeed, beauty is in the eye of the beholder.

No one will deny the fact that advertising is, in fact, a carefully crafted form of illusion. A French ad for Robusta adjustable beds, for example, highlights the Swiss brand's identity with a Swiss flag inspired logo and mention of Swiss craftmanship (*Garantie Qualité suisse*) but quite ironically features a popular mountain hiking destination in the United States, the Maroon Bells-Snowmass wilderness near Aspen, Colorado, in the visual. This choice of imagery is all the more astonishing when one considers the variety of similar landscapes found in Switzerland, the country in which the product originated. Clearly, stock images such as these, which are often used when shooting a film on location is not feasible for budgetary reasons, are included in advertising purely for their socio-psychological appeal, associating positive concepts (beauty, reliability, modernity, elegance, simplicity, and so on) with the product being advertised, and do not necessarily reflect reality.[33] They also, as in this case, are inserted to reinforce the brand identity (assuming the readers of this ad mistakenly believe that the scenery in the illustration is from Switzerland).

Advertising agencies will also sometimes shoot a commercial in a foreign location. In such cases, careful attention is paid to the overall 'look and feel' of the background environment. In search of fair weather locations that will appeal more to their intended audiences, Canadian ad agencies, for instance, will sometimes shoot their commercials in warmer climates during the winter months. Whereas Florida has been the most convenient location in previous years, Canadian product teams are now filming in places such as Uruguay, Mexico, Prague, and Budapest (Pinard, 2004). Argentina, used recently in a Canadian commercial for Danone's Silhouette yoghurt, is another popular location. According to Stéphane Raymond from La Fabrique d'images, who produces television commercials for audiences in Quebec (Pinard, 2004: 37):

Ce pays est particulièrement apprécié du fait qu'en plus d'être abordable, ses étés (qui ont lieu durant nos hivers), comparativement aux tropiques, ressemblent davantage à ceux du Québec ... C'est plus facile alors de donner l'impression qu'une pub a été tournée chez nous.

Engilsh translation (mine)

Argentina is particularly popular. Not only is it affordable but also the summers (which coincide with our winters) resemble summers in Quebec, contrary to those in the tropics ... Thus, it's easier to give the impression that the commercial was filmed here at home.

Thus, in certain cases, the use of global imagery may in fact be motivated by a desire to create an atmosphere that appears to be 'local', especially if one is constrained by local weather conditions and other factors (including production costs).

Occasionally, a creative team will also insert global imagery from several different countries as a way of presenting the product or service as combining 'the best of both worlds'. Lapeyre, for instance, uses this strategy in their home improvement ads, advertising the fact that the products they sell (doors, windows, shutters, and so on) are made with materials imported from Sweden, Finland, Poland, Brazil, Indonesia, and Malaysia. This intercultural (and sometimes rather odd) 'collage' of imagery is also evident in a recent French ad for Teisseire Cuisines & Bains which features an American style kitchen (*Cuisine Californie*), inhabited by a woman with an Anglosaxon name (Linda), who is apparently living in Japan (as indicated by the Kyoto-inspired scenery outside her kitchen window). Another multicultural reference is the time of day displayed in the copy (3.10pm). This example of 'paralinguistic code-mixing' includes elements from both French (period punctuation between the hour and minutes as seen, for instance, on train schedules) and English (*pm* to denote afternoon and evening). One also notices, however, careful highlighting of the French origins of the brand, as in the mention 'made in France' (*fabrication française*) visibly displayed in the copy. Whereas the cultural images chosen for this particular ad reflect the French appreciation for large (and well-designed) kitchens they have encountered in America, as well as Japanese elegance and simplicity, one is reminded of the importance of taking into account local cultures and sensibilities when addressing local consumers. Here the underlying message is clearly that the French are capable of producing the same quality workmanship found in American cabinetry and that this company brings the best the world has to offer (efficiency, modern design, simple elegance, and so on) to your home.

The 'best of both worlds' theme is also evident in a recent print campaign for Kellogg's Special K cereal distributed in France. Magazine ads for the brand offer personal trainers from Brazil (Paolo), Australia (Jim) and Sweden (Karl) (depicted in the visual), who will 'encourage' readers by emailing them 'advice, exercises, and customized menus'. Positioning the brand as a weight loss solution, this ad, which appeared in *Modes & Travaux*, a women's magazine in France, targets female consumers who will likely find the idea of external motivation coming from gorgeous, muscular men with sexy accents quite appealing. Having the possibility of a personalized service provided via the Internet further

intensifies the sense of being 'pampered' while addressing women as intelligent, technologically-savvy consumers.

The most entertaining 'global mix' of imagery in the data, however, can be found in a television spot for VISA, which is known in France as Carte Bleue Visa (Martin 2005). The commercial opens with a man and a woman (both nomads) seated in the sand outside their tent in a remote desert location watching the sun set. In their local language (subtitled in French), the man asks his companion how she would like to spend the evening. She replies 'How about a movie?', to which he responds quite nonchalantly 'Sure, why not?' Each then puts on a pair of glasses which double as portable computer screens, with controls located on the sides of the glasses. After the ultra modern eyewear quickly scans their eyes to verify their identity, they click on the controls (marked in Arabic) to select a movie (electronic payment by visa, of course). The movie they select (*Singing in the Rain*) only adds to the commercial's irony and humor: the futuristic combined with a simple nomadic existence far from civilization, singing about rainfall in a desert climate, 'ordering up' Hollywood in Arabic, and so on. The commercial ends with the couple happily watching the film, singing along with the screen character in their heavily accented English as they sway to the music: *Singing in the rain, just singing in the rain. What a glorious feeling, I'm happy again!*

Global references in French print advertising also include the mention of cities located around the planet (typically listed at the bottom of the ad) that appeal to the rich and well-traveled: Paris, London, New York, Tokyo, and so on. Each is carefully chosen to reflect prestige, status, and wealth. Typically, advertisements that fall into this category are for fashion designer clothing and expensive jewelry, both of which appeal to the French elite. To lend additional status to the product and brand name, and to avoid translation costs for different markets, the cities are sometimes listed in English rather than French, as was the case in a recent Ralph Lauren Polo ad, which indicated Paris, London, Brussels, New York, Beverly Hills, Hong Kong, and Tokyo as places where Ralph Lauren fashions are sold.[34]

Cultural identity, stereotypes, and foreign languages

In order to emphasize concepts such as regional identity, authenticity and tradition, however, advertising campaigns more typically feature cultural images that the French commonly associate with the country or region where the product was created. Examples from the present corpus mostly include advertisements for food items, such as Carapelli

Firenze (olive oil), San Pellegrino (sparkling mineral water), and Barilla Passioni Italiane (cookies). All of these ads feature scenes from the Italian countryside, and Italian-sounding product names, making them all the more appealing. The same technique, of course, applies to other brands being advertised around the world. A classic example is the French mineral water brand Evian, which has been using images from the French Alps in its global campaigns for years (Mueller, 1996: 32).

Other images, relayed either verbally or visually and imported from around the world, are highly stereotypical in nature and are clearly inserted for their entertainment value. Those who designed the French ads for Tetley herbal teas, Figure 2.2, for example, were very clever in choosing the slogan: *Enfin un produit anglais qui vous veut du bien* ('Finally an English product that does you good') (Martin, 2005). While it may seem counter-intuitive for a company in the UK to evoke French stereotypes regarding England when advertising its own products, this was a brilliant advertising strategy for the French market, where such a slogan is very likely to produce a smile given French attitudes towards *haute cuisine*.[35] This form of 'self-stereotyping' is also evident in recent ads for Foster's beer, which exploit whimsical images associated with Australia, such as kangaroos and crocodiles. One of their more indelible illustrations seen in recent French poster and magazine ads is that of a

Figure 2.2   Tetley advertisement

baby kangaroo resting comfortably in its mother's pouch, which ironically happens to be the label on an ice-cold bottle of Foster's – Australia's Famous Beer. Ballantine's Scotch Whisky adopts a similar approach in a recent campaign distributed in France, with the infamous Loch Ness monster identifying the brand as Scottish. In this advertisement (Figure 2.3), we see the creature's body looping in and out of the water with one of the 'loops' appearing in an angular fashion, as opposed to the curves one would normally associate with a snake in motion. The slogan reads: *Obstinément différent* ('Stubbornly different'). Another Scottish brand, Glenfiddich Single Malt Scotch Whisky, uses Scotland's capital city, Edinburgh (notoriously shrouded in fog) as the visual theme of their print campaign in France. Bavaria 8.6, a beer brewed in Holland, on the other hand, is advertised in France using Dutch windmills in the background visual. As they are typically associated with the country being depicted in the ad, 'tourist snapshot images' such as these are likely to reinforce the brand's origins in the French consumer's imagination.[36]

The same stereotypical imagery can also be found in French television commercials. A recent spot promoting the Eurotunnel, which is sponsored by the British Tourist Authority, features a series of mirror images from both the British and French countryside to imitate the change of scenery, language and culture one experiences when crossing the English Channel. The commercial opens with three French individuals crossing the cow-dotted landscape of Normandy in their convertible. Before reaching the tunnel that will lead them under the English Channel into the UK, they pass a bed and breakfast sign displaying a rooster and the name '*Cocorico!*', both of which are commonly recognized as symbolizing French pride. In their popular book on French culture, Gilles Asselin and Ruth Mastron (2001: 11) explain this French icon in some detail:

> The rooster is to the French what the bald eagle is to Americans. Yet a rooster does not fly high in the sky, and it does not soar to reach high peaks and discover new horizons. Rather, a rooster wakes up the entire village at dawn, attracts attention from others, and never retreats from his defiant and domineering attitude toward the rest of the coop. Nowadays, French influence is certainly not as far-reaching as it used to be, and the world is much larger and more complex than a single coop. Still, some French roosters like to remind everyone that France has awakened the entire world to the beauty and grace of its civilization, culture, and language.

Figure 2.3   Ballantine's advertisement

Other images reminiscent of the French countryside included in this segment are a church steeple rising above the roof tops of a village, tree-lined country lanes, and a man riding his bicycle with a basket strapped to his back. After exiting the tunnel on the British side of the Channel, the same travelers are seen driving on the opposite side of the road, passing sheep (instead of cows), several bright red London-style phone booths, plus an Inn whose sign (also depicting a rooster) reads 'Cock-A-Doodle Doo!'. This cultural border crossing is further accentuated by the switching from French to English heard in the accompanying music soundtrack (*Downtown*, originally recorded by British singer Petula Clark) as the couple reach the mid-way point between France and England:[37]

J'ai beau cherché mais j'ai plus rien trouvé
J'ai beau cherché . . . mais j'ai cherché en vain, tu sais
Downtown . . .

(language switch)

Downtown – things will be great when you're
Downtown – no finer place, for sure
Downtown – everything's waiting for you.

The Eurotunnel logo (*UK OK*) and closing slogan featured in this commercial – *Great Britain, in its (very) original version* – further underscore the authenticity of the border-crossing experience. The combination of cultural icons, stereotypical imagery and French-English mixing make this advertisement particularly interesting from a sociolinguistic perspective, highlighting the way in which multimodal references can impart meaning.

Foreign languages may also be used as visual attention-getters in advertising, particularly when the language displayed is unlikely to be understood by the targeted consumer. Magazine ads for Bouygues Telecom used in France make liberal use of this technique, featuring 'exotic' languages written in various scripts. In one ad, the visual depicts a wooden signpost indicating twelve different destinations in Russian. The other features road signs on a highway near Beijing, presented in Chinese characters. The headline in both cases reads: *A l'étranger, votre portable aura moins de mal que vous à s'adapter* ('When you're traveling abroad, your cell phone will have an easier time adapting than you will'). The copy accompanying these images outlines Bouygues

Telecom's two-way international calling plan for 'over 150 countries or destinations'.

France Télécom, on the other hand, approached the 'calling from overseas' dilemma from a different angle, using an entirely different type of global imagery. Their magazine advertisements, for instance, featured pay phones in various countries which are notorious for frustrating foreign tourists who may lack change in the required currency, or who may find the dialing instructions and local language(s) confusing. France Télécom, of course, offers the perfect solution:

Où que vous soyez, téléphonez sans monnaie comme si vous étiez chez vous.

English translation (mine)

No money? No problem. With your France Télécom calling card, wherever you may be on the planet, it's just like calling from home.

Another observation to be made here, however, is that certain regions of the world are typically presented to French consumers as 'exotic', 'distant', or 'foreign', such as Asia. The slogan in the Bouygues Telecom campaign mentioned earlier seems to suggest that the average French tourist or business traveler for that matter would find such environments very unfamiliar and baffling, if not intimidating. Although other representations of Asia appear in the data, such as the attractive Asian model for Clarins mentioned earlier, and Nokia's use of sushi in their print campaign for cell phones, one does notice different visual and textual treatment for various parts of the world in advertisements targeting French consumers. Recent French television commercials for Menthos Cool breath mints featuring a Hindu walking over hot coals and the Amazon Indians contemplating their European visitor as their main course in a recent spot for Apéricubes cream cheese appetizers are prime examples.

Europe, on the other hand, particularly those countries that are closest to France, is typically portrayed as something more familiar. A recent ad for BMW (Figure 2.4) is an interesting case in point. Filling the page is a map of Europe, with France slightly left to center. In the upper left-hand corner the legend reads: *Plan de la Banlieue* (likely to be interpreted by the French as 'map of the Paris suburbs'). A motorcycle enters the page from the bottom left-hand corner accompanied by a text detailing the

82

Figure 2.4 BMW advertisement

product specifications. With the simple 'suburb' reference in the photo caption, and European cartography, this advertisement is insinuating that all areas depicted in the visual are within easy driving distance from Paris if one owns a BMW motorcycle. Unlike China and Russia depicted in the Bouygues Telecom campaign described earlier, the European countries seen in this ad are presented as neighbors and easily accessible. The introduction of the euro in 2002 and the growing membership of the European Union have further accentuated this feeling of solidarity.[38]

Visual references to the United States, on the other hand, fall into an entirely different category both in terms of their sheer ubiquitousness in French advertising across media and the motivations for inserting them into advertising campaigns for certain products and consumer groups. We will therefore devote the following chapter to an analysis of Americana in television, poster, and magazine advertising in France (for instance, American landscapes, cultures, lifestyles, symbols, celebrities, fictional television and movie characters, and so on).

The picture emerging from this juxtaposition of the globalization 'debate' with global images appearing in advertising copy is one of two universes representing opposing realities. Whereas French consumers are well aware of the proliferation of global brands and the anti-globalization movement (personified by individuals such as José Bové and fueled by anti-globalist activist groups), they are experiencing globalization on an entirely different level as consumers and audiences of print and broadcast media. Indeed, the advertisements featured in these pages position the French as 'global consumers', connected to the rest of the world's population through technology and shared tastes, with equal access to products sold internationally. They are also encouraged through these images and discourse to envision themselves as part of the 'global village' where equality reigns regardless of one's ethnicity or religious persuasion, and where children are the future of the planet. Within this 'global' universe, however, the French cultural identity remains very much intact, as evidenced by the use of cultural stereotypes and foreign languages to represent 'Otherness' in some of the advertisements included in this study.

As Barthes (1977) so clearly demonstrated in his own analyses of advertising, audiences are continually guided towards preferred readings of text and imagery. Through 'mythical inversion', services or objects of any nature may appear more accessible or desirable, whether it be the use of global imagery to reflect global business practices (Microsoft), depict a global village atmosphere (Benetton, Volkswagen, Aventis), the 'best of both worlds' (Kellogg's, VISA), or as a sign of exclusivity or

mood enhancer (Roche Bobois). The persuasiveness of this discourse is enhanced through an interaction of several modes of communication, including illustrations and slogans, each of which relies on the other to produce the desired interpretation on the part of consumers. In this regard, advertising is a world of illusion, seduction, and positive associations that continually play on the consumers' perceptions of language and society and their relation not only to objects, but also to the world on a global scale. Among these 'global' images one sees in French advertising, however, the ones that most frequently appear in advertising across media are American-inspired, a phenomenon that will be examined in detail in the following pages.

3
Seducing the French
with Americana

This chapter will examine the role that American imagery plays in advertising and globalization as manifested in France. To contextualize these images, we will begin this discussion with an overview of French perceptions of the US, moving from imported cultural traditions (such as Halloween) and Americans who are well known in France (including film makers, movie stars, and politicians) to America's reputation as a global superpower and the representation of America in the writings of French intellectuals (for example, Tocqueville, 1835; Baudrillard, 1986/1988). Also discussed here are various reactions to American television and film imports as images from these particular media are among those appearing in French advertising today. The remainder of the chapter is devoted to 'slices of Americana' found in billboard, magazine, and television advertising in France organized according to various categories (for example, landscapes, celebrities, lifestyles, fiction television and movie characters, symbols, and other representations of American culture). It will be demonstrated that, whereas some anti-American sentiment has been expressed over the years (in the writings of some French intellectuals, for instance), in the context of advertising, America symbolizes positive concepts such as freedom, modernism, technology, adventure, and glamour.

French perceptions of the US (and vice versa) reflect a 'love–hate relationship' (see, for instance, Kuisel, 1993; Mathy, 1993; Gordon and Meunier, 2002; Sardar and Davies, 2002; Revel, 2002). In certain contexts, especially advertising, these perceptions are quite positive. The same conclusion applies to English borrowings into French, as will be illustrated in the discussion on language-mixing and translation in Chapter 5. With regards to illustrations used in French advertising, a predilection for certain aspects of the 'American way of life', at least as

a source of entertainment, is undeniable. The images presented here provide a glimpse of the many American cultural references that ad makers utilize for the purposes of symbolism to evoke certain positive emotions and associations in the French consumer's imagination. Although cultural stereotypes are very often involved, this is not always the case. The role of American imagery in French advertising across media is much more subtle and complex than one might imagine. Before cataloguing these images according to their various sources of inspiration (Hollywood, tourism, and so on), however, an overview of French attitudes towards the United States is useful to better contextualize these images within the framework of advertising.

French perceptions of 'America'

American culture as experienced in France

The average French citizen is bombarded by American cultural images through not only advertising, but also television programs, movies, the press, and other local media. American traditions are also making their way to France and, just like so many other American cultural exports, they have been used as a marketing tool for addressing French consumers. Garnier (2000: 77), for instance, describes an advertising campaign for France Télécom featuring a Halloween-inspired pumpkin carved with the initials OLA, representing its latest line of cell phones. As part of its campaign in France, the telephone company placed 4000 of these sculpted works of art at the base of the Eiffel Tower, all of which were apparently snatched up by pedestrians. The OLA pumpkin was also prominently displayed in their poster advertising, highly visible throughout the Paris subway system at the time. As for North Americans who are popular in France, a 2004 article in the leftist magazine *Le Nouvel Observateur* (Boulet-Gercourt *et al.*, 2004: 12–33) is rather enlightening. Appearing in the article are several individuals known for 'bucking the establishment', including Michael Moore, Howard Dean, Ralph Nader, and Naomi Klein (whose book *No Logo* has fueled the anti-globalization debate, as mentioned in Chapter 2). Although they lack the 'star appeal' necessary for the advertising industry, their inclusion along with many others in the article is indicative of the respect the French have for those who dare to speak out against their government and other authorities to propose an alternative solution to the 'status quo'. Also featured are several movie stars whose appearances on the silver screen have won them a place in the hearts of French audiences and in their advertising. Just as Americans are

enamored by many aspects of French culture, not the least of which is their food, the French are also intrigued by the American way of life and worldview, whether or not they agree with it. The popularity of books aimed at business executives heading for overseas assignments, whether in the US (for instance, Lawrence, 1996; Engel and Peterson, 1997) or France (for instance, Carroll, 1988; Johnson, 1996; Barsoux and Lawrence, 1997; Platt, 1998; Asselin and Mastron, 2001) should therefore come as no surprise. Photography books and travel guides showcasing different regions of the US are by no means in short supply either.

As anyone who has browsed bookstores in France can attest, however, there are also scores of publications outlining the reasons why America has become so unpopular in recent years. Coming from both sides of the Atlantic, these writings (some of which are meticulously documented) point to a certain US cultural, political, and economic hegemony that many around the world find threatening. This perceived 'American cultural imperialism' is addressed at length in Sardar and Davies' (2002) book, whose title (*Why do People Hate America?*) is as provocative in English as its translated French version (*Pourquoi le monde déteste-t-il l'Amérique?*, éditions Fayard). Citing the Indian film industry (generally known as 'Bollywood') as one of the very few to have resisted the cultural influence of the US, for instance, these authors present developing nations as victims of a global US invasion claiming that the very cultural values and identities of these nations are, as a result, in serious danger of erosion (Sardar and Davies, 2002: 166–7). From Hollywood and hamburgers, to America's response to terrorism, their examples suggest that American consumerism, US cultural exports, and American foreign policy very much reflect America's own interests, ignoring the impact of the American way of life on the rest of the world. The US is often portrayed by those of similar opinions as a country turned in on itself with little awareness of the influence it has on less powerful countries across the globe.

One must also acknowledge, however, the sympathy expressed towards the United States and its citizens in the wake of the 9/11 terrorist attacks. Accompanying the famous headline appearing in *Le Monde* two days later that read '*Nous sommes tous des Américains*' ('We are all Americans') was an outpouring of solidarity and support towards Americans. Indeed, French attitudes towards the US defy categorization as they vary considerably depending on the time period, topic, and individual. Notes historian Richard Kuisel (1993: 7) in his discussion on anti-Americanism in France:

Most discourse about America is difficult to classify as either 'for' or 'against,' and extreme stances are extremely rare – though they exist. Affirmative and critical postures are not rigid categories and often overlap or merge into one another.

Nevertheless, certain stereotypes persist, some of which Kuisel clearly articulates in the following passage (*ibid.*: 9):

> French perceptions of America have been and continue to be highly patterned. There is a certain repetition associated with stereotypes even if the same images are evaluated in contradictory ways. America is a 'young' country. This may mean either that Americans are open, curious, and lively or else that Americans are immature and naïve. In general Americans are supposed to be youthful, dynamic, wealthy, pragmatic, optimistic, and friendly, but they are also seen as materialistic, puritanical, vulgar, and even racist and violent. They are *les grands enfants*.

The US is also seen as a nation of immigrants, many of whom are contributing to its global economic reach in a very meaningful way. The following comment regarding the IT (information technology) industry made by Alan Shipman (2002: 219) is revealing:

> Without a plentiful supply of foreign physicists and software engineers, America would have struggled to keep its new technology lead. Silicon Valley is reported to have become so multilingual that programming language is the only one that its inhabitants have in common.

But alas, the image projected by US president George W. Bush has done little to improve America's reputation abroad. The following quip from Shipman alluding to the president's oratorial skills, although humorous, unfortunately reflects the opinions of many English-speaking media audiences around the world (*ibid.*: 219):

> The presidency is probably the only skilled American job still always to be filled by a US citizen. But in 2000 even this post passed to a man who gave every appearance of speaking English as a second language.

The American president's knowledge of the world outside the US doesn't appear to have impressed members of the advertising industry in France

in any case, one of whom remarked during my 2002 advertising agency interviews:

> Bush in his recent trip here . . . came across as the Texas ranchman visiting Europe. He said [to French president Jacques Chirac], 'Jack, they tell me the food here is fantastic.'

In a country where *la haute cuisine* is not only a great source of pride and inspiration but also an element of French culture that has been enjoyed in countries across the globe, this comment on the part of 'GW' was a monumental *faux pas*, revealing an alarming ignorance of French culture and *savoir vivre*.

French intellectuals' visions of America

Anyone who is perplexed by this reaction on the part of the French will find valuable insight already in the early writings of French intellectuals who have shed copious amounts of ink discussing life in America. One of the references *par excellence* in this regard is Alexis de Tocqueville (1835) who detailed his perceptions of the New World in the early nineteenth century. His observations regarding America's morality, patriotism, consumerism, and overall self-obsession continue to reverberate in later writings of the French cultural elite (for example, Duhamel, 1931; Sartre, 1965; Camus, 1978). He also noted a certain pragmatism and a general lack of interest in the intellectual side of life in America, a national characteristic that is in sharp contrast to the French propensity for Cartesian logic and intellectual reasoning. In a more recent publication, social theorist Jean Baudrillard (1986/1988) presents the US as a land of 'hyperreality' where 'life is cinema' (*ibid.*: 101) and the American way of life is 'spontaneously fictional' (*ibid.*: 95). In describing American culture, he contrasts it with the European notion of 'high culture', a world that involves ministries (such as the French Ministry of Culture and Communication), government subsidies, and various promotional initiatives (such as *le Printemps des Poètes, la fête du cinéma,* and *la semaine de la langue française et de la francophonie*).[1] American culture for Baudrillard, unlike its European counterpart, should be seen rather as a collection of 'mores' and an overall 'way of life' (*ibid.*: 100):

> There is no culture here, no cultural discourse . . . One should speak rather of an 'anthropological' culture, which consists in the invention of mores and a way of life. That is the only interesting culture here, just as it is New York's streets and not its museums

or galleries that are interesting. Even in dance, cinema, the novel, fiction, and architecture, there is something wild in everything specifically American, something that has not known the glossy, high-flown rhetoric and theatricality of our bourgeois cultures, that has not been kitted out in the gaudy finery of cultural distinction.

One senses in Baudrillard's writing a certain fascination with American landscapes that have since become a staple of French advertising, including American cities whose 'sparkle and violence' (*ibid.*: 16) distinguish them from their Canadian neighbors just north of the border, and the desert Southwest, 'where the air is so pure that the influence of the stars descends direct from the constellations' (*ibid.*: 6). The wide-open vistas of the American continent so often used in French advertisements as a form of seduction also appear in Baudrillard's description of the US. In one of his passages on New York City (*ibid.*: 16), he contrasts this open, airy feeling with similar spaces typically found in Europe:

> In Paris, the sky never takes off. It doesn't soar above us. It remains caught up in the backdrop of sickly buildings, all living in each other's shade, as though it were a little piece of private property. It is not, as here in the great capital of New York, the vertiginous glass façade reflecting each building to the others. Europe has never been a continent. You can see that by its skies. As soon as you set foot in America, you feel the presence of an entire continent – space there is the very form of thought.

As for Monument Valley, Utah, so often depicted in French advertising for every product imaginable, his description sheds considerable light on the reason this type of imagery is so popular in France. It is, in fact, a landscape that encapsulates the surrealist rock formations and stark emptiness of the American west, the plight of Native Americans, which is an historical fact often mentioned by the French in their criticisms of American culture, and the awe-inspiring and entertaining background imagery of Hollywood westerns (*ibid.*: 70):

> Monument Valley is the geology of the earth, the mausoleum of the Indians, and the camera of John Ford. It is erosion and it is extermination, but it is also the tracking shot, the movies. All three are mingled in the vision we have of it.

Other French thinkers' perceptions of the US are outlined by Jean-Philippe Mathy (1993: 137) who notes:

Between World War II and Vietnam, the perception of American culture and society in French intellectual circles changed considerably. During the moment of euphoria following the liberation of France, a period marked by the political alliance of the various ideological streams (communists, socialists, Christian Democrats, Gaullists, and liberals) that had resisted fascism, the United States appeared as a nation of liberators who had made the key contribution to the victory over Nazi barbarity. The onset of the Cold War, on the other hand, rekindled the anti-Americanism of many in the French intelligentsia, regardless of their political persuasion. The United States had become, with no serious rival, the largest industrial nation (producing half the world's manufactured goods), the self-appointed 'leader of the free world', and the police officer of the planet.

Mathy describes the attitudes of French intellectuals during that time period as reflecting one of three basic points of view: (i) 'opposition to American civilization and foreign policy . . . and overall support of the Soviet Union'; (ii) a refusal to wholeheartedly support either of these 'superpowers'; or (iii) an acceptance of American protection and leadership as 'the only chance for weakened European countries to regain their rank among leading nations and to preserve freedom and humanism' (p. 138). Whether it be in the writings of Georges Duhamel (1931), Simone de Beauvoir (1952), Jean-Paul Sartre (1965), Jean-Marie Benoist (1976), Albert Camus (1978), or that of many other members of the French intellectual elite, a certain list of typically American characteristics continually resurfaces. These include references to everything from violence in American cities and an emphasis on wealth and material possessions, to American pragmatism and anti-intellectualism, a 'humanization of nature', and a general lack of authenticity. Many also point to America's economic imperialism and cultural hegemony. However, as Mathy readily admits, even the harshest critics of the US have always been seduced by the grandeur of American landscapes (Mathy, 1993: 163):

While America's industrial, urban civilization found few supporters among the French intelligentsia up to the 1960s, the unsoiled, unspoiled beauty of the land has always inflamed the French imagi-

nation, prompting a host of impassioned, lyrical celebrations of unlimited space and exhilirating vistas.

Reactions to American media

One would be remiss to not also mention authors who have countered some of the arguments made by French intellectuals mentioned above. Jean-François Revel (2002) notes, for instance, that although Disneyland Paris, which opened in 1992, has been dubbed by some intellectuals in France as a 'cultural Chernobyl', many of its themes and characters are European-inspired, including *Snow White and the Seven Dwarfs*, *Sleeping Beauty*, and *Pinocchio*. The musical score of the feature film *Fantasia* also features several European composers (*ibid.*, 2002: 202–203). As for American cinematic works in general, Revel is not convinced by the argument that Hollywood's financial resources and marketing wizardry are the sole reasons American movies so often become box office hits in France. In this regard, he notes (*ibid.*: 194):

> *On n'impose jamais par la contrainte ni même par la publicité une oeuvre littéraire ou artistique, encore moins une oeuvre de simple divertissement, à un public qu'elles ne séduisent pas.*

One can never impose, by force or even advertising, a literary or artistic work, and even less so a simple form of entertainment, on a public that doesn't like it. (translation mine)

A similar remark was made by Abrate (2004: 29):

> *Malgré toutes les discussions sur 'l'impérialisme culturel' et des remarques désobligeantes sur la qualité du cinéma américain, il faut se rendre à l'évidence et reconnaître que le public français apprécie ce cinéma.*

Despite all of the discussion on 'cultural imperialism' and disagreeable comments about the quality of American cinema, one has to face facts and recognize that the French public appreciates this cinema. (translation mine)

Regarding American movies, he writes (*ibid.*: 29):

> *ils sont en général très bien faits, ils abordent des thèmes qui plaisent à un public très vaste et ils sont conçus pour plaire au plus grand public.*

generally they are very well made, they use themes that appeal to wide-range of audiences, and they are designed to please the masses. (translation mine)

Still, the battle for screen space has been going on for almost 60 years, and shows no signs of abating. Notes Barber (1996: 92):

> With its 150 films a year, of which perhaps two dozen are exportable, France still has one of the world's great cinema cultures; indeed, it still controls nearly half of what appears on its screens, and still makes films that are both parochially French and globally distributed as well as universally acclaimed . . . But major studios are closing and for all the rancorous expletives no one knows how to stop the American tidal wave. A group of European directors wrote an open letter to 'Martin' (Scorsese) and 'Steve' (Spielberg) imploring them to recognize that the Europeans were 'only desperately trying to protect European cinema against its complete annihilation.'[2]

Denise Bombardier addresses this same issue from a somewhat different angle. From her French–Canadian perspective, she has noticed that despite their criticisms of the US, the French seem to have an insatiable appetite for American media imports. She implores her French counterparts to embrace their own cultural roots instead of blindly adopting the American model, imitating everything from the Oscar ceremonies to reality shows in their television programming in France. These French 'copies' are, in her opinion (a) no match for the original, and (b) an insult to French society where screenwriters and others involved in these American-inspired made-for-TV productions would create programs of a much higher quality if they used formats that were more in tune with the French culture and mentality (Bombardier, 2000: 21–3):

> *D'entrée de jeu, je le proclame, jamais j'aurais cru que votre pays marqué de tradition culturelle où les intellectuels et les écrivains ont joué le rôle que l'on sait, la dégradation de la télévision ait été si subite. La vulgarité, l'insignifiance, l'ineptie ont envahi les chaînes et, en ce sens, la télévision française n'a plus rien à envier à la télé américaine . . . N'essayez pas d'imiter les Américains car dans les émissions qu'ils créent, haut ou bas de gamme, ils sont imbattables. Regardez vos soirées des Césars, copie déprimante de leurs Oscars, regardez vos Victoires de la musique, shows indigents à côté de leurs Grammys. Trouvez donc des formules qui vous ressemblent, qui s'inscrivent dans vos traditions, votre esprit, votre esthétique. Un Français qui joue l'Américain décontracté provoque toujours un malaise chez moi tellement il m'apparaît faux.*

English translation (mine)

Let me proclaim, right off the bat, that I never would have imagined, in a country so marked by cultural tradition, where intellectuals and writers have played an enormously important role, such a sudden degradation of television offerings. Vulgarity, triviality, and ineptitude have invaded your television channels so much so that French television looks just like American television . . . Don't try to imitate the Americans because the quality of the programs they produce, whether grandiose or simple, will be far superior. Your *Césars* and *Musical Victories*, for instance, pale in comparison with their American counterparts, the *Oscars* and *Grammys*. Instead, find formats which suit you much better, reflect your traditions, your spirit, your sense of aesthetics. A Frenchman who poses as a casual American always stirs up in me a feeling of uneasiness, he looks so fake.

Notes French film maker Daniel Toscan du Plantier (1995: 46–7), on the other hand:

> *le cinéma français est le seul qui ait réellement survécu au cinéma américain; c'est une réussite extraordinaire par la variété des talents, la diversité des genres, l'intelligence du système qui le fait vivre, l'audace, l'énergie.*

English translation (mine)

French cinema is the only one to have really stood up to American cinema; it's an extraordinary success given the variety of talents, the diversity of genres, and the intelligence behind the system which keeps it alive through its audacity and energy.

He does, however, feel a certain admiration for American film makers who produce films with a more artistic or intellectual bent, such as Woody Allen and Robert Altman, whom he places in a category of their own, which he calls *l'Amérique minoritaire* (*ibid.*: 110). He also bestows this honor on Steven Spielberg for having produced *Schindler's List*, '*le plus beau cri de dénonciation antihollywoodienne qu'on puisse imaginer*' ('the most beautiful denunciation against Hollywood that one could possibly imagine') (*ibid.*: 98). As for his own movies, Toscan du Plantier finds his inspiration in the works of colleagues from countries all around the world, including Ingmar Bergman, Federico Fellini, Werner Herzog, Akira Kurosawa, Satyajit Ray, Roberto Rossellini, Carlos Saura, and Andredi Tarkovski (*ibid.*: 103). This embracing of *la diversité culturelle* for the sake of art, he beautifully sums up in the following sentence (*ibid.*: 103):

Ce qui fait l'art, c'est l'universalité des émotions, ce n'est pas la couleur du passeport.

English translation (mine)

The beauty of art is the universality of emotion. It has nothing to do with the color of your passport.

Scott Olsen (1999) attributes the global popularity of American television programs and movies to their ability to transcend cultural barriers, providing multiple meanings to multiple audiences worldwide. These 'transparent texts' are, according to this view, interpreted differently depending on the cultural and social values of the viewing public and thus produce strikingly different readings in different contexts. As Olsen (1999: 34) notes: 'The process of decoding a media text, as in decoding any message, has a cultural bias.' This is not to say that Americans are the only ones generating media with international appeal (*ibid.*: 37):

> Brazil, Mexico, and Peru all successfully produce and export soap operas, many of them to the Spanish-language market in the United States. India and Hong Kong are successful exporters of motion pictures, and of course, Great Britain and France still produce international box-office hits. Nevertheless, few transnational media exports match the American ones for versatility, ubiquity, and sustainability.

The real advantage of American television productions, however, is price. American producers can undercut any Western European production agency, particularly if GATT rules subsidies illegal.

Nevertheless, the French remain infatuated with certain aspects of American culture (such as Hollywood movies and the American Southwest) despite criticisms expressed by certain members of the French intelligensia, disagreement with American foreign policy, and debates surrounding the 'American cultural invasion'. As the examples presented throughout the remainder of this chapter illustrate, this infatuation with the 'Far West' and other landscapes, American media and other elements of American life are reflected in advertising directed at French audiences.

'Slices of Americana' in French advertising

In addition to the visual elements drawn from various parts of the world examined in Chapter 2, American-inspired imagery is extensively

used in French advertising.[3] These 'slices of Americana' typically fall into one of several categories: (i) locations in the US that carry particular (positive or negative) associations for the French (certain cities and landscapes, for instance); (ii) American celebrities (for example, movie stars, recording artists, athletes, fashion models); (iii) American cultures, faces, and lifestyles (Native Americans in traditional dress, cowboys, corporate executives, farmers, small town shopkeepers, scenes from football and basketball games, cheerleaders, and so on); (iv) American symbols (such as 'Uncle Sam' or the 'stars and stripes') and various other elements of American culture (including popular food items, use of miles and inches as opposed to the metric system, US-based organizations, the American space program, and so forth); (v) fictional television and movie characters (such as Batman, Superman, Bugs Bunny); and (vi) excerpts or 'spoofs' related to the entertainment industry (for example, syndicated television programs, Hollywood movies, Hollywood musical comedies).

American landscapes

As with every other aspect of advertising (which can be a very expensive proposition), the selection of illustrations for a print campaign and/or location for shooting a television commercial is, of course, a very careful one. Well-known advertising executive and author David Ogilvy (1985) offers an insider's view of the industry. With his typical tongue-in-cheek delivery, he refers to European advertising designed to draw tourists to the US:

> When we started advertising the United States in Europe, we used research to find out what the Europeans would most like to see. The answer was Manhattan, Grand Canyon, San Francisco, Niagara Falls and cowboys. So these were the attractions we featured in the advertisements – until the US Travel Service instructed us to feature scenes of South Dakota. One of the Senators from that State was on the Senate Committee which voted the advertising budget. (Ogilvy, 1985: 127)

This referencing of the United States is not limited to products and services originating in the US. Indeed, brands from all over the planet are being marketed through American-inspired images such as these, including French products sold in France. A recent print advertisement for French automaker Renault's Kangoo, for instance, uses the caricature of a Native American wearing a deer skin, moccasins, and feather

headdress in a landscape closely resembling Monument Valley. Several cacti are included to further identify the scenery as belonging to the American 'Far West'.[4] Every item in the visual, including the product, is constructed of brightly colored modeling clay, adding to the advertisement's originality and appeal. The two product features mentioned in the copy, the Kangoo's quiet motor and excellent mileage per gallon, are underscored by the vast open spaces depicted in the illustration and the rather compromising position of the Native American who finds himself completely flattened against the pavement having failed to detect the arrival of the Kangoo automobile. His kneeling position, with one ear placed on the ground (another stereotype), suggests that he had been listening for possible intruders when the automobile ran him over. In the copy, this turn of events is described as 'most fortunate' for (French) tourists traveling in such wild and remote areas of the American West as 'Cheyenne Indians are supposedly very easily offended'.[5]

In a print advertisement for Umarex rifles appearing in a French magazine for hunting enthusiasts (*Le Chasseur Français*), we find a similar 'Far West' theme. In this case, scenes closely resembling those found in Arches National Park in Utah form the backdrop for a horse-drawn wagon led by rugged-looking men in cowboy hats. To remain consistent with the 'American pioneer' atmosphere in the illustration, the copy refers to this style of 'speed-loading' rifle as an 'American legend'. Also appearing in the copy is the English phrase, 'made in Germany'. This particular expression was first adopted by the British in the late nineteenth century when they began to indicate the country origin of a brand on labels as a way of distinguishing quality products from lower-quality imitations. During World War I, on the other hand, the labels 'made in Germany' and 'made in Austria/Hungary' were required on all products made in these 'enemy' countries so that the British could boycott them if they so desired.[6] More recently, 'made in Germany' has come to symbolize quality engineering and technology in advertising distributed around the world (for example, Haarmann, 1984; Piller, 2001; Kelly-Holmes, 2000):

Ce modèle unit de manière idéale la technologie de pointe 'made in Germany' à la ligne classique d'une légende américaine.

English translation (mine)

This model flawlessly combines the latest German technology with the classic style of an American legend.

A desert park in California known as Joshua Tree National Monument appears to be the inspiration for a print campaign for New Balance Running Shoes for men (identified as '*New Balance Chaussure de Running Homme*' in the copy). American desert landscapes also appear in ads for the fast-food chain McDonald's, Marlboro cigarettes, the Jeep Grand Cherokee automobile (whose product name 'Grand Cherokee' also reinforces the American origins of the brand), the Mitsubishi Montero car, Algeco warehouse storage, AirPlus business travel, and the film Crossroads on DVD. These types of images are extremely appealing to French audiences who associate them with Hollywood westerns and positive concepts such as adventure, freedom, and independence (Baudrillard, 1986/1988). American songwriter and balladeer John Denver, whose music so often spoke of the American wilderness, described this common emotional response quite eloquently:[7]

> There's nothing in the world like the American West: the wide open spaces, these mountains, the desert, the incredible beauty of the landscape everywhere you look. In all the places that I've traveled, everywhere that I've been, there's something about the American West that personifies personal freedom, adventure, a frontier, the opportunity to make our own world, to make it what we dream it can be.

The copy of a Jeep Grand Cherokee automobile advertisement captures the spirit of these 'wide open spaces' quite well while highlighting the 'off-road' versatility of the automobile:

> *l'aventure commence là où les autres s'arrêtent . . . Plus d'autoroute, plus de route, juste un paysage sans limite.*

English translation (mine)

> Where others stop, the adventure begins . . . No more highway, no more road, just an endless horizon.

It is also important to note that landscapes used in French advertising are often filmed or photographed in such a way as to be unmistakably American but unidentifiable in terms of precise location (for instance, corner grocery store in a small southern town, rock formations indicative of the American desert Southwest, urban landscapes with skyscrapers and American-style police cars and sirens, and so on). Such images can serve several purposes, such as create a particular mood for the campaign, inform the consumer about the product (a jeep's durability

in tough terrain, for instance), reinforce the brand image (particularly if the brand is normally associated with the United States) and so forth.

Additional landscapes that frequently appear in French advertising include popular tourist destinations in other parts of the US. The recently inaugurated Walt Disney Concert Hall in Los Angeles, which is 'home to the LA Philharmonic' as the copy carefully informs us, is featured in an advertisement for the French steel industry, presumably as an example of what can be accomplished with this type of construction material. Los Angeles is also proposed visually and verbally as a possible destination in an advertisement for Air Tahiti Nui. Other products evoke certain locations in the US as a means of reinforcing their brand identity. Advertising for Florida orange juice distributed in France, for instance, makes liberal use of orange tree groves in its illustrations and repeatedly mentions the state of Florida.

The American city that appears most often in French advertising, however, is New York. As the observations made by Jean Baudrillard (1986/1988) and others suggest, the magic and significance of this location for the French is not to be underestimated. In a very elegant poster advertisement for Nicolas Feuillatte champagne (Figure 3.1), for instance, we find a reference to New York City that is quite striking. Directly beneath the brand name at the top of the poster are listed, in bold lettering, three geographical locations: Epernay • New York • *ailleurs* (*ailleurs* meaning 'elsewhere'). The illustration denotes a mountain lion intently watching the arrival of the cork from a bottle of Nicolas Feuillatte champagne which is flying through the air in her direction. The simple elegance of this copy is eye-catching enough, but close inspection reveals several layers of meaning. From the text, we gather that the champagne, produced in the relatively small French town of Epernay, is making its mark in the world by first targeting New York City. The arrival of the French product on American soil is connoted by the champagne cork dropping from the sky like a space capsule returning from orbit. One can predict from its trajectory and speed (subtly represented by the speed lines indicating a wake behind the 'tail' of the cork) that it will very shortly hit the animal (who seems to anticipate its landing) right between the eyes. Given the New York City reference in the headline, it is quite possible that the cougar as it is used here is symbolizing the United States where wild animals of this nature still freely roam the backcountry in certain regions. This particular campaign features many different wild animals (www.feuillatte.com), but the referencing of New York City in the poster advertisement suggests that the cougar was

100

Figure 3.1   Nicolas Feuillatte advertisement

selected with the US in mind. It is also an image that is extremely well chosen for its beauty and elegance, making it (and other wild felines) a popular element in advertisements for luxury products such as this.[8] Following the textual reference to New York and the visual reference to North America, however, we encounter one additional reference to location: *ailleurs* ('elsewhere'). A possible reading of this juxtaposition of places (Epernay • New York • Elsewhere) is that the champagne has won international acclaim due to its popularity in the 'Big Apple', the location from where its global reputation of excellence was launched (or 'uncorked' as it were). The expression *partout ailleurs* ('everywhere else') would have accentuated this symbolism more strongly but would have destroyed the symmetry of the slogan (one word • two words • one word). The bar serving Nicolas Feuillatte champagne mentioned in fine print vertically along the right-hand edge of the poster contributes to the American 'look and feel' of the advertisement:

Le Champagne Nicolas Feuillatte est servi au bar du LIVING ROOM, 671 Washington Avenue • Miami • Florida • USA

English translation (mine)
Nicolas Feuillatte Champagne is served at the LIVING ROOM bar, 671 Washington Avenue • Miami • Florida • USA

As all of the locations mentioned in this address are immediately recognizable to the French (including the name of the bar which is a highly assimilated English borrowing into French, its street address, and the city of Miami), this string of text is by no means coincidental and adds significantly to the advertisement's American-inspired 'dream-like' appeal.

In another French advertisement, for DKNY, this one appearing in a magazine, New York City is referenced in an entirely different manner. Highlighting the brand (Donna Koran International) with its company headquarters located in New York City, the advertisement consists entirely of a photograph of a street scene in the city, immediately recognizable by the Empire State Building in the background. Other American elements in the illustration include the American flag and road signage (marked 'one way', and, in very fine print 'DEPT OF TRANSPORTATION'). The product being advertised, a watch, is displayed as an integral part of the city, where flashing pedestrian walk signs read 'DKNY Time' and a skyscraper in the foreground is 'wearing' a gigantic DKNY watch. Graffiti appearing in the ad (in the form of a sticker on the sign post)

also bears the DKNY logo. By presenting the product in this context, the advertisement clearly identifies the American origins of the brand.

American celebrities

A second category of American images commonly found in French advertising consists of celebrities of different sorts: actors, athletes, recording artists, and so on. The export of American television programs, Hollywood movies, music recordings on CD, video and DVD, and televised international sports competitions have brought the faces of American celebrities into every French household. Media such as radio, television, and cinema have made these individuals easily recognizable symbols of success and entertainment. Depending on their livelihood, and the contexts in which they are seen (music videos, movies, sports broadcasts, and so forth), they are often associated with such concepts as achievement, glamour, adventure, and the lifestyles of the rich and famous.[9] Although advertising research has shown that audiences are more likely to recall the celebrity in an advertisement than the brand (Ogilvy, 1985: 83), American celebrities continue to be a popular strategy in international advertising (Kilbourne, 1999: 59–61).

Of all the famous Americans appearing in French advertising across media, the faces of Hollywood movie stars greatly outnumber those of other types of celebrities. A poster advertisement for the French cable company NOOS displayed in the Paris subway, for instance, features Julia Roberts and Susan Sarandon starring in the Hollywood movie 'The Stepmom'. Voted as two of the 'nicest' Anglophone women in the movie industry by French readers of the magazine *Marie Claire* (Malagardis, 2002), these two heroines are appreciated in France not only for their personalities and the spunky film roles they have played (Julia Roberts' *Erin Brockovich* and Susan Sarandon's 'Louise' in *Thelma and Louise*, most notably), but first and foremost for their social activism (opposing environmental pollution, the death penalty, and their various other causes).[10] It is thus not surprising that NOOS chose these American actresses in particular for the illustration of one of their advertisements. The copy of this particular poster ad is also interesting in that it involves an English expression ('best of') borrowed into French:[11]

Pour 15 euros / mois
L'essentiel du cinéma est dans les chaînes du 'Best of'

Best of Noostv, la meilleure sélection de chaînes de cinéma, de sport, d'information, de jeunesse . . .

English translation (mine)

For only 15 euros a month
Find the best movies on our 'Best of' channels
Best of Noostv. The best selection of channels dedicated to movies,
sports, news and younger viewers can be found on Noostv.

A fair number of Hollywood movie stars also offer celebrity endorsements for particular products and/or services. As Andie MacDowell is a spokesperson for L'Oréal, for instance, she appears in both the magazine and television data included in this analysis. In the television version, her American identity is foregrounded by her thick American accent as she delivers the famous l'Oréal slogan in French:

Parce que je le vaux bien.
Because I'm worth it.

The commercial also highlights a passion of hers which happens to be archery. Thus, the spot opens with the actress shooting an arrow with a bow after which the efficacy of the product is demonstrated with various visuals (including a very scientific-looking graph similar to the one alluded to in Chapter 1 for another facial cream). Another interesting phenomenon in this instance is the 'identity switching' that occurs when Andie MacDowell's French counterpart (presumably the voice used when dubbing her films in French) delivers a line for her off camera (with no American accent whatsoever):

Ce que je vise, moins de rides, plus de fermeté, avec Revitalift Action Profonde.

English translation (mine)

My goal is to have fewer wrinkles [and] firmer skin, so I use Deep Action Revitalift (product name)

Andie MacDowell does, however, deliver the punch line herself, returning to her heavily accented French (as with the slogan mentioned earlier): *Objectif atteint* ('Bull's eye!').

A celebrity endorsement for Gemey-Maybelline delivered by television actress Sarah Michelle Gellar (Figure 3.2) is another example.[12] Here, we also see English in the copy, including the product name (Water Shine), its 'Shine Reflect' coating detailed in the descriptive copy, and several colors of nail polish featured in the ad (Juicy Bubblegum,

Figure 3.2   Gemey–Maybelline Water Shine advertisement

Mango Delicious, French Kiss Pink). To better appeal to French audiences, the line 'delivered' by the actress appears in quotation marks in the form of a pun: *'J'ai des miroirs au bout des doigts!'* Reminiscent of the idiomatic expression *Jusqu'au bout des doigts*, (meaning '100 percent' or literally 'right to the tip of one's fingers'), this expression could be interpreted in several ways:

1. I have mirrors on the tips of my fingers (literal meaning);
2. This nail polish I am wearing is as smooth and shiny as a mirror (connoted meaning derived from *'cette brilliance effet miroir'* appearing elsewhere in the copy); or possibly
3. I am 100 percent Gemey-Maybelline (additional connotation, one step further removed).

In another print advertisement for TAG Heuer watches (Figure 3.3), we see the late American movie legend Steve McQueen gazing into the camera with the TAG Heuer Monaco watch appearing directly beside him. The photo caption in the bottom left-hand corner of the ad reads: 'Steve McQueen and his Monaco'. This text appears with a French translation (*'Steve McQueen et son Chronographe Automatique Monaco'*) as required by the 1994 Toubon Law in France. (This legislation will be discussed in detail in Chapter 6.) The strength, determination, style, and cool sophistication associated with this actor and the characters he brought to life on the silver screen blend perfectly with the headline ('What are you made of', also translated as *'De quoi êtes-vous fait?'*) used in this campaign, drawing the readers into a world of adventure and intrigue.[13] Other American actors who fall into this 'endorsement' category in the data include George Clooney (Running Heart Foundation), Jennifer Garner (The Gap), and Martin Sheen (Mandarin Oriental Hotel Group).[14]

American recording artists are another group of celebrities one sees, and hears, quite frequently in French advertising across media. A print ad for Skechers USA, for instance, features American pop singer Britney Spears, whose popularity in France is such that this ad is very likely to appeal to its intended readers, French teenagers targeted by *Star Club* magazine.[15] The slogan reads *'Pure Fun!'* (translated in the copy as *'Fun à l'état pure'*). The fact that the English borrowing 'fun' appears in the translation as well is intriguing but not at all unusual as this particular word is widely used and understood by a significant portion of the population in France.[16] Another American recording artist appearing in the French television data is Barbara Streisand, whose album including song titles such as 'Woman in Love', 'Tell Him', and 'Memory' is fea-

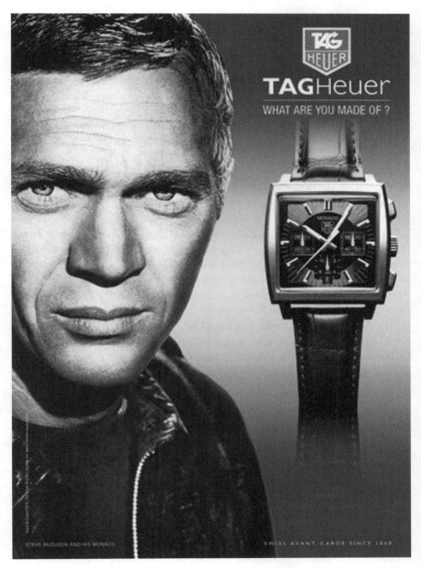

Figure 3.3 TAG Heuer advertisement

tured in a TV commercial for the French radio station Chérie FM (www. cheriefm.fr). The English-language album title used in France ('The Essential') is pronounced with a French accent by a male voice off camera. This hyperbolic expression in English connotes the uniqueness and remarkable quality of this album and is immediately understood as it is very close to its French equivalent ('*l'Essentiel*'). It is also very typically used by the French when referring to entertainment in advertising (readers may recall the '*Best of Noostv . . . L'essentiel du cinéma*' example cited earlier).

In a print advertisement for the same radio station (Chérie FM), we find one other face 'exported' from the US, the singer Whitney Houston, plus British icon Elton John, with the remaining individuals depicted in the illustration being Francophone. These include French Canadians Isabelle Boulay, Céline Dion and Garou, along with two local French recording artists, Patrick Bruel and Florent Pagny. The Francophone majority represented here is, in fact, quite refreshing given the overwhelming presence of English in entertainment across media and reflects the diversified listening tastes of French radio audiences today as well as Chérie FM's commitment to promoting French music.[17] Chérie FM is also one of the few radio stations in France with this audience (for example, Fun Radio, Skyrock) that has a station identification name that is 100 per cent French. The use of celebrities here (as well as the Barbara Streisand example) differs from the celebrity endorsements mentioned earlier in that Chérie FM is featuring in this advertisement recording artists whose songs are played on the radio station. Other American musicians referenced in this manner throughout the television and magazine corpus include James Brown, Ray Charles, Bob Dylan, Duke Ellington, George Gershwin, Barbara Hendricks, and Elvis Presley.

As for American athletes, we find, for instance, tennis champion Venus Williams in French advertising for Reebok, as well as world-renowned cyclist Lance Armstrong for the Mandarin Oriental Hotel Group (Figure 3.4). The choice of Lance Armstrong for the French market is particularly brilliant given the special status this athlete has in France. Having won the grueling bicycle race known as the Tour de France seven times, breaking all previous records, Lance's athletic achievements have won him tremendous respect in France. According to *France-Amérique*, a French-language newspaper published in the US, a common nickname for him in France is 'le boss', a title that reflects the French appreciation for his perseverence and determination.[18] Who better to represent this international hotel to French audiences? The

Figure 3.4 Mandarin Oriental Hotel Group advertisement

copy below his image reads, in a very stylish and understated fashion, *'Il apprécie'* ('He appreciates [Mandarin Oriental hotels]'), reflecting the refinement and elegance of the hotel group, and its popularity among celebrities with discriminating tastes.

One additional famous American appearing in the corpus is Thomas Jefferson, one of America's forefathers and the third president of the US. In an advertisement for Click & Trust that ran in a French magazine for business executives (*Management*), his familiar signature acts as a guarantee that the service Click & Trust provides in securing information on the Web is trustworthy and dependable.

American way of life

Although celebrities certainly have tremendous appeal in advertising for certain products directed at certain consumer groups, there is no doubt that glimpses of average American citizens seen in 'distinctly American' contexts are also images used in advertising to 'seduce the French'. Indeed, snapshots of American culture, from tobacco farmers to high school football players, are not an uncommon occurrence in the French media. An article appearing in a women's magazine in France features choreographer Alexandra Roche sporting pom poms commonly used by cheerleaders in the US to demonstrate various typical cheerleading movements one can use to stay in shape.[19] The photo caption, indicating where one might find such an unusual item, reads:

> *Beaucoup plus legers que des poids, les pompons renforcent le travail musculaire des bras. Vous en trouverez dans les magasins de farces et attrapes.*

English translation (mine)

> A lot lighter than weights, pom poms develop your arm muscles. Available in joke and novelty shops.

The minority group in the US most often featured in French advertising, however, are Native Americans. In addition to the very stereotypical images such as those described at the beginning of this chapter, we also find in French advertising members of the Native American community in more 'respectful' settings. Their cultural identity is, however, always (and not so subtly) referenced through clothing, music, or other means. In a television commercial for Afflelou progressive lenses eyewear (*Verres Progressifs Cent pour cent d'Afflelou*), for instance, we see a group of Native

Americans standing in a circle, each holding a bow and arrow. All are wearing items one might associate with this ethnic group (bandanas in the hair, Native American silver and turquoise jewelry, and so forth) as well as the product being advertised (prescription eye glasses). With Native Americans chanting to the beat of a drum in the background music soundtrack, all but one of the members of 'the circle' take aim at their respective targets (totem poles painted with a bull's eye), shoot their arrows, and hit their bull's eye dead center. The one remaining, visibly much older than the others, takes more time, carefully studying his target as he draws his arrow, before also hitting the center of the bull's eye. While his arrow is 'in flight', a brief image of a Native American in full feather headdress flashes across the screen. The dialogue that follows is entirely in French:

> Male voice-off: *En 1995, j'ai lancé un nouveau verre progressif: le cent pour cent. Je suis opticien et je pense à tous ceux qui ont besoin de voir de près comme de loin mais avec la même paire de lunettes. Mais surtout mon verre progressif s'adapte vraiment au plus grand nombre. D'ailleurs, vous êtes des centaines de milliers à l'utiliser.*

> Female voice-off: *Le cent pour cent, c'est une exclusivité d'Alain Afflelou.*

English translation (mine)

> *Male voice-off*: In 1995, I launched a brand new progressive lens on the market: my '100 per cent' ['20/20' line of eyeglasses]. As an optometrist, I think of all those who need to see up close as well as at a distance with the same pair of glasses. What makes my glasses unique is that they really work for everyone. As a matter of fact, there are already hundreds of thousands of satisfied customers.

> *Female voice-off*: The 100 per cent, exclusively from Alain Afflelou.

This commercial is, of course, full of symbolism and cultural references that enhance this 'Native American experience' for the viewing audience. The circle formation, the bow-and-arrow theme, the totem poles, clothing, and music are all part of the Native American heritage and that which makes them unique from a French perspective. The respect felt toward the older gentleman by his younger counterparts (symbolized by the flash image of a Native American in a traditional feather headdress one might expect to see worn by a tribal chief), coupled with his steady patience and concentration, are also derived from Native American culture.[20]

Still, the 'pioneer days' appear to hold a certain mystique for French consumers who are accustomed to seeing in their advertising 'cowboys and Indians' made popular in Europe through Hollywood or 'spaghetti' westerns. The Renault Scénic, for example, was recently marketed in France using a magazine ad that showed the automobile crossing a rugged landscape resembling the American desert Southwest. The presence of Indians is indexed by some twenty-five or so arrows sticking out of the tires indicating a recent attack. Thanks to the Scénic Pax system, which helps one maintain control in the event of a flat tire, however, the automobile is able to continue its perilous journey through the American wilderness. The cowboy hat worn by the person behind the wheel further enhances this Western movie atmosphere.

Basketball players, an image that immediately evokes American culture, also appear in several advertisements in the corpus, including a series of television commercials for IBM. One spot opens with a referee blowing a whistle to launch 'the action', after which we see two opposing teams grappling for control of the ball using various muscle tactics, such as pinning the opponent's arms to his side to prevent him from retrieving it. On the players' jerseys are written technical computer terms in place of names, leaving no doubt as to who are the 'bad guys' (*spam*, *hacker*, *virus*) and the 'good guys' (*firewall*, *mainframe*, *pc*, *back-up*, *linux*). Fans of the blue team (the IBM corporation) cheering in the bleachers are then shown holding up signs to show their support that read 'Unix', 'Linux', and 'I love Mainframe' as a member of their team scores a final dunk and wins the game. Halfway through the commercial, which was originally recorded in English and dubbed into French for the French market, the camera cuts to another scene where the coach is outlining game strategy on a blackboard. An off-camera voice narrates the images (my translation):

> E-business is like a [basketball] game. There are players, there are leaders, and there are opponents who don't always play by the rules. In this kind of game, strategy is what counts, plus the ability to relay information to team players, just as you would pass them the ball. But there's a lot more money at stake here than in any other game. E-business is much more than a game, it's a very serious investment. So if you want to play, play to win.

In the French version, however, there are two words near the end that rhyme, encapsulating the message of this commercial quite well (*jeu*, or 'game', and *enjeu*, 'stakes'). This mnemonic device is, unfortunately, lost

in the English translation I have just provided. Here, then, is the version of the dialogue broadcast on French television. (The use of the borrowing 'e-business' will be discussed in Chapter 5):

> *Le 'e-business', c'est comme dans un match. Il y a des joueurs, il y a des dirigeants, et il y a des adversaires qui ne respectent pas toujours les règles. Dans ce genre de match, ce qui compte, c'est la stratégie et la capacité à transmettre l'information comme on se passe le ballon. Mais il y a beaucoup plus d'argent en jeu que dans un autre match. Le 'e-business', ce n'est pas seulement un jeu, c'est l'enjeu. Alors, si vous voulez jouer, jouez gagnant.*

This 'basketball' theme also appears in another IBM commercial in the corpus, where the exceptional skills of a new recruit (whose name is Linux, reflecting one of IBM's latest products at the time) are emphasized. The scenes in this commercial, which is also narrated in French, involve two men in business suits who have come to 'assess' the team in which they have invested.[21] The coach introduces them to the newest member of the team as they watch him in action. As in the other commercial, the players' jerseys display text such as 'mainframe', 'firewall', 'pc', and 'wireless'.

Dialogue (dubbed in French):

> Coach: *Bon, les gars, je vous présente le nouveau. Son nom c'est Linux, c'est un as. Il va faire progresser toute l'équipe.*
>
> 1st executive: *Ça démarre plutôt bien.*
>
> 2nd executive: *Ouais . . . Ce Linux fait un super boulot.*
>
> 1st executive: *Et il nous coûte combien?*
>
> 2nd executive: *Presque rien.*
>
> 1st executive: *Un si bon joueur, pour presque rien?*
>
> 2nd executive: *Il adore le jeu.*

English translation (mine)

> *Coach*: Ok guys, here's our latest. His name is Linux and he's one of the best. He'll push the entire team further.
>
> *1st executive*: Looks good so far.
>
> *2nd executive*: Yep, this Linux guy is doing a great job.
>
> *1st executive*: And how much is he costing us?
>
> *2nd executive*: Next to nothing.
>
> *1st executive*: Such a good player for so little money?
>
> *2nd executive*: He loves the game.

Although the message behind these commercials is certainly clear (that if you want to succeed in business, you definitely want IBM on your team) and reinforces the American origins of the brand (through the basketball imagery most notably), the French advertising executives interviewed for this study tended to agree that the basketball theme is not something with which European consumers can easily identify. Several commented that soccer, for instance, would have been a better choice for this market. Another difficulty that French audiences apparently had with these commercials was the complexity of the English appearing on the players' jerseys. Although English computer terms (such as *e-mail*, *e-business*, *Internet*, *PC*, and so on) have certainly become a staple of business communication in France and throughout Europe, in France, words such as 'firewall' and 'mainframe' are not yet part of the general lexicon and therefore lead to some confusion. Nevertheless, snapshot images such as these of life in America are fairly common in French advertising today.

Elements of American culture

Other 'Americana' that has crept into the discourse of advertising in France include various symbols of patriotism, including the American flag. In addition to the DKNY advertisement described earlier, which includes the 'stars and stripes' as part of a scene from New York City, the Tommy Hilfiger clothing line also prominently displays the flag in its advertising distributed in France. In one instance, two young models involved in a rather innocent flirtatious act are dressed in red, white, and blue with the American flag filling the background. The woman is reaching around her male counterpart's right shoulder from behind, pulling up his polo shirt (bearing the Tommy Hilfiger logo) ever so slightly to reveal his Tommy Hilfiger underwear. A bottle of Tommy Hilfiger 'eau de toilette' figures in the lower right-hand corner of the page immediately beneath the copy, which reads:

> *T pour lui*
> *Votre nouveau parfum*
> *Tommy Hilfiger*

English translation (mine)

> T for him
> Your new perfume
> Tommy Hilfiger

Whereas the copy is written entirely in French, and includes one element that could be construed as a French pun (*T pour lui*, producing 'You are [perfectly suited] for him', or *T'es pour lui*, when the letter 'T' is pronounced in French), the advertisement has a distinctly American flavor due to the flag, overall color scheme, and the 'American look' of the models (facial expressions, perfect teeth, hairstyles, casual dress).

A poster advertisement in the Paris subway for a temporary employment agency, GR intérim, uses another American symbol, Uncle Sam, as the main visual theme. Displayed in huge red lettering against a background image of Uncle Sam pointing his finger directly at the reader is the English-language headline:[22]

I WANT YOU *

In smaller (black) print appears a description, in French, of the type of career professionals they are seeking:

> *Si vous êtes*
>
> *Assistante*
> *Secrétaire Bilingue*
> *Hôtesse/Standardiste Bilingue*
> *Comptable (tous niveaux) Bilingue*
> *Contrôleur de Gestion, etc.*

English translation (mine)

> If you are
>
> an office assistant
> a bilingual secretary
> a bilingual receptionist or phone operator
> a bilingual accountant (any level)
> a management controller

Immediately following is an additional line of text in English in a somewhat larger font:[23]

COME AND APPLY **

The English and Uncle Sam imagery in this poster advertisement have several functions. Both are certainly operating as attention-getters in this context, where the rather domineering stance of Uncle Sam facing

the camera and the color and size of the English phrase 'I WANT YOU' (one foot high, occupying approximately one-sixth of the surface of the poster) are sure to catch the eye. With his glaring stare and right forefinger pointed directly at the reader, Uncle Sam is also depicted as someone who 'means business'. Although the copy makes no specific reference to being bilingual in French and English, as opposed to other languages, this American symbolism, coupled with the language most prominently displayed on the poster, make it perfectly clear that fluency in English is one of the skills required for these 'bilingual' positions. Unfortunately, however, it is also an advertisement that smacks of cultural imperialism (rather ironic coming from a French firm recruiting English speakers), treating English more as a language of dominance and control than as a window to the international world of business. Nevertheless, the copy and illustration certainly meet their objectives of attracting the attention of commuters in the metro and conveying a need for French–English bilingual job candidates.

Another element of American culture appearing in French advertising that may come as some surprise are certain food items that are gaining popularity in France. These include such American treats as pancakes, muffins, brownies, cookies, and milkshakes. A magazine advertisement for the chocolate–hazelnut spread Ferrero Nutella (an Italian brand), for instance, mentions both pancakes and muffins in the descriptive copy. Elsewhere in the corpus, Francine (a French brand) is selling their pancake mix using a combination of American imagery (a stack of pancakes with maple syrup on the packaging and on a plate in the background illustration) and French–English code-mixing:

Des pancakes prêts en 5 minutes . . . Ça vous brunche?

English translation (mine)

Pancakes ready in 5 minutes . . . How does that strike you?

The 'Frenglish' blend in this case involves another American concept, the Sunday brunch, which has started to take root in France. Here, the English borrowing has been transformed into a French verb (with the characteristic final [-e] ending for the 3rd person singular) to evoke an idiomatic expression in French (*'Ça vous branche?'* meaning 'How does that strike you?') By substituting the letter [u] in place of the letter [a] in the middle of the word, the team creating this ad was able to produce a pun that evokes both the American origins of the recipe and the intended use of the product.

Original French expression	Expression with modified spelling
Ça vous branche?→	*Ça vous brunche?*
(How does that strike you?)→	(How does [the idea of pancakes for brunch] strike you?)

Indeed, in France where the typical breakfast is a much lighter affair (toasted bread with jam, for instance), the idea of devouring a stack of pancakes is inconceivable unless presented within the context of a late breakfast/early lunch combination (*le 'brunch'*). Both the recipe (pancakes) and the meal format (brunch) alluded to in the advertisement are, therefore, American-inspired concepts used to market this French product in France. The Rocky Mountain scenery on the packaging and the maple leaf above the Francine logo (with the mention: *Avec du sirop d'érable*, 'with maple syrup') further contribute to the American look and feel of the advertisement.[24] Pancakes also appear in the poster advertising for McDonald's displayed in their restaurants in Paris who, it should be noted, also serve breakfast *croissants, pains au chocolat,* and other French pastries to appeal to consumers in this market. The French company Lefèvre Utile (widely known as LU) has also perfected several 'American recipes' such as cookies and brownies which it prominently displays in its advertising for the French market. These examples illustrate that despite the 'love–hate' relationship between the US and France described in the opening pages of this chapter, imported food items and concepts are one type of commodity that flows freely between the two cultures and is embraced rather enthusiastically.

There have also been several visual references to the US space program in advertising distributed in France. The French company Saint-Gobain used a pen-and-pencil drawing of the space shuttle in one of their magazine advertisements as one example of the way their materials and technology were being utilized around the world. In another magazine ad for a French hair conditioning product (Garnier Fructis), an attractive young female model appears wearing a white space suit with two NASA-inspired decals depicting the space shuttle with its famous 'solid rocket boosters' in action and characteristic flap wings designed for a 'glide landing'. The model's reddish brown hair is floating upwards as if she were indeed an astronaut in a gravity-free environment. To her left, the product, in a nature-inspired bright green bottle surrounded by slices of lime and lemon, is also 'floating' as indicated by the air bubbles surrounding it, suggesting its total submersion in water. The 'weightless' atmosphere connoted by these various elements of the illustration (NASA imagery, model's hair movement, floating bottle) reinforces the claim

in the copy that the product 'untangles your hair without weighing it down' (*'pour démêler vos cheveux en toute légèreté'*). The headline reads:

Le 1er après-shampooing qui défie les lois de la pesanteur

English translation (mine)

The 1st hair conditioner to defy the law of gravity.

Whereas this referencing of NASA in a French advertisement for a French brand of a hair conditioner may appear as an anomaly, there are also several American organizations alluded to in the corpus, including the National Geographic Society and the Wildlife Conservation Society, both of which are mentioned, for example, in a print ad for Rolex watches.[25]

Very occasionally one also encounters American measurement references in ads distributed in France. A typical example is the use of 'miles' in referring to frequent flyer programs, as seen in a recent French magazine ad for *Sky Team* (a global airline alliance that includes Air France). Included in the copy is the following sentence:

Avec les Miles accumulés, SkyTeam vous offre des destinations de rêves

English translation (mine)

With accumulated Miles, SkyTeam offers you dream destinations

This use of 'miles' instead of kilometers in addressing French consumers is most likely motivated by the desire to ensure product name recognition. The symbol for inches ("), as opposed to centimeters, appeared in another ad in the corpus, this one for the discount hypermarket chain Carrefour. This ad featured several office products, including a 14" flat screen desktop computer, which is described in the French-language copy as an *écran plat 14"*.

Fictional TV and movie characters

Images drawn from American television programs, Hollywood movies, and other forms of entertainment (such as Broadway musicals) are also quite prevalent in the advertising landscape of France. Nokia, for instance, ran a campaign featuring characters from the Star Wars film series. In one of their magazine advertisements appearing in the French sports magazine *L'Equipe*, Obi-Wan Kenobi stands defiantly holding his 'lightsaber', staring directly into the camera.[26] Superimposed on this

image is the mobile phone being advertised, the Nokia 3410, with the title of the film STAR WARS displayed in large capital letters on its LCD screen. The fact that the copy is geared toward younger audiences is evidenced by the use of the informal form of 'you' (*tu*). The reference here to the 'Nokia Club' is also likely to appeal to this age group:

> *Club Nokia. Tu as aimé le film? Vis l'expérience jusqu'au bout grâce aux jeux, aux logos et aux sonneries de la saga Star Wars à télécharger en exclusivité sur www.club.nokia.fr.*

English translation (mine)

> Club Nokia. Did you like the movie? Live the experience to its fullest with games, logos, and custom ringers from the Star Wars saga, available for downloading exclusively on www.club.nokia.fr.

A Batman poster, on the other hand, is featured in a print advertisement for a Nissan automobile. Pinned to the wall of a child's room with thumbtacks, the poster depicts Batman and his sidekick Robin posing next to the Batmobile under a full moon with Gotham City looming in the background. The owner of the poster, the child shown in a Polaroid photograph, also tacked to the wall, has presumably cut out an image of the featured Nissan model and taped it directly on top of the Batmobile so that only the Batmobile's 'bat wings' at the rear are showing. Directly beneath the illustration, which also includes a blue teddy bear, a bag of Haribo candy, and other objects one might find in a child's bedroom, the caption reads:

> *Nissan Tino Haribo. Le Monospace que les enfants vont adorer.*

English translation (mine)

> Nissan Tino Haribo. The minivan that children are really going to love.[27]

In a French magazine advertisement for Mini automobiles, the presence of another superhero is connoted by the red and yellow Superman cape seen protruding from the automobile's engine. Set against an elegant dark gray background, the brightly colored cape immediately draws attention to the ad, symbolizing the power and dependability of the automobile while referencing the name of the model being advertised, the Mini Cooper S. A 'hero' of a quite smaller stature appears in French advertising for Hertz rental cars. Accompanied by a Walt Disney cast of

characters at the newly opened Walt Disney Studios Park outside Paris, Mickey Mouse is an image that is immediately recognizable and offers a suggested vacation destination to tourists renting cars in France.[28]

The American television cartoon characters 'Wile E. Coyote and Road Runner', on the other hand, are depicted in a magazine advertisement for Amora bottled sauces.[29] In the illustration, we find a typical 'Western' scene from the television cartoon in which the roadrunner has just narrowly escaped the crushing weight of a huge boulder dislodged by his archenemy, Wile E. Coyote. The copy that appears in bold directly beneath this image 'anchors' (Barthes, 1977) the scene, providing a desired 'reading' of the illustration:

> *Sauce Curry Royal Amora. Si vous en avez assez de la volaille, mettez du poisson.*

English translation (mine)

> Royal Curry Sauce by Amora. If you're tired of eating poultry, serve it with fish.

Whereas 'Roadrunner' would have been a more precise description of the rather crafty character depicted in the illustration, 'poultry' (*de la volaille*) was a lexical choice that enabled the copywriters to allude to other domesticated fowl one might eat in France, such as chicken and Cornish hen. References to other possible uses of the product are sprinkled throughout the rest of the copy, underscoring the idea that Amora has something for everyone:

> *Si vous n'aimez pas le poisson, mettez de l'agneau, si vous n'aimez pas l'agneau, mettez du riz. Et si vous n'aimez pas la sauce Curry Royal, essayez la Sicilienne, la Créole, l'Aigre Douce ou la Marocaine.*

English translation (mine)

> If you don't like fish, try lamb. If you don't like lamb, use rice. And if you don't like the Royal Curry Sauce, try the Sicilian, Creole, Sweet and Sour, or Moroccan sauces.

Of all of the television and movie characters in the corpus, however, none pulls the heartstrings like ET, the lovable extraterrestrial made famous by the Hollywood movie by the same name. In a French magazine advertisement for Perrier, ET (who appears on the tee-shirt of someone opening a refrigerator door) gazes intently at a bottle of the

sparkling water with his brightly glowing fingertip innocently pointing in its direction. One gets the distinct impression that the ET character is trying to relay his desire for the Perrier to his human companion, much as he 'communicated' with the little boy who adopted him in the film.[30]

Hollywood musicals and TV dramas

Hollywood musical comedies are another popular theme in French advertising and appear in several television commercials in the corpus. In a spot for Evian bottled mineral water, for instance, the television viewing audience is treated to a full-fledged water ballet performed by an adorable team of babies moving in synchronized fashion. As the infants carry out their various choreographed movements in the water, the very festive music soundtrack and harmonies sung in English heard over the images further contributes to the Hollywood musical atmosphere:

> *Bye bye baby*
> *Remember you're my baby*
> *When they give you the eye*
> *Although I know that you care . . .*
> *[voice-off commentary]*
> *But send that rainbow to me . . .*

Interspersed with the lyrics is a voice-off commentary that presents the product as a sort of 'fountain of youth', emphasizing its rejuvenating properties:[31]

> *Boire chaque jour une eau pure et équilibrée en minéraux entretient la jeunesse de votre corps. Evian. Déclarée source de jeunesse de votre corps.*

English translation (mine)

> Drinking pure mineral water on a daily basis keeps your body young. Evian is your body's natural source of youth.

American-style musical comedies seem to have inspired a recent television commercial for Rexona deodorant shown in France as well. The spot opens with a woman with disheveled hair and ratty clothes walking her dog in a city park. Suddenly her 'ex' appears with a gorgeous, stylish woman on his arm. The ensuing dialogue is short on words but speaks volumes nonetheless:

Ex-boyfriend (looking surprised and happy): *Anna?*
Woman walking dog (looking humiliated): *Mathieu?*

The viewing audience is then drawn into the scene by a simple question inviting them to imagine themselves in a similar situation:

Quel effet ça fait de tomber sur son ex?
(How does it feel to run into your ex?)

Suddenly, the park explodes with activity with everyone else in the immediate vicinity breaking into a song-and-dance routine exactly as one might see in a made-for-Hollywood musical. With the park fountains pulsating in rhythm to the upbeat music soundtrack, the onlookers-turned-entertainers (who include tennis players, a delivery man, little girls with cotton candy, a cotton candy vendor, tree trimmers suspended from tree branches, and women in 1950s garb prancing in unison down the park steps for the finale) burst into song, performing a lively choreographed number rehearsed for this very occasion. Their message, sung in French, but nevertheless in true Hollywood musical fashion, is that Rexona deodorant will help you appear calm in even the most stressful situations (my translation):

Music soundtrack

T'es dans un état. T'es ridicule, regarde-toi! Il nage dans le bonheur et toi tu aimerais bien être ailleurs. Tu sais que tu vas bientôt craquer. Comment fais-tu pour ne pas transpirer?

You're a mess. Look at you, you look ridiculous! He's on cloud nine and all you want to do is disappear. You know you're losing it. How come you're not sweating?

Voice-off

Parce que le stress provoque des soudains excès de transpiration, avec Rexona Source, c'est cliniquement prouvé pour vous offrir une protection imbattable.

Because stress can cause sudden excess perspiration, Rexona Source has been clinically proven to offer you the utmost protection.

Music soundtrack (continued)

Ton Rexona Source! (Your Rexona Source!)

Voice-off

> *Ne laissez pas vos émotions vous trahir.*
> (Don't let your emotions give you away).

As counter-intuitive as it may seem, this 1950s Hollywood musical atmosphere is very appealing to French audiences who find in these nostalgic images and music a certain humor and irony. It is, to say the least, a very entertaining commercial for a product category (deodorants) that does not necessarily inspire humor, nor the *joie de vivre* atmosphere that the designers of this commercial were so cleverly able to create.

Occasionally, chase scenes reminiscent of American TV dramas will also surface in French television commercials. Canal Satellite, for instance, ran a commercial in France featuring police officers in pursuit of a criminal suspect who is finally apprehended in a 1950s style diner typical of those still found in the US. This commercial is particularly interesting for its symbolism and the manner in which it 'switches' the criminal suspect's identity to that of the consumer. As one of the officers handcuffs the individual, he yells to his partner (my translation):

> *Jean-Paul, on l'a attrapé!*
> (We got 'em, Jean-Paul!)

Another officer on the scene then addresses the man who is now in police custody, using the informal 'tu' form of 'you' to show a lack of respect:

> Policer officer (to criminal suspect): *Alors, ton abonnement à Canal Satellite tu en es content?*
> (So, are you happy now with your Canal Satellite hook-up?)
> Suspect: *Bien sûr j'en suis content. Ça me permet de m'évader.*
> (Of course, I'm happy. It helps me escape [from reality].)

At this point, the apprehended suspect 'morphs' into a clean-cut father figure washing his car with his young son outside their suburban home. The 'dad' continues the dialogue initiated in the diner:

> Father (addressing his son): *Eh oui, avec Canal Satellite on a six grandes chaînes de cinéma. Il y en a vraiment pour tous les goûts.*
> (With Canal Satellite, you get six major movie channels. There's really something for everyone.)

The next portion of dialogue alludes to the frequent exposure to English one experiences in France through entertainment media. This presence of English, on cable television, in this case, is highlighted by both the son (apologizing in English for demonstrating his karate kick on one of the car's tires) and the father (noting that watching movies in their original version with French subtitles is a way to improve one's English):

Son: *Moi, ce que j'aime, c'est les films de karaté.*
(What I like are the karate movies) (gives one of the car's tires a karate kick).
Oops, Sorry Daddy! (subtitled as *'Désolé, Papa'*).
Father: *Tu vois, avec le choix entre la VO et la VF sur Canal Satellite tu parles déjà anglais, enfin, presque. On se fait une petite comédie ce soir?*
(You see, with the language viewing option (original version or French version) you already speak English. Well . . . almost. How about a little comedy tonight?

This brief switch to English in the middle of their conversational exchange is rather interesting in that its primary function is to under-score, albeit in a tongue-in-cheek fashion, the widespread use of English in the media. This idea is reinforced by the movie titles flashed across the screen at the end of the commercial (for example, *Notting Hill*, *The Matrix*, *The Mummy*). Indeed in a country where many of the movies on cable television channels are imported from the US, the option of watching movies on cable in either French or English is a selling point that is often used when marketing this type of service to French con-sumers.[32] The final scene, where the family dog unceremoniously relieves himself on one of the wheels of the freshly washed automobile, is also worth noting in that it is very typical of the type of humor that appeals to the French, some of whom find *happy endings à l'américaine* rather unsatisfying.

To summarize, American images seen in French advertising include landscapes, celebrities, movies, television programs, comic strip charac-ters, musical comedies, American symbols, lifestyles, and other aspects of American culture. It is undeniable that the French continue to hold a certain fascination for Americana when it comes to advertising. As these many examples suggest, much of this 'Americana' is carefully selected to specifically appeal to this market and is limited to elements and individuals who are easily recognizable in France. They may be

chosen to symbolize certain positive concepts that are to be associated with the product or service featured in the campaign (for example, Steve McQueen for TAG Heuer watches) and/or to create a certain atmosphere (chase scene blended with suburbia in Canal Satellite commercial). They may reinforce the origins of the brand (scenes of New York City for DKNY, or the remote Southwestern landscapes for the Jeep Grand Cherokee) or be used as a form of humor (Hollywood musical renditions performed in television commercials for Rexona and Evian). They may also be celebrity endorsements (for example, Andie MacDowell for l'Oréal) that appeal to French consumers to whom certain Hollywood movie stars, American athletes, musicians, and other 'famous faces' are extremely familiar due to the global reach of the American movie, television, and recording industries.

Furthermore, there is an unmistakable preference for symbolism in French advertising where, for instance, an image such as the space shuttle orbiter can be easily inserted to depict weightlessness in an advertisement for a hair conditioner, or opposing teams of basketball players may symbolize the protection against computer viruses and other problems afforded by a certain computer software. This American-inspired iconic discourse mirrors not only French perceptions of the United States, but also relies quite heavily on the intended audience's cultural values and knowledge of the world. It is a carefully constructed montage of images, music soundtracks, dialogue, and text that speaks directly to French consumers in a language they understand. However, whereas one might be tempted to assume that this limited portrayal of American landscapes, faces, and lifestyles accurately depicts the reputation of the United States in France, this is certainly not the case, as the opening section of this chapter clearly demonstrates. The Americana featured in French advertising is merely one of many tools employed by the advertising industry to convey their message in a way that is highly effective and appeals to the intended audience of the campaign as much as possible.

Despite the commonly held belief that American corporate power and the global dominance of American media are the main driving forces behind globalization, the 'America' depicted in advertising is experienced on an entirely different level. Seen from the French consumer's perspective, these images transcend their American origins, producing an emotional response that advertisers use to their advantage. In the world of advertising, these elements reflect a certain vision of the world, creating an atmosphere conducive to selling dreams and ideas. Applied to products and services in the carefully crafted discourse of advertising,

the Americana seen in these examples is far removed from the anti-globalization rhetoric discussed in the previous chapter. Indeed, viewing these images through their own cultural lens, the French are projecting their own values into the advertisement, transforming it into something indigenous, a message that speaks to them directly. Whether it be Uncle Sam claiming 'I want you', Native Americans, or Hollywood musicals, these snapshot images of American culture have very specific meanings for the French, who interpret them according to their own cultural perceptions and experience. This is not to say that American images will be well received in French advertising for every type of product. Indeed, the difficulties of designing advertising that will appeal to local audiences are not to be underestimated. To gain a better understanding of the techniques used in advertising to entice French audiences, we turn our attention now to adaptations of international campaigns.

4
Adaptations for the French Market

The aim of this chapter is to explore local adaptations of international campaigns with specific reference to France. We begin this discussion with an overview of approaches to international advertising, examining the advantages and disadvantages of tailoring global campaigns to individual markets. To gain a better understanding of how these strategies are applied to advertising distributed in France, testimonials from advertising executives working on international accounts for agencies in Paris (such as Publicis Conseil, Ogilvy & Mather, McCann-Erikson, among others) are also included in this discussion. Following this brief introduction to international advertising is a section outlining various concepts that appeal to French consumers. Included here will be an overview of the advertising creative strategies (emotional appeals, use of humor and sex, information content, and so on) most commonly used in French advertising as reported in the literature (for example, Biswas, Olsen and Carlet, 1992; Zandpour, Chang, and Catalano, 1992; Taylor, Hoy, and Haley, 1996). The final section of this chapter illustrates how multinational corporations are adapting their advertising for the French market using samples drawn from the corpus. Examples in the data include visual and textual references to elements of French culture, popular media, and the metric system. International campaigns used in France also emphasize other concepts that generally appeal to the French, including logic, intelligence, word play, natural ingredients, and environmental protection. We will also explore multilingual labels used to address European consumers and the discourse used to market global brands as products that specifically respond to the needs and desires of local consumers. This examination of French advertising across media provides evidence that those who design international advertising for multinational corporations are well aware that their messages must be tailored to local audiences in order to be effective.

Approaches to international advertising

The adaptation of global advertising campaigns for local audiences (a process referred to as 'localization') has received considerable attention in the research literature on advertising.[1] Whereas the advantages of developing specific national campaigns are numerous and will be illustrated in this chapter with examples from France, one should also note certain objections voiced by those who favor standardized 'global' campaigns over localization (Levitt, 1983). Claiming that the tastes of world consumers have become 'homogenized' due to the influence of global media, those who oppose individualized country strategies emphasize the fact that modifying the execution for local markets invariably results in higher production costs and delays. Indeed, modifications required typically include the shooting of subtitles, dubbing films with local languages, inserting a different close-up of the product (or 'pack shot') for each market to accommodate linguistic and cultural differences and adhering to specific country regulations with regards to filming children, commercial timeslots, use of media for advertising certain products, and so forth. Facing such obstacles (along with the pressure to produce quicker product roll-outs than ever before), some corporate executives feel that the disadvantages outweigh the advantages. Others simply fail to appreciate the subtle cultural differences that can impact an audience's perception of a campaign. Consider, for example, the following comment made by an executive working for a multinational corporation (cited in Vardar, 1992: 18): 'Why do I need eight different advertising campaigns in Europe? From a ten-foot pole in Brussels I can see all of Europe!' Having interviewed advertising executives in London about this very issue, Vardar (1992: 1) discusses a host of other factors that can influence the decision of whether or not to tailor a particular global campaign to local markets, including 'a lack of management support, agency commissions, local-authority/local-responsibility dilemmas and chaotic agency–client relationships'. From her research on international advertising, she concludes, however, that 'there is a clearly felt need by corporates to differentiate their global campaigns across borders' and that 'stereotyped decision-making processes are not advisable' (*ibid.*: 22).

Indeed, advocates of localization argue that a universal approach does not take into account country-specific variations, a good number of which are enumerated by Vardar (*ibid.*: 16):

The opponents of international advertising generally emphasize the difference across countries regarding language barriers (even in

the regions of the same country), religion, tastes, culture, standards of living (discretionary income), the literacy rate, advertising legislation, media availability, distribution channels and a lack of international advertising agencies. It is also stressed that local execution should be the norm – not the other way around.

To this list, Kanso and Nelson (2002: 80) rightfully add 'consumers' resentment of international corporations' attempts to homogenize their differing tastes and cultures'. Having reviewed the literature on standardization versus localization, Chen (2003: 13) agrees that those who favor customized approaches in advertising reject 'the unwarranted belief that the world consists of homogeneous consumers' claiming that 'the process of globalization may also have strengthened consumers' desire to hold on to their unique cultural heritage and national identity'.

Other current trends in international advertising include the use of pan-regional campaigns (such as advertising aimed at the European market) in lieu of global campaigns and 'pattern standardization' (a concept first introduced by Peebles, Ryans, and Vernon, 1977). Kanso and Nelson (2002: 80) describe the distinction between 'prototype standardization' and 'pattern standardization' as it is practiced today:

> Under prototype standardization, as it has been historically understood, the international firm in various countries would use the same advertisement or campaigns with the only differences being appropriate translations and a few idiomatic changes. On the other hand, under pattern standardization – a trend that seems now to be toward a more flexible form of standardization – the campaign, including the overall theme and individual components, is originally designed for use in multiple markets. Thus, the campaign is developed to provide uniformity in direction but not necessarily in detail. In other words, pattern standardization calls from the outset for the development of a single promotional theme along with flexibility in campaign execution to adapt to various local markets.

It has also been reported by members of the advertising industry that certain products are more likely to require country-specific campaigns (food products, for example) and that advertisements for 'high-tech' items (such as computers, stereo equipment, and so forth) do not necessarily require adaptation to local markets (Vardar, 1992). As the follow-

ing section will reveal, however, it is extremely important to take into account the local consumer's mentality and worldview when redesigning international campaigns for multiple audiences.

Testimonials from ad agencies in Paris

Providing local executions for an international campaign is, in the words of linguist Greg Myers (1999: 60) 'as complex as translation of poetry, for it involves, not just finding equivalent words, but also thinking about equivalent practices and interpretations.' This becomes particularly evident when one discusses the issue directly with those who design local advertising copy. Indeed, recent interviews in some of the leading advertising agencies in Paris have yielded some insightful commentary regarding the adaptation of global campaigns for the French market.[2] One of the most common observations made during these interviews was that advertising designed for the US market is often unappealing to French consumers who cannot always easily identify with the 'look and feel' of the advertisement. Referring to television commercials sent to Paris ad agencies from the US, one strategic planner noted:

> Sometimes it's just so American that you can't use it ... The American advertising we tend to get here [in the Paris office], sometimes it is extremely patriotic so it doesn't work. You can get that on any account ... It's interesting to see because it's supposed to be advertising that comes out of the US but from an international account and that's supposed to be used in all countries: Latin America, Australia, Asia, etc. And obviously it won't be used. It's just not possible.

Another pointed out cross-cultural differences with regards to notions such as 'success' and 'strategy' that can impact a campaign's design. This individual noted, for instance, that the French respond better to advertising messages that are less aggressive about 'beating the competition' than they might be in the US, preferring an emphasis on careful planning and 'strategy-building':

> A lot of the [advertising] messages that come out of the US are about being more successful [emphasizing] that major companies need to be more competitive. Those are issues in France as well. It's just that [the French] are not as straight to the point. It's not all about success.

It's all about building the right strategy [and] the right team to make your business more profitable.

In order to adapt international campaigns to local markets, ad agencies whose clients include multinational corporations often rely on multicultural, multilingual teams who can think 'outside the box'. Ad executives interviewed in Paris also applauded this 'blinders off' approach. As one American employed in one of the agencies put it:

Working on an international account, in my opinion, the only way to make it work right is having a multicultural background. If you only have Americans, it's not going to work. They're never going to see past the American viewpoint. In fact, sometimes I have to step back and ask other people what their opinions are [regarding a particular campaign] before I even form mine, because I have this natural tendency to see things [from an American perspective]. I need to see how these other people are reacting to it. So it's a challenge.

An account director in another agency in Paris underscored the importance of communicating local variables that can impact an advertising campaign's message back to the head office. Translating an international campaign into the 'language' of a particular market is, in this respondent's view, the responsibility of the local agency handling the account:

It's not [the head office's] problem. It's our problem. And we try to feed as much information as we can to New York and try to make them understand that, in the end, France is not Brazil, it's not Australia and even [that] France is not Germany and France is not Italy.

Indeed, those who fail to recognize the importance of local perceptions when distributing their advertising worldwide may seriously tarnish their brand's image.[3] Johnston and Beaton (1998: 67) provide some additional examples:

The Greek people were very angry and made strong representations to Coca-Cola about what an outsider might consider quite a harmless and witty advertisement. The design of the advertisement was a drawing which showed the Parthenon in Athens supported by four typical Coke bottles instead of Greek Corinthian columns. This

trivial approach to a cherished national monument made the Greeks very indignant and eventually forced Coca-Cola to withdraw the advertisement, although not before losing many sales and much goodwill in Greece. Similarly, the Christian Dior fashion house caused much consternation in the Arab world because of a dress design that had verses from the Koran as a decoration. Such lapses in judgment, or insensitivity towards cultural feelings, can cost companies dearly.

Generally speaking, the best advice to multinational corporations redesigning their international advertising for local markets is to choose visuals that are neutral or specifically adapted to the local culture. Dubbing on-camera voices in television commercials is also to be avoided as it is both awkward and expensive (Mueller, 1996: 156–7). Music, on the other hand, has universal appeal, particularly when sung in English due to the popularity of British and American pop recording artists (Martin, 1998a: 296–7). Those who are designing campaigns for the French market, however, would be wise to also take into account certain messages that appeal to this particular audience. Indeed, to effectively communicate with French consumers, one must look well beyond the mechanics of advertising design and consider various cultural perspectives that shape this audience's mentality. To address this issue, the following section provides an overview of French advertising for different products and services with a special emphasis on concepts that generally appeal to the French.

Advertising à la française

A typical example of adaptation can be found in a French print campaign for a French liqueur known as *Grand Marnier* (Figure 4.1) designed for the American market. In their effort to appeal to American consumers, those who designed this advertisement planted the Eiffel Tower (beloved symbol of France for the average American tourist) in a desert landscape (representing the United States). Scattered around this immediately recognizable French icon are the classic Saguaro cacti often used in French advertising to create an American 'Far West' atmosphere (as in the Renault Kangoo advertisement described in Chapter 3). The most interesting element, however, is the margarita recipe provided along the bottom edge: *1 oz. super-premium tequila, 1 oz. Grand Marnier™, 1 oz. fresh-squeezed lime juice (sugar to taste)*. To the right of the recipe sits a cocktail glass filled with the ice-cold mixture

Figure 4.1   Grand Marnier advertisement

nestled beside a bottle of Grand Marnier. A word borrowed from the French brand name (Grand Marnier) produces the slogan (*The Margarita goes GRAND*), drawing the reader's eye to the top of the Eiffel Tower and implying that a French product 'has arrived' in the 'land of Uncle Sam'. The word 'grand', however, can in fact be interpreted in several other ways as well. American audiences are likely to understand the word as 'impressive' or perhaps 'magnificent', whereas native speakers of French may also associate the word with size (motivated perhaps by the notion that everything is so 'big' in the US) as reflected by the Eiffel Tower filling the page of this ad. The most immediate association in this context, however, would most likely be 'GRAND' as in Grand Marnier. This entire Franco–American blend of dreamscapes is packaged as a postcard (presumably sent from the US back to France) bearing a postmark that combines all of the elements of the advertisement's intended message (*Grand Marnier Margarita*). Appearing in a design magazine specializing in home furnishings, this ad contains an attention-getter (the Eiffel Tower) that would likely appeal to the magazine's readers and presents the product in a context familiar to Americans.[4] Indeed, many of the cultural elements included here (the mixing of tequila with Grand Marnier to create margaritas, cocktails 'on the rocks,' and so on) would never be associated with this product when advertising it to the French. Audiences in France would expect a more subtle and sophisticated message for Grand Marnier geared towards the upper class, not to mention their aversion to ice cubes and mixing expensive French liqueur (a cultural icon in and of itself) with tequila. Indeed, wrapped in red ribbon with the French distiller's seal (Marnier–Lapostolle) stamped in a matching colored wax just above its very traditional and elegant label, the bottle looks oddly out of place in this arid, cactus-dotted American wilderness. A deeper analysis, however, reveals another possible interpretation. Grand Marnier is positioned here as a product that can be used to improve upon a well-loved recipe in America (imported from Mexico), news that is being reported back to France through the US postal system.

This technique of presenting a French improvement on a foreign recipe has been used for marketing French products in France as well. In the mid-1990s, for instance, the French company Lefèvre–Utile (represented as LU on its packaging) produced a TV spot for its latest cookie product, *'Hello!'* (Martin, 1998a: 288–90). The dialogue of the commercial (delivered entirely in American English, with French subtitles) was as follows:

French TV commercial for Lefèvre-Utile

A: (American model): Hello de LU? Incredible. A French cookie better than an American cookie? Ahhh. 30 per cent more chocolate chips. I get it! Do the French do everything with 30 per cent more?

B: (another woman, conservatively dressed, reading a book): Yes . . .

A: Oh Jennifer!

Voice-off: Hello! The cookie made in LU.

As in the Grand Marnier example, we see in this campaign a certain French pride (Martin, 1998a: 289–90):

> While mocking the arrogance of the French, the commercial advertises the fact that a French company has finally mastered a recipe that thus far only Americans could execute successfully: that of the notorious 'American chocolate chip cookie' . . . The fact that an American is making this claim in the commercial makes it even more appealing to French consumers.

This 'self-stereotyping' is one of many strategies used to evoke humor in advertising and may also operate as an attention-getter as illustrated in these examples (see Chapter 2).

Symbolism and cultural references

Studies on French advertising indicate that certain other strategies and concepts are frequently employed to appeal specifically to the French. It has been reported, for example, that audiences in France respond well to the use of symbols in advertising. In their analysis of French, Taiwanese, and American advertisements, Zandpour, Chang, and Catalano (1992: 35) made the following observation:

> French commercials work very hard to entertain the public through symbolism, humor and drama. Dramatic events often unfold without any apparent attention to the audience. The symbolism and drama may not even be related to the product.

Taylor, Hoy, and Haley (1996: 4) provide some interesting commentary in this regard from those who design advertising copy for the French market:

One strategic planner described the process of mentally examining all of French literature and culture to find an appropriate symbol for the protection plastic wrap gives prepackaged salad. The planner chose the screen (*paravent*) used by the little prince to protect a rose in Antoine de Saint-Exupery's *Le Petit Prince*.

Many additional examples of French cultural references in advertising are provided by Angelini and Federico (1998: 120) who note:

> The universe of reference for the French consumer is all of France: its regions, its history, its art, its literature, the character of the people who live there and their mentality. French advertising continually makes reference to French culture rather than just simply to the product itself.

This referencing of local culture can be integrated in various ways. French advertising for Kanterbräu beer, for instance, appeals to the French sense of regional pride. Kanterbräu magazine ads appearing in the corpus feature the famous *Flammeküche* (sic), a thin pizza-like Alsatian specialty topped with onions, bacon and *crème fraîche*. By focusing their ad on the Flammeküche (featured in both the text and the visual) and its quirky pronunciation, they draw the consumer's attention to the Alsatian origins of the beer brand (La Taverne de Maître Kanter), while emphasizing values that are extremely important to the French (such as *savoir-faire*, tradition and quality of life):

> *Flammeküche*: difficile à prononcer mais facile à apprécier. Que vous la mangiez à plusieurs en entrée ou comme plat principal, la flammeküche, servie sur sa pâte fine, fine, fine a les moyens de vous chatouiller l'appétit. Accompagnée d'une Kanterbräu, agrémentée de petits lardons, de crème fraîche et d'oignons, vous aurez du mal à ne pas vous laisser tenter. C'est normal, que voulez-vous, notre flammeküche suit la recette que Maître Kanter appliqua dès le jour où, il y a une centaine d'années, il décida d'ouvrir sa toute première brasserie: associer la qualité et le savoir-faire, la tradition et le savoir-vivre.*

English translation (mine)

> Flammeküche*: difficult to pronounce but easily appreciated. Whether you share it as an appetizer with friends or eat it as your

main dish, flammeküche, served on an ultra thin crust really whets your appetite. Accompanied by a Kanterbräu, sprinkled with bacon, crème fraîche and onions, you will have a hard time resisting. It's no wonder. Our flammeküche is made according to the very same recipe used by Maître Kanter when he opened his very first bar nearly a hundred years ago. A winning recipe that combines excellence with savoir-faire, and tradition with quality of life.

One also notices in the copy certain modern conveniences – such as pre-packaged foods ready to serve at anytime (*midi/minuit – 7/7 jours*) – presented as an alternative to more traditional eating habits from 'a hundred years ago'.

Coupled with this symbolism seen across the French advertising landscape is often a patchwork of imagery designed to be as aesthetically pleasing as possible. Advertising has, in fact, risen to somewhat of an art form in France, where at least one weekly documentary-style television program (*Culture Pub*) is devoted entirely to the topic, and cult audiences flock to area cinemas for 8-hour-long marathon projections (known as *La Nuit des Publivores*) of award-winning TV commercials from around the world (www.nuitdespublivores.com).[5] For French consumers, a picture tells a thousand words. Note Hall and Hall (1990: 95) in their cross-cultural comparison of the French, Germans, and Americans: 'image in advertising is far more important to the French than factual details'. Their description of a French theater is helpful in understanding the French appreciation for style (Hall and Hall 1990: 95):

> When you walk into a French theater, you may be overwhelmed by its elegance and ornate décor: gorgeous chandeliers, plush carpeting, elegant antiques. But if you look carefully, you'll notice that the baseboards need painting and the seats are frequently rickety . . . The French appreciate the overall effect and dismiss a bit of genteel decadence. This relates directly to the French preference in advertising.

This is not to say that quality and perfection are overlooked, however. On the contrary, any focus on quality workmanship and excellent materials is a successful strategy when addressing the French, regardless of the context (Zandpour, Chang, and Catalano, 1992). In a country where self-employed craftsmen (or *artisans*) are revered for continuing centuries-old traditions, and where in the world of business the pursuit

of quality and precision often takes precedence over the 'time is money' philosophy adopted by many Americans (Martin, 2003), any mention of excellence in terms of engineering or product components is likely to appeal to consumers.[6]

Humor and sexual appeals

Other aspects of French culture that are evident in their advertising include their sense of humor (Graby, 2001) and attitudes towards sexuality (Biswas, Olsen, and Carlet, 1992; Angelini and Federico, 1998). The use of emotional appeals has also been described as a successful means of addressing the French market. In their comparison of American and French print advertisements, for instance, Biswas, Olsen, and Carlet (1992) found that French advertisements conveyed more emotion than advertising in the US and were more likely to contain sexual humor. Their advice is simple (*ibid.*: 80):

> Multinational corporations attempting to advertise in France should be aware of the greater use of emotional appeals, sex appeals, and humor in French advertising and adapt accordingly.

One of the most notorious campaigns involving nudity in France was a series of poster advertisements for *Avenir* (an outdoor advertising contractor) depicting a very attractive young woman on a sunny beach smiling into the camera with her back to the ocean (Ogilvy, 1985: 26–7). In the first round of posters the model wore a two-piece bikini. The slogan, in bold capital letters, read 'On September 2nd, I will take off the top.' On precisely that date, another poster appeared with the same model standing topless next to the slogan 'On September 4th, I will take off the bottom.' After much anticipation, the French public saw the same model in a third version of the poster on September 4th, as promised, only this time completely naked from head to toe (with her back to the camera, alas). The closing slogan read 'Avenir. The poster contractor who keeps its promises.' Referring to the likely reaction of Americans to the use of nudity in this campaign, advertising guru David Ogilvy noted: 'Few Parisians were shocked. But I would not advise you to put up these posters in South Dakota' (Ogilvy, 1985: 26).

This appreciation for sexual humor is, in fact, evident in French advertising for every product and service imaginable. A kitchen sponge (with one abrasive side for scrubbing) marketed in France as *Spontex Diabolic*, for example, is depicted in a recent French television com-

mercial as a desirable lover for hedgehogs who enjoy rubbing their bodies against its rough, scratchy surface (Martin, 2005). The accompanying music soundtrack is in English:

Give me love, give me all that you've got
Give me love, give me all that you've got
Give me love, give me all that you've got

A sexy male voice (off-screen) alludes to the durability and high performance one might expect of a condom in his sensual description of the sponge (emphasis and italics added indicate words emphasized during the commercial):

Spontex présente Diabolic. Une éponge **très** *maniable avec une nouvelle texture grattante pour durer encore* **plus longtemps.** *Nouvelle Diabolic de Spontex. Aussi efficace, c'est Diabolic.*

English translation (mine)

Spontex introduces its *very* flexible sponge with a new rough texture that lasts *even longer.* It's Diabolic, and it's from Spontex. If it works that well, it's gotta be Diabolic.

Making similar sexual innuendos, a French bank (Banque Populaire) uses the English-language slogan 'Sleeping Partner' in their magazine advertising campaign promoting financial services for companies. The term 'sleeping partner' (or 'silent partner' in the US) as it is used in business is the English equivalent for *commanditaire* in French, referring to partners who invest in a company without having any direct role in management nor liability beyond their own financial contribution. The pun, of course, conjures up images of sharing one's bed with someone (presumably a business partner in this case) in an intimate manner, and requires the English translation ('sleeping partner') for humorous effect. A recent ad for ADA rental cars also appeals to the French sense of humor and directness in matters related to sex. It features a woman dressed in business attire picking someone up at the airport. In order to identify herself to the right gentleman as he exits the baggage claim area and customs, she holds up a sign with her party's name printed on it in large bold letters: Mr. P. NISS. The most unfortunate surname featured in this advertisement is interpreted in a similar fashion in both French and English due to its orthographical representation.

Word play

As was noted in the research presented in Chapter 1, a copywriter's palette includes any intricate array of linguistic devices, each of which serves to reinforce the semantic link between the copy, brand, and illustration in the advertisement. Given the French inquisitiveness and appreciation for clever word play, it is not surprising that linguistic creativity is another primary feature of their advertising. The copy used in a recent Goldy magazine advertising campaign is a prime example. Promoting watches, this campaign uses various invented homonyms for existing French words, all of which contain the French equivalent for 'time' (*heure*) as the final syllable in the very prominently displayed advertising slogan. As is very common in French advertising, where humor and linguistic creativity are often intertwined, an analysis of both the subtext and the visual are required to fully appreciate the pun in each advertisement. In one example, we find the slogan *'CREAT'HEURE'* (reminiscent of *créateur* in French, or 'creator') written horizontally in bold capital letters across the center of the page, after which the following text appears in fine print: *Bonne fête à tous les hommes qui ont eu la riche idée de se faire appeler 'papa'*. (Happy Father's Day to all the men out there who had the splendid idea of being called 'daddy'). The visual depicts the faces of two babies peering over the shoulders of their *'papa'* who is facing away from the camera. At the bottom of the page is a rather small representation of the product being advertised: a Seiko watch. Using the text as a support to the visual, at first glance, one might interpret the slogan literally as 'creator' (as in 'procreator', or he who begets offspring). This 'reading' is, of course, encouraged through both the image and the second line of text (alluding to Father's Day). This unusual hybrid also projects another 'reading' as *'créateur'* (the French word which automatically springs to mind when hearing the slogan's pronunciation) is also used as an adjective in French, meaning 'creative', which also refers back to the 'splendid idea' (*la riche idée*) in the slogan. This second level of association is certainly a positive one that the company would not object to on the part of its advertising audience. Other inventions of this nature featured in the campaign include *BON'HEURE, BOUD'HEURE*, and *VAINQ'HEURE*, all of which are likely to be understood in the following manner:

BON'HEURE → *bonheur* ('happiness')
BOUD'HEURE → *boudeur* ('sulky, sullen person')
VAINQ'HEURE → *vainqueur* ('victor, winner')

The unusual punctuation (apostrophe placed in center of word) further identifies each word as a whimsical creation on the part of copywriters. As for the use of imagery in these latter examples, the ad featuring 'BON'HEURE' ('happiness') as its slogan depicts a (very) pregnant woman with copy that reads: *Bonne fête à toutes les mamans et à celles qui vont le devenir dans . . . quelques heures* (Happy Mother's Day to all you moms and to those who are going to be . . . in a few hours). Thus, the slogan in this case is alluding to the joy (*'bonheur'*) of becoming a mother while at the same time recalling the product being advertised (*'heure'* or 'time'). 'BOUD'HEURE' ('sulky'), on the other hand, describes a child who is pouting in the visual of another ad. The slogan 'VAINQ'HEURE' ('winner') in yet another ad included in the campaign is reinforced by the image of a tennis ball heading straight for a player's face (the consumer). This campaign is a classic example of what Schmitt, Tavassoli, and Millard (1993) refer to as brand name, copy and picture relation, whereby the copy (puns derived from the French word for 'time'), visual elements of the ad (illustrating the pun), and the product (watches) reinforce one another, one of many strategies employed by copywriters to enhance product brand recall.

Another form of word play encountered in French advertising is the back slang involving creative processes such as syllable-inversion and spelling reversal known as *verlan* (Azra and Cheneau, 1994). Popularized through rap music and other entertainment media, this complex cryptic language game is primarily used by France's younger generation and thus does not appear in any of the advertising in the corpus for other audiences.[7] In a magazine ad for cell phone rings and logos, however, we find two examples of *verlan*:

Je te kiffee à donf
Kiff ta meuf

Considered as examples of 'monosyllabic verlan' (Goudailler, 1997: 24), the items *'à donf'* and *'meuf'* are derived from *'à fond'* (or *'vraiment'*, meaning 'really') and *'femme'* ('woman') respectively. There is much more to the word formation processes of verlan than meets the eye, however. The word *'meuf'*, for example, involves affixation (with the addition of a word-final schwa), followed by syllable-inversion, and truncation (that is, removal of the final vowel):

femme → *meufa* → *meuf*

The verlanization of the word *'fond'*, on the other hand, involves a switching of the word-initial consonant [f] and the word-final consonant [d], producing *'donf'*:

$$fond \rightarrow donf$$

As for the words *kiffee* and *kiff*, these items are slang words derived from the verb infinitive *kiffer* (Goudailler, 1997: 118) meaning *'aimer beaucoup'* or *'adorer'* ('to really like or appreciate'), giving us the following interpretation:

Je te kiffee à fond → Je t'adore
Kiff ta femme → Aime (ou apprécie) ta femme

English translation (mine)

You rock! (I really dig you!)
Rock your woman! (Love your woman!)

Tejedor de Felipe (2004) provides another example of a discourse resembling *verlan* used in a French advertisement for SNCF, France's national railway company. The dialogue involves a group of young people purchasing tickets in a train station. Both the young travelers and the SNCF ticket salesman with whom they interact express themselves using syllable-inversion and spelling innovations typical to this language variety (Tejedor de Felipe, 2004: 19):

Teenager:	*Eh! Keum, mon tepo et wam,*
	on veut partir à la rém.
Employee:	*Chètcou ou place assise?*
Teenager:	*Euh! C'est pas possible.*
Employee:	*Mais si, c'est blesipo.*

French translation (Tejedor de Felipe, 2004: 19)

Teenager:	*Eh! Mec, mon pote et moi,*
	on veut partir à la mer.
Employee:	*Couchette ou place assise?*
Teenager:	*Euh! C'est pas possible.*
Employee:	*Mais si, c'est possible.*

As Tejedor de Felipe points out, however, the language used in this context could more aptly be described as an imitation of *verlan* (invented

specifically for the advertising campaign) as several elements in the conversational exchange do not reflect the reality of *verlan* as it is spoken by urban youth, including the words chosen for verlanization. Consider, for instance, the syllable reversal in the word *couchette* (*chètcou*) 'sleeping berth' or the consonant inversion applied to the word *mer* (*rém*) 'sea', neither of which is attested in *verlan* as it is commonly used by the urban youth. Furthermore, as *verlan* operates as an in-group code, it is inconceivable that young people would express themselves in this manner when addressing a presumably unknown SNCF ticket salesman, whose use of *verlan* in responding to them is therefore even more conspicuous. Nevertheless, by displaying what appears to be *verlan* in their advertising, SNCF does the unexpected and is thus able to better attract the attention of younger audiences.[8]

Natural ingredients

Anyone wanting to design an advertising campaign for food, personal care, or household products for the French market would also be wise to emphasize natural ingredients, a concept that is of utmost importance to French consumers. Indeed, in France, ads for everything from face cream, deodorant, shampoo, and laundry detergent to chickens and ice cream stress the avoidance of chemicals and additives as much as possible. Given the rejection of genetically modified crops in France, Picard's reference to organic foods in their advertising is hardly surprising. Specializing in frozen foods, Picard offers a line of products made solely from organically grown produce which they call '*Bio*' after the term used by the French when referring to organic produce or health food stores.[9] In their advertising for the French market, they stress the fact that Picard is serious about offering as natural a product as possible. The slogan in one recent campaign reads:

'*Mes envies de bio, c'est mon besoin de naturel, alors . . . Picard, c'est plus sûr.*'

English translation (mine)

'My desire for organic foods reflects my need for all that is natural, so Picard is a sure bet.'

The use of quotation marks for the slogan in this particular ad implies that the remarks printed in the campaign are coming from a satisfied Picard customer, a woman whose cupped hands, holding a clump of dark rich soil with a single seed starting to sprout in the center, are featured

in the visual. Also pictured is a spoonful of 'organic' broccoli (*Fleurettes de brocolis Bio*) and a tub of 'organic' strawberry sherbet (*Sorbet fraise Bio*). The nature theme continues throughout the rest of the copy:

> *Retrouver le goût du vrai. Rechercher le naturel. Aider au respect de l'environnement. Possible avec Picard et sa gamme Bio, allant de l'entrée au dessert: plus de 30 produits issus de l'agriculture biologique. Envie de changer? Connectez vous sur Picard.fr . . .*

English translation (mine)

> Rediscover the taste of real food. Find natural ingredients. Respect the environment. Picard makes it all possible with its Bio product line, featuring everything from appetizers to desserts: more than 30 products grown organically. Feel like changing? Log onto Picard.fr . . .

This 'bio' strategy was a wise choice for Picard's advertising campaign as frozen foods tend to be regarded by the French as less desirable as compared to meals prepared from scratch using natural ingredients gathered at a local farmer's market.[10] Those adapting international campaigns for this market should note that underscoring the organic properties of various foods is likely to be much more effective with French consumers than low carbs, low sugar, or low fat, all of which are used to sell similar products in other markets, such as the United States.

A very similar (verbal and textual) copy strategy is used in ads for the French supermarket chain, E. Leclerc. The visual features a woman about to put a sizable clump of dirt and grass into her mouth. The slogan reads:

> *Pour s'assurer qu'un poulet est bio, il faut s'assurer que la terre qui l'a nourri l'est aussi.*

English translation (mine)

> If you want to be sure that a chicken is 'all natural', you have to know that the earth that produced its feed was as well.

In smaller print, we find the *Agriculture Biologique* (*AB*) label used in France for organic foods interpreted for the discerning consumer:[11]

> *Ce label vous garantit qu'un produit est réellement bio, c'est-à-dire élaboré sans engrais chimique, désherbant ou insecticide de synthèse.*

English translation (mine)

   This label guarantees that a product is 100 per cent organic, developed without chemical fertilizers, weed killer nor synthetic insecticide.

The 'all natural' approach extends to cosmetics as well. In a recent ad for an Yves Rocher face cream line (marketed as *Soin Auto-Défense Ville*, or 'Auto-Defence Care for City Life'), we find references to plants (*100% végétal . . . biologie végétale . . . extraits végétaux . . . Ginkgo Biloba*), a female model dressed in a nature-inspired mossy green top, green product packaging, plus a pun involving the word 'nature' in the company signature line: *Yves Rocher. On n'a jamais autant respecté la nature des femmes* (Yves Rocher. No one respects the nature of women more). Other companies specializing in body care products also use natural ingredients as the focal point of their advertising. The first thing one notices in a recent Garnier Ultra Doux hair mask cream ad is the lemon peel wrapped around a bottle of olive oil and cream, presumably evoking 'the perfect recipe for well nourished hair' (*la recette préférée des cheveux bien nourris*). Grape seeds figure both visually and textually in an ad for a face cream by Nivea (Nivea Vital) as well.[12] Roger & Gallet shower gels, on the other hand, are advertised as containing lettuce extract, grape extract, and linden blossoms and as being 'rich in essential oils, vitamins, and minerals'.[13] French brands (for example, Garnier) are using a similar 'nature' theme in their advertising for foreign markets, claiming that vitamins and minerals drawn from vegetables, fruits, and herbs are among the 'natural' ingredients in products such as shampoo.

Environmental protection

The French are also generally concerned about pollution and protecting the environment, a philosophy highlighted in a good deal of their advertising. There have been several recent campaigns, for instance, that use recycling as the primary theme. Responding to the French consumer's love for bottled water, Evian was one of the first companies to introduce collapsible plastic bottles that could be flattened (much like a soda can) for easier recycling, saving valuable space in the kitchen. Protecting the environment is the main theme of a recent French television commercial for the local gas company (Gaz de France). The spot features a series of snapshot images from around the world interwoven with glimpses of daily life in France. Television viewers are left with the impression that the energy they consume is directly linked to the environment, both in terms of origin and human impact on existing

resources. The off-screen narration and visual images are listed below in the order of their appearance in the commercial:

French TV commercial for Gaz de France (voice-off and images)

Original voice-off in French as it is heard during the commercial	Voice-Off in English (translation mine)	Images seen during commercial
La chaleur est là	→ The heat is over there	• Desert sand dunes
On en a besoin ici	→ We need it here	• City traffic in winter storm • Snowing at night • Little girl wiping condensation off a window from lighted interior of her home
Les glaçons sont là	→ The ice cubes are over there	• Icebergs in Antarctica
On les consomme ici	→ We consume them here	• Ice cubes falling into a glass
Nos réserves sont là	→ Our reserves are out there	• Woman smiling with her family. Children giggling in the ocean surf • Oil rig in ocean
Nos clients sont ici	→ Our customers are here	• Stove top flame with pot boiling • Kids coming out of school • Birds flying, eagle soaring
L'air pur est là	→ The air there is pure	• Himalayas with Tibetans on horseback driving yaks • Indian woman with child on bus in the mountains

		• Men talking on bus
Il faut le défendre ici	→ We must protect it here	• Pedestrians
		• Close-up of back of public bus in France where it is written '*Je roule au gaz naturel*' (I am running on natural gas)
		• Woman with child in stroller walks behind bus
Gaz de France. Nous inventons un monde fait pour vous ici, là-bas, pour vous, pour demain.	*Gaz de France.* We invent a world made for you . . . here, over there, for you, for tomorrow. (Voice-off. Translation mine)	

By weaving together in this manner a stream of images from both the consumer's immediate environment and locations around the planet, the company places environmental issues in a global context and assures the viewer that they are doing everything they can to protect the planet's natural resources, while providing a valuable service to its customers. With its international flavor, intertwining images of nature, and visual reminders that Gaz de France is concerned about environmental issues, this ad is appealing in that it positions the environmentally-conscientious French consumer as a member of the global community while assuring them that their energy needs are being met.

Logic and intelligence

Those who have analyzed the French mentality and made cross-cultural comparisons between the French and Americans (Zeldin, 1984; Hall and Hall, 1990; Platt, 1998; Asselin and Mastron, 2001; Nadeau and Barlow, 2003; among others) have also noted that a key characteristic of the French psyche is an appreciation for logic and intelligence. As Asselin and Mastron (2001: 147) put it: 'Rational thought is the highest expression of French intelligence, and thinking about something rationally can be an end in itself.' A decade earlier, Hall and Hall (1990: 105) seem to have reached the same conclusion: 'The most persuasive argument to the French is always the logical, practical argument.' The following

anecdote these authors provide regarding the adaptation of a French advertising campaign for the German market illustrates this cultural trait quite clearly (Hall and Hall, 1990: 105):

> One French executive who had worked successfully in both France and Germany had great difficulty persuading his French home office to use German-style ads in Germany for its French products. For many years he tried unsuccessfully to explain to his superiors why French ads had no appeal to Germans. 'Germans don't care about mood or emotional appeal,' he would say, but the French office could not believe this and continued running their mood-laden ads. Finally, he turned to logic: 'Since German shopping hours are severely limited, Germans naturally prefer ads that are full of information and facts about the product. They are also very value-conscious. But because there is not enough time to shop around and compare products in the stores, Germans are in the habit of doing their comparisons on the basis of information gleaned from ads. It is logical, therefore, that if a French firm is to sell in Germany, it must provide the buyer with enough information so he can make up his mind.' This approach reached his French superiors.

This preference for logic extends to advertising copy directed at French consumers where one also finds references to intelligence and education.

The importance placed by the French on academic achievement, logic and intelligence, coupled with their love for the French language and the pleasure they derive from word play, explain in large part the enormous success of the annual spelling competition in France known as *Les Dicos d'Or* (Garnier, 2001). Aired on major television networks, *'la dictée nationale'* is led by popular literary television talk show host Bernard Pivot and draws enthusiastic audiences who listen to the dictation on television (or in person by attending the star-studded event) and test their spelling prowess by writing out the text.[14] Cross-cultural trainer and author Polly Platt underscores the significance of the event in her popular book *French or Foe?* (1998: 158–9).

An institution since he started it in 1986, Pivot's *dictée* is known as the Spelling Championship of France. Its popularity is up there with the Tour de France (the bicycle race) and the world soccer championships. It consists of two or three paragraphs of extremely difficult prose riddled with traps ... Each year the *dictée* mobilizes over 300,000 officially registered candidates around the world, and perhaps

seven million more taking it by television ... The winner and the full text, the esoteric words and grammatical traps carefully explained, are in all the newspapers the next day. A spelling bee? 300,000 candidates? Yes! Writing and speaking French perfectly is as crucial as getting the right wine to match the cheese you're serving.

Anyone who has witnessed this phenomenon cannot deny that intellect enjoys a certain prestige in France, making it a popular theme in advertising campaigns for the French market. Consider, for example, the concept of '*la dictée*' featured in a television commercial for *Jour après Jour* by Lactel. In this case, the milk product is presented in the voice-off as a beverage rich in fiber for mothers who must deal with the many challenges of raising children (such as learning that your son failed his dictation):

> *Flash info: Votre fils a eu un zéro en dictée, mais ce n'est pas une fatalité. Jour après Jour de Lactel: des fibres, et du bien-être.*

English translation (mine)

> News flash. Your son got a zero in dictation. So, it's not the end of the world. Jour après Jour ['Day after day'] by Lactel, for fiber and a sense of well-being.

As the following content analysis of adaptations of international campaigns for the French market will reveal, advertising agencies are incorporating these and other creative solutions for addressing French consumers, appealing to their regional and national identity, sense of humor, intellect, and culture-specific attitudes regarding the product being advertised. These adaptations for the French market provide proof that customizing advertising campaigns for local audiences is an entertaining but daunting task which requires an in-depth knowledge of the French mentality and worldview. One size, indeed, does not fit all.

Global campaigns tailored to French audiences

Addressing the French as Europeans

One of the ways in which advertising agencies tailor international campaigns to the French market is to simply adapt a 'regional' approach, addressing French consumers as Europeans. Recent ads for IBM appearing in French magazines (Martin, 2005), for instance, feature IBM repre-

sentatives whose European-sounding names (for example, Christophe Menant, Antje Kruse-Schomaker) imply that they are locally employed Europeans and are therefore better able to communicate with IBM's European customers. Following the name of the individual depicted in each ad is a brief description of the specific business solutions he or she has implemented for IBM clients. The slogan written in bold capital letters across the forehead of each employee further reinforces IBM's claim to meet local demands: 'Who do you need?' ('*De qui avez-vous besoin?*'), while supporting the 'symbolic' message expressed by the illustration. Young and engaging, and distinctly European, the IBM employee depicted in each ad exudes a certain energy and professionalism (and readiness to please) while offering a level of comfort through a 'familiar' face. In contrast to other IBM campaigns which have focused on the interconnectivity of today's global market and 'solutions for a small planet', this approach is clearly targeting Europeans in particular, placing the multinational corporation squarely behind faces with which French consumers can easily identify. This campaign also features a fair amount of English in the copy (for example, SOFT2YOU, e-business) which the French are likely to associate with the notion of exclusivity (software designed specifically for your needs) as well as the latest trends in global business (such as online purchasing).[15]

In another IBM campaign for French consumers, we find a wall-mounted thermostat featured in the illustration (with degree markings ranging from 0 to 30), obviously geared towards Europeans who prefer their temperature readings in Centigrade (as opposed to Fahrenheit). Next to the thermostat appears the phrase '*A régler selon vos besoins*' ('Set according to your needs'). The rest of the copy alludes to IBM's 'e-business on demand' as being a basic necessity, comparable to utilities such as gas, electricity and water, for which IBM provides the hardware, installation, and servicing:

Découvrez e-business on demand. The next utility (slogan). Besoin de chaleur? Montez le thermostat. Besoin d'eau? Ouvrez le robinet. Besoin de plus de ressources informatiques? Vous achetez des serveurs, vous construisez une solution, puis vous les installez, les intégrez, les paramétrez . . . Ou bien optez pour e-business on demand. Il vous évite de lourds investissements et vous permet d'être rapidement opérationnel. Il couvre l'ensemble de vos besoins, des matériels aux applicatifs. Il est fiable et évolutif. Avec 'The Next Utility', vous faites face en toutes circonstances. Découvrez e-business on demand: visitez ibm.com/e-business/fr/ondemand . . .

English translation (mine)

> Discover e-business on demand. The next utility (slogan). Need heat? Turn up the thermostat. Need water? Turn on the faucet. Need more computer capability? You can buy servers, come up with a solution, then install everything, reconfigure it, and set all of the parameters . . . Or you can choose e-business on demand. You will save yourself a lot of money and be operational in no time. It will meet all your needs, whether it is hardware, software, or technical support. It's reliable and adaptable to your situation. With 'The Next Utility', you will be ready for anything. Discover e-business on demand: visit ibm.com/e-business/fr/ondemand . . .

French advertising for the Ford Mondeo (Figure 4.2) also displays a sensitivity to the European context. In this case, the product, sold by a US-based automaker, was first developed in Europe for the European market before being marketed in the US. Here, to address European audiences, the Ford Motor Company uses an image that Europeans will find familiar (Martin, 2005). The main selling point of this campaign is a safety feature in the Ford Mondeo (referred to as the *Intelligent Protection System*, or IPS) that electronically adjusts the deployed airbag size, seat belt length, and head rest height to fit the car's occupants. In the visual, two tape measures (marked with centimeters rather than inches) serve as seat belts taking measurements of both the driver and the front seat passenger, thus protecting them in the event of a collision. By simply referencing the metric system, the ad speaks directly to Europeans while providing a key visual that encapsulates the entire selling point (that the Ford IPS system will protect you) into one neat package. The slogan (*Protection sur mesure?* IPS: Intelligent Protection System) also contains elements that are appealing to the French, such as the references to intelligence and protection, as well as the claim (as in the IBM example) that Ford is providing a feature that is specifically tailored (*'sur mesure'*) to the client's situation. The measuring tape in the illustration clearly symbolizes this 'customization' while alluding to the added level of security that these electronically adjusted seatbelts (and other features) provide. The use of an English acronym (IPS) and accompanying English slogan is also significant in that this type of technical jargon, when borrowed from English into French, is often associated with modern technology and/or quality engineering.[16] The fact that the French translation is more prominently displayed, however, suggests that the Ford Motor Company wanted to place the product firmly within a French context, addressing French consumers directly.

Figure 4.2   Ford Mondeo advertisement

Television commercials for American brands distributed in France may also use imagery that appeals more to Europeans. Coca-Cola, for instance, chose soccer as its theme for a campaign used in the French market (Martin, 2005). Aired just before the 2002 World Cup, hosted by Korea and Japan, the spot features two sports announcers, one Asian, the other from South America. The Asian arrives unannounced at the home of his South American counterpart, asking for advice as to how to become a great sportscaster in time for the World Cup. Relying on stereotypes that paint Asians as reserved, 'soft-spoken' individuals, the storyline involves the more 'expressive' Latino teaching the Asian how to pronounce the word 'goal!' with more gusto and enthusiasm. After several unsuccessful attempts, the Asian finally 'nails' the pronunciation after his 'coach' suggests that he take a swig of Coca-Cola. *Et voilà!* This commercial was well received in France because of the familiar cultural references (such as soccer) and use of humor (based, in this case, on stereotypes involving other countries). No reference whatsoever is made to the American origins of the brand. (English translation mine.)

French TV commercial for Coca-Cola

South American sportscaster:	Oui? (*Yes?*)
Asian:	*Je voudrais devenir un grand commentateur de la coupe du monde.* [I would like to become a great sportscaster for the World Cup]
South American:	*OK. Mais vous devriez faire comme je vous dis . . . (screaming) GOL!!!!* [OK. But you'll have to do as I say . . . GOAL!!!!*]
Asian (trying to approximate the pronunciation):	*Gol . . . gol . . . gol . . . * [Goal . . . goal . . . goal . . .]
South American (hands him a can of Coca-Cola):	*Tenez* [Here, try this]
Asian (smiling):	*GOL!!!!!!!* [GOAL!!!!!!!] * Subtitled as '*But*'

Advertisements distributed in France will also sometimes feature multilingual product labels to avoid the cost of translating the campaign
into several languages for the European market.[17] The following chart
provides the example of text featured on the product labels for two hair
products recently advertised in French magazines:

Brand name	Product type	Languages appearing on product label	Text on product label (excerpt)
Kérastase Oléo- Relax	Shampoo	1. French 2. English 3. Spanish	• Shampooing détente cheveux secs et très rebelles • Smoothing shampoo dry and rebellious hair • Champú relajante cabello seco y muy rebelde
Roger & Gallet Gels Douche Doux Nature	Shower gel	1. French 2. English 3. German	• Gel bain douche dermoprotecteur • Gentle nature bath & shower gel with Grape extract • Dusch- & Badegel mit Traubenextrakt

Another ad, this one for a sunscreen lotion by Nivea, features both a
trilingual (French, English, German) label and a slogan involving a
bilingual (French and German) pun: *'Tout schuss sur la protection
maximale. Anti-froid / Anti-UV'*. With the young female snowboarder in
the visual, the product (*Nivea Sun Alpin*) is positioned as a skin lotion
designed to prevent chapping due to exposure to cold weather and
sunburn, both of which one is likely to experience while skiing at
high altitudes. Here, the German word *schuss* (which onomatopoeti-
cally depicts the crouching position downhill skiers use to gain
speed) sounds very much like *juste* (as in *tout juste* in French), producing a slogan approximating 'Just the right amount of maximum
protection from both the cold and the sun's ultraviolet rays': *Juste ce*

qu'il faut pour la protection maximale. The text appearing on the product label mixes all three languages (English, French and German) as well:

Languages used	Text appearing on label
Brand name + English	Nivea Sun
French or German	Alpin 26
French–English mix	Combi crème-stick
German	Kälteschutz
German	Sonnenschutz
French	Mousse contre le froid
French	Protège des coups de soleil

Advertising specifically designed for the French

Other advertisements distributed in France are obviously designed for the French market as they contain verbal, visual, and cultural elements that appeal specifically to French consumers (as opposed to Europeans in general). Consider, for example, a recent French advertising campaign for the Toyota Yaris. Capitalizing on the fact that this particular model was designed in France (where it is also manufactured), the company ran a television commercial for the French market featuring a French–English code-mixed dialogue that essentially identifies the product as being 100 percent French.[18] This French version of the similar 'Made in USA' strategy used in a good deal of American advertising is interesting in that French consumers are generally well aware of the Japanese origins of the Toyota brand. To create a French (as opposed to Japanese) atmosphere in the commercial, however, the dialogue (accompanied by a typically French accordion music soundtrack) alludes to the superiority of French cuisine, as well as their general pride in all things French (in this case, the car). Also interesting is the use of heavily accented pigeon-like English in the dialogue which appears to serve a triple function: (i) poking fun at the required use of English with non-Francophone international guests despite the difficulty of learning English as a foreign language, (ii) making the English dialogue accessible to a wider (French-speaking) television-viewing audience, and (iii) modifying the *lingua franca* (English in this case) so as to give the commercial a 'French flavor', much as the Japanese-brand automobile is presented here as '*la French voiture*' ('Toyota Yaris France. The French car'). Using this code-mixed version in lieu of a monolingual expression ('*la voiture française*') draws attention to the spot, is humorous, and is an effective strategy for placing France on the global stage through the medium of English:

TV commercial for Toyota Yaris

Visual: A foreign dignitary with entourage aboard a private jet is heading somewhere in France. The Frenchman whose English is rather limited tries to make him as comfortable as possible, doing everything he can to emphasize French hospitality. The dignitary (busy reviewing his itinerary with his personal assistant) totally ignores his French host until he catches a glimpse of the car awaiting him on the runway, a Toyota Yaris. (*indicates subtitles appearing in the commercial)

Frenchman:	Excellency, the French petit déjeuner *Votre excellence, petit déjeuner français*
Dignitary:	(Does not respond. Ignores breakfast tray.)
Frenchman:	Excellency, cuisine française *Votre excellence, cuisine française*
Dignitary:	(Does not respond. Ignores lunch tray.)
Visual:	They land and open the cockpit door, seeing the Toyota Yaris parked beside the plane.
Frenchman:	Excellency . . . *Votre excellence . . .*
Dignitary:	(holds up hand signaling that he understands) French car *Voiture française.*
Frenchman:	Oh yes! *Et oui.*
Voice-off:	Toyota Yaris France. La French voiture. A partir de 9160 euros aux journées Yaris France. (Toyota Yaris France.The French car. Starting at 9160 euros during Yaris France Days) (my translation)

The commercial closes with accordion music in the background, further symbolizing French culture.

Any mention of the French culinary expertise in the commercial, highly prized in French society, however, remains entirely in French ('*petit déjeuner*', '*cuisine française*'). Although it is designed for a Japanese brand, through its imagery, music, dialogue, and symbolism, this commercial is a celebration of the French culture and identity and highly entertaining for audiences in this market.

Similar references to French culture appear in advertising in other media as well. A magazine ad for Amadeus business travel solutions, for instance, features a breakfast croissant prominently displayed in the visual, with the following headline: *'Si vous décrochez le contrat du siècle, les croissants de votre hôtel à Zanzibar et Amadeus y sont sûrement pour quelque chose . . .'* (If you get the contract of the century, the croissants from your hotel in Zanzibar and Amadeus surely had something to do with it). Here, the image of the croissant (lying on a white tablecloth) symbolizes any number of concepts that are appealing to the French. First of all, it reflects a certain level of comfort and familiarity, providing a 'touch of home' to a French business executive traveling to an island off the East coast of Africa (now part of Tanzania). It is a slice of French culture, a snapshot of domesticity and contentment, that evokes positive associations with family life, the security and comforts of home, and the pleasure of dipping a buttery croissant into a steamy cup of *café au lait* while reading the morning newspaper. This visual symbol of 'Frenchness' also connotes a certain energy as 'fortifying' oneself with croissants before attacking the duties of the day might be seen as a type of *'ravitaillement'* (or 'refueling') given the 'contract negotiations' theme of the slogan. Thus, the product is positioned as a catalyst for success much as a croissant is a fuel source that helps one 'jumpstart' the day. The image also exudes a certain elegance and formality (also indicative of the French business culture) as the white tablecloth background is likely to be associated with dining in expensive restaurants. Thus, an additional layer of meaning emerges: the executive who purchases this service can dazzle his or her client over breakfast at a hotel (found by Amadeus) that serves croissants that are just as exquisite as those one might find in France. From this perspective, an appreciation for the French cultural identity of the advertisement's intended audience is as evident here as it is in the Toyota example presented earlier.

In an Italian advertising campaign in France promoting tourism in Vallée d'Aoste, Italy, on the other hand, we find a reference to the fashion industry which is also likely to appeal to the French. One ad describes the highest mountains in the region (Mont Blanc, Mont-Rose, Cervin, Grand Paradis) as 'top models' whose impressive measurements (in meters) appear in large bold print in the copy (with alpine scenery appearing in the background):

4810, 4632, 4478, 4061. Voici les mensurations des 4 top-models valdôtains.

English translation (mine)

4810, 4632, 4478, 4061. These are the measurements of the four top-models in Vallée d'Aoste.

Another features a full-page photo of cheese on page one, an image that is also very likely to attract French consumers who have a special relationship with cheese, and whose own country has produced over 400 varieties, each associated with a particular region in France (www.fromages.com). The cheese shown here is Fontina, commonly used in making cheese fondu, a dish the French associate with the Alps. A description of other culinary specialties of the Vallée d'Aoste region appears on the second page of the ad (for example, *polenta, jambon de Bosses, lard d'Arnad*, plus 22 different locally produced wines). While capitalizing on the French tourist's fascination with food, the copy in this very same ad also takes into account their appreciation for history and ancient architecture, inviting readers to explore the ruins of one hundred or so castles dating from the Neolithic Period, the Roman Empire, and the Middle Ages. The cheese pictured in the ad is also presented with a reference to both history and archeology, increasing its appeal: *Fontine. Ce monument gastronomique date de 1270!* (Fontina. This gastronomic monument dates back to the year 1270!). The signature line accompanying the logo at the end of the ad further imbues the ad with a sense of reverence for historical preservation and cultural traditions while making use of a pun that is likely to appeal to this audience: *Vallée d'Aoste, Italie. Elle ne change pas, ça change tout!* (Vallée d'Aoste, Italy. It doesn't change and that changes everything!)

GrimBergen beer ads in France also contain familiar images that appeal to the French consumer's sense of history and architectural heritage. In the land of gothic cathedrals, a gargoyle hanging off the side of a church (with duct tape over its mouth, in this case) is likely to have some appeal. At the top of the page, a foaming glass of GrimBergen beer greets the consumer, followed by the slogan *Bière d'Abbaye depuis 1128. GrimBergen. Et le silence se fait.* ('Abbey beer since 1128. GrimBergen. And then there was silence'). In the crease of the magazine appears an explanation for those who remain puzzled (English translation mine): *Le silence: règle qu'observaient les prémontrés à l'Abbaye de Grimbergen.* (Silence: rule observed by monks at the Abbey of Grimbergen). Indeed, French consumers are likely to find this advertisement entertaining for its use of subtle humor but also its visual and textual treatment of monasteries, a popular weekend destination for many French people who enjoy the architecture and history of such places, and appreciate

their centuries-old tradition of brewing beer. This advertisement also appeals to their inquisitiveness, as in France any advertisement that requires a little analysis on the part of the consumer is always welcome.

As for companies advertising deodorant in France, they have the special challenge of convincing the French consumer that their product contains no harmful chemicals. Having analyzed the product from a medical/health perspective, the French view deodorants (with their cocktail of unpronounceable ingredients) with a bit of suspicion, opting for the most natural product available on the market. A recent French ad for a deodorant sold under the brand name Dove Sensitive is a case in point (Martin, 2005). The headline clearly takes into account typical French attitudes towards deodorant: *Ce n'est pas ce qu'il y a dedans qui le rend différent. C'est ce qu'il n'y a pas.* (It's not what's in it that makes it different. It's what's not in there.) Centered on the page is the product with text to either side indicating that it contains neither alcohol, coloring, nor perfume. The copy at the bottom of the page, in bold, assures the consumers that the product is both natural and effective: *Hypoallergénique, efficace et c'est tout* (It's hypoallergenic, it works, and that's all there is to it). Worth noting here as well is that the product name (Dove Sensitive) not only implies that it is gentle on the skin, but it is also an interesting example of a recently adopted English borrowing (the more commonly used French equivalent being *sensible*). Commercials for other products appearing on French television also feature the English word *sensitive* (such as the toothpaste marketed in France as Signal Sensitive Extra), offering additional evidence that the original meaning of the borrowing in English is gaining recognition in France. Additional examples of recent English borrowings used in French advertising copy will be discussed in greater detail in Chapter 5.

A recent French television commercial for an automobile (the Audi A2), on the other hand, emphasizes environmental protection. The spot opens with the close-up of two men dressed in dark business suits peering through the window of a parked Audi in a chic Parisian-style neighborhood. The on-screen dialogue implies that they consider owning an Audi as an impossible dream, associating it with a higher social status:

French TV commercial for Audi

1ˢᵗ man: *Quand t'as une voiture comme ça, t'es au top!*
2ⁿᵈ man: *Ouais, tu dois suivre le salaire, les filles.*
1ˢᵗ man: *T'es le roi.*

2nd man: *Remarque, si j'avais une voiture comme ça, moi, je sais ce que je ferais.*

1st man: *En même temps, t'es jamais tranquille. Tout le monde te regarde.*

2nd man: *Elle est belle, hein?*

English translation (mine)

1st man: When you drive a car like that, you've got it made!

2nd man: Yeah, you must really be raking in the money, and the girls.

1st man: You're the man!

2nd man: You know, if I had a car like that, I know what I'd do.

1st man: Yeah, but it'd be a drag, everybody always staring at you.

2nd man: (admiring car) She sure is a beauty.

Soon thereafter, the owner of the Audi (whose camel hair coat and tan pants differentiate him from the conservatively-dressed 'admirers'), walks up to the car, gets in, and drives off, exposing the real reason these gentlemen were looking through the car's windows. Rather than examining the Audi A2's interior, they are, in fact, staring in admiration at a purple pick-up truck (on over-sized tires complete with bright yellow flames painted down its side) parked in a courtyard behind the automobile. An off-camera voice and on-screen text reveal the punch line: *Audi A2. La voiture qui va plus vite que les mentalités.* (The Audi A2. The car that is evolving faster than people's mentalities.) The commercial closes with a written promise that the automobile is made of recyclable aluminum, and is therefore environmentally friendly:

100 % aluminum
95 % recyclable

This referencing of environmental protection in advertisements for automobiles has not, however, affected consumer purchasing behavior in any significant way. Whereas the positioning of certain brands as 'non-polluters' (such as Toyota's *Pruis*) continues to be a popular strategy when creating campaigns for the French market, consumers in France are reluctant to pay higher prices for 'cleaner' technology. Indeed, the failure of this Audi campaign to significantly increase sales (as reported in Girard, 2004) is an indication that, for French consumers at least, pricing is just as important as ecology. This attitude is reflected in

Citroën's latest campaign *'les journées écolonomiques'* ('affordable ecology days at Citroen') where price reductions are being offered on their 'clean automobile' line.[19] Nevertheless, there is a growing concern in France about protecting the environment. Notes Isabelle Saïd, strategy planner for Renault at Publicis Conseil:

> Today, everyone's talking about clean automobile engines to save the environment. But the big revolution on the horizon is a change in attitudes in regards to the role of automobiles. We're moving away from the pursuit of happiness and individualism towards a consideration of the common good of society. (Quoted in Girard, 2004: 17. My translation.)

Appealing to the French appreciation for intelligence and academic achievement, on the other hand, is a recent Nestlé's ad for chocolate syrup (Martin, 2005). Both the copy and illustration insinuate that Nestlé's *Nesquik Sirop* will, in fact, awaken a child's intelligence and creativity. Although relating chocolate to intelligence is a bit of a stretch, with its reference to language and the emphasis placed on studying in a French child's life, this ad is very likely to appeal to French mothers. Indeed, anyone who has raised children in France is well aware of the very strenuous preparation required of students in the French educational system, particularly when approaching the dreaded national high school exam (known as the *baccalauréat*, or *le bac*). Clearly alluding to the importance of education, this advertisement features a little girl practicing her alphabet (and penmanship, another important requirement in French schools where papers and assignments must be impeccably handwritten) by writing letters on slices of bread with her Nesquik chocolate syrup as she and her mother prepare her afternoon snack. Next to the 'bread composition' sits a glass of chocolate milk, presumably made with the Nesquik syrup as well. The copy reads:

> *Nesquik, éveille les enfants, émerveille les parents. Une page d'écriture improvisée . . . Il n'y a rien de plus beau pour une maman que de découvrir que son enfant est un artiste qui s'éveille. Le sirop Nesquik est plein d'imagination gourmande pour qu'il se régale à l'heure du goûter. Et pour vous, c'est un régal de le voir grandir. Nesquik, le goût de l'enfance.*

English translation (mine)

> Nesquik, stimulates a child's interest, making parents marvel. An improvised composition . . . There is nothing more inspiring for a

mother than to discover that her child is a budding artist. Nesquik syrup is such an imaginative food that your children will thoroughly enjoy themselves during their afternoon snack. And for you, it's simply a pleasure to watch them grow up. Nesquik, the taste of childhood.

To summarize, this chapter highlights strategies adopted by the advertising industry in addressing individual markets and the importance of tailoring one's message to local cultural perceptions and sensibilities. It is a field of inquiry that has received considerable attention (for example, Biswas, Olsen, and Carlet, 1992; Zandpour, Chang, and Catalano, 1992; Zandpour *et al.*, 1994; Mueller, 1996; Taylor, Hoy, and Haley, 1996; among others) and continues to inform advertisers about consumer reactions to specific creative strategies, levels of informativeness, and advertising styles in different markets. We have seen, for instance, how advertising agencies in Paris work with copy and commercials sent to them by agencies in other countries (including the US) that they must then adapt for distribution in France.

For those who want to address the French specifically, this chapter also provides a description of advertisements from different media that feature concepts and appeals that are popular among the French, including symbolism and references to French culture, sexual humor, word play, organic farming and natural ingredients, environmental protection, Cartesian logic, academic achievement, and intelligence. By incorporating such elements in advertising intended for the French market, advertisers are much more likely to convey their message successfully within the French context.

This chapter also includes examples of international advertising campaigns adapted for French audiences that use these same types of appeals (cultural references, word play, natural ingredients, intelligence, and so on) to communicate more effectively with this particular market (for example, IBM, Ford, Coca-Cola, Nivea, Toyota, Amadeus, Vallée d'Aoste, GrimBergen, Dove, Audi, Nestlé). In examining these print and television commercials that specifically address French consumers with imagery and discourses that are particularly meaningful to them, one is constantly reminded of the importance of 'context of situation' (Firth, 1935; Hymes, 1972; Halliday, 1973, 1978; Halliday and Hasan, 1985) when describing human communication. Indeed, each of these messages has been skillfully crafted to appeal to local audiences, taking into account such contextual variables as the media in which the ad will appear, the market in which it will be distributed (some of which may require foreign language translations, for instance), the cultural sensi-

bilities and worldview of the intended audiences in those markets, and, most importantly, the overall message of the campaign. Unlike any other genre, however, the 'meaning potential' (Halliday and Hasan, 1985) of these advertisements is largely in the hands of advertisers. Indeed, the success or failure of an advertising campaign will depend heavily on a creative team's ability to predict the reactions of certain groups of consumers to the messages they construct. Thus, those who designed the Grand Marnier print campaign for the American market were very clever in choosing to present their product as a margarita ingredient, as was the IBM advertising team who used distinctively European faces in their print ads as a way of reassuring customers in Europe that IBM provides customized solutions for their specific business environment.

A certain 'multivoicedness of meaning' (Bakhtin, 1981) is also evident across all modes of discourse displayed in these messages. Thus, for instance, a simple word such as 'French', when inserted in a television commercial for a Japanese product directed at audiences in France (Toyota Yaris France – *La French voiture*), evokes humor (due to its irony), masks the foreign origins of the brand, and operates as an attention-getter, while the French–English switching throughout the dialogue draws attention to the commercial. The word 'French' as it is used in this context, although it is presented in English, also connotes a certain French national pride, further underscored by the mention of the art of French cooking (*cuisine française*) and the accordion music soundtrack.

French advertising is also notorious for exploiting puns, a few of which are described in these pages. With their multiple layers of interpretation, these elements derive meaning from their immediate context, whether it be the expressions constructed with the French word for 'time' (*Creat'heure, Bon'heure, Boud'heure, Vainq'heure*) to reflect the illustrations in an advertising campaign for watches (Goldy), the 'sleeping partner' slogan used for a French bank (Banque Populaire), or the mountains described as 'top models' to draw French tourists to Italy. This 'multiplicity of meaning' (Voloshinov, 1929) is also apparent in the use of visuals, where a croissant in a print advertisement aimed at French business executives who travel abroad, for instance, can connote 'Frenchness' and all the comforts of home, but may also be interpreted as a catalyst for successful business negotiations (Amadeus). Regardless of the strategies used to draw audiences into these advertisements, an awareness of local perceptions, and a willingness to reshape one's message into a discourse that is more palatable for local markets, will

greatly contribute to a campaign's success. Having examined advertising from this perspective, it is time now to turn our attention to the very complex issue of language-mixing which is a common feature of French advertising across media. Included in this discussion will be an analysis of the French translations required in advertising distributed in France (as stipulated by the 1994 Toubon Law, discussed in more detail in Chapter 6).

5
Language Mixing and Translation in French Advertising Copy

The aim of this chapter is to explore the impact of English on French advertising discourse across media through an analysis of product names, dialogue, jingles, signature lines, and slogans, with specific attention to lexicogrammatical features, phonology, semantics, and issues related to translation.[1] This discussion will begin with an overview of the motivations for inserting English in French advertising copy, noting, for instance, the role of English as a link language in international campaigns. Transcending cultural and linguistic barriers, English may appear (in product names, slogans and jingles, for instance) in advertising addressed at multiple audiences around the world, regardless of the country origin of the brand. English used in music soundtracks may also function as a mood enhancer, contributing to the overall atmosphere of the campaign. Brand names, labels, slogans, descriptive text, and jingles may also feature English to associate the product with notions such as global access, exclusivity, modernity, and sophistication. Exporting one's *savoir faire*, language and culture (as is the case with Francophone recording artists) is also facilitated through the use of English as it enables one to reach a global audience. In order to establish an international reputation, some French musicians are indeed marketing their craft through the medium of English, both in print advertising and television commercials. English may also serve to enhance brand recall and may reinforce the country origin of the brand (for example, Glenfiddich Single Malt Scotch Whisky, Foster's – Australia's Famous Beer).

The product categories favoring English will also be discussed, citing specific examples of English in different areas of the copy (product names, slogans, jingles, dialogue, and so on). Closer examination reveals, however, that certain English borrowings are being directed at specific audiences in France as determined by gender and age group. A number

of English borrowings, for instance, are more frequently encountered in advertisements aimed at women, many of which are associated with concepts such as glamour, beauty treatments, and weight control (*diet, lifting, body, peeling*, and so on). French teenagers are another group of consumers whose advertising displays specific types of English borrowings, including musical genres (for instance, *rap, trance, hiphop*) and lexical items such as *fun, groove, hits* and so forth. These examples will illustrate how the advertising industry is tailoring their use of English not only to a national market (in this case, France) but well-defined segments of the population as well. Included in this discussion will be some commentary on English in advertising directed at tourists.

To further explore the cultural specificity of much of the English displayed in French advertising copy, we will examine different forms of language-mixing used by advertisers who have found ingenious ways of tapping into the cultural and linguistic perceptions of their intended audience. Viewed from a local perspective, bilingual puns and other linguistic innovations are carefully crafted for their entertainment value, imparting multiple layers of culture-specific meaning supported by the illustrations and surrounding text. The bilingual creativity displayed in these examples is a clear indication that indigenous varieties of English are an integral part of the advertising landscape of non-Anglophone countries. Although the French public is continually exposed to 'global' English in product names, slogans, descriptive text and jingles, they are also experiencing an additional 'local' variety in their advertising that very much reflects their own cultural identity and worldview.

We will also explore in this chapter the many strategies used to translate English elements inserted into French advertising copy. Whereas the French translations provided are often mirror images of the English text (for example, Mont Blanc. Is that you?* *Est-ce bien toi?*), in other cases, translations may be slightly modified to appeal more to the French market. One notices (most ironically) that French translations sometimes contain English elements as well, despite the 1994 Toubon Law (discussed in detail in Chapter 6) requiring that all foreign language text in advertising distributed in France be translated in its entirety. These examples illustrate how translations of English text in French advertising produce several layers of meaning much like product names, slogans and illustrations, and may contribute considerably to the overall message of the campaign.

Throughout this analysis, English is functioning as both a global and local language. Distributed worldwide in a universal format in global campaigns, it is also being adapted to specific markets by advertisers

who are refashioning it in an effort to appeal to local audiences. As consumers of advertising discourse, the French, therefore, are experiencing English as both a *lingua franca* and a locally brewed variety that specifically reflects their own linguistic and cultural identity. These data clearly demonstrate the delicate balance involved in tailoring international advertising to the European market while highlighting the impact that globalization has had on the European's consumer's perception of language.[2]

Motivations for using English

English as a global language

When English appears in advertising distributed in multiple markets, it is often operating as a *lingua franca*, a global link language across cultures that is not associated with any particular area of the world (such as the UK, USA, Canada, Australia, or New Zealand). Consider, for example, a campaign for Evian mineral water (a French brand) that ran in Japan (Mueller, 1996: 32). The headline appearing in one of the print ads for the campaign (printed in large letters displayed entirely in English) read 'MADE IN FRENCH ALPS'. The illustration depicting a bottle of Evian set against a background of Alpine scenery is very characteristic of the company's advertising. The use of English, however, is not, and was obviously inserted here as an attention-getter that would (i) likely be intelligible to a world audience, and (ii) convey certain positive concepts regarding the product, such as its French (and therefore, chic) origins, and the pure 'alpine source' quality of the water. English is also operating as a global link language in a TV commercial for Emmentalier (sic) cheese from Switzerland in the present corpus. The commercial opens with an image of the Swiss flag and a young couple. The man is hand-feeding his female companion a bite of cheese. The rest of the spot features a kaleidoscope of Swiss imagery: a woman pulling a milk cart on the side of a mountain, a young man carrying a full round of cheese up the mountain on his back, an artisan tapping a round of cheese in the final stages of its maturing process, a woman tasting it, a group of young people on the roof of a skyscraper feeding each other cheese, and so. The voice-off, delivered in French with a thick Swiss accent, positions the cheese as a Swiss product:

> *Ce qui distingue notre emmentalier suisse ce n'est pas seulement son incomparable goût de noisette. Non, non, c'est la Suisse. Fromages de Suisse. Plus de Suisse dans le goût.*

English translation (mine)

> Its unmistakable chestnut flavor is not the only thing that sets our Swiss Emmentalier apart. It's far more than that. It's a piece of Switzerland. Swiss cheese. For a taste of Switzerland.

Although the images on the screen and voice-off commentary clearly identify the brand origins as Swiss, the commercial concludes with a close-up of the product accompanied by the following word (presented in English):

Switzerland

By presenting the brand's country of origin on-screen in a *lingua franca* (English), those who designed this commercial could avoid reshooting the film (lowering costs) and simply provide a different dubbed version (i.e., foreign language soundtrack) for each market.[3]

English as a mood enhancer

In other cases, English is used as a mood enhancer to create a particular atmosphere or express a certain lifestyle. The English appearing in French print advertising for Roche Bobois, for instance, was carefully chosen to reflect a certain vision of the world with décors designed around their leather sofas and other furnishings. One ad, featuring a canopy bed made of solid cherry and walnut, for instance, depicts a bedroom filled with an eclectic mix of decorative items from distant places (handwoven rugs from North Africa, elephant figurines evoking the African continent, silk fabrics, and so on). The Morrocan slippers (known locally as *babouches*), the 'ancient' weathered look of the walls and ceiling, and potted plants (including a fan-shaped palm tree as one might see in Southeast Asia, for instance) complete this 'exotic' imagery. The name of the product line, Médina (a term used to describe the old section of cities in the Maghreb), adds to the overall atmosphere. The attention-getter is a simple two-word English-language slogan:

> Imaginary journey*
> (subtitled as *voyage immobile*)

Other English slogans used in Roche Bobois advertising (each of which reflect the décor depicted in the illustration) include the following:

Black Story* (*Histoire de cuir noir*)[4]
charming days* (*ambiance de charme*)
natural chic* (*chic naturel*)
peaceful time* (*moment paisible*)
simply chic* (*simplement chic*)

Whereas English in this case may also be operating as a link language in an international campaign, the fact that Roche Bobois (a French company) uses French slogans to communicate with audiences outside of France (in the US, for example) indicates that English was consciously chosen for the French market for its positive connotations.

The following music soundtrack for Iberia airlines was also clearly used as a mood enhancer, alluding to the warm sunny climate of Spain (and other tourist destinations served by the airline), an image that is particularly appealing to at least half of the French population who experience rainy weather much of the year. One notices in this example, as in many of those that follow, that songs from Broadway musicals and other American recordings from the 1960s are rather popular:[5]

Let the sunshine, let the sunshine in, the sunshine in. . . .
Let the sunshine, let the sunshine in, the sunshine in . . .
Let the sunshine . . .[6]

The English-language jingle for Aquafresh toothpaste is also rather upbeat, and contains several phrases ('you're smilin'. . . . you're laughin' . . .') that directly reflect the scenes depicted throughout the commercial (passengers on a city bus singing along with the lyrics and smiling ear to ear, showing off their gleaming white teeth):

When you're smilin', keep on smilin'
The whole world smiles with you.
And when you're laughin . . . keep on laughin' . . .
The sun comes shinin' through . . .
The whole world smiles with you.[7]

Although the English music soundtracks heard in these commercials are likely to be unintelligible to most French television viewers, they are certainly recognizable as English in most cases, and therefore contribute to the overall atmosphere of the campaign. As these examples illustrate, however, the English is sometimes chosen to reflect certain

benefits of purchasing the product or service (for example, toothpaste producing a brighter smile), suggesting that some of these TV spots may be used in other markets where audiences have a better comprehension of English.

English as a vehicle for cultural export

English may also be employed as a vehicle of expression for exporting the French culture and (most ironically) French language. In a TV commercial for recording artist Patricia Kaas appearing in the corpus, several song titles from her featured CD *Piano Bar* are presented on the screen in both English and French:[8]

If you go away. Ne me quitte pas.
The summer knows. Un été 42
I wish you love. Que reste-t-il de nos amours?

Addressing her audience, Patricia Kaas clearly states her motivation for recording the album: '*Par ce disque, j'ai voulu rendre hommage à la chanson française.*' ('With this album, I wanted to pay tribute to the French song writing tradition'; translation mine). The English used in this case is obviously included (in both the commercial and the recording itself) to appeal to audiences beyond the borders of France. It is a vehicle of expression that enables artists to 'extend' the reach of their artistry to a global scale, making it more accessible to audiences in other markets. Indeed, throughout the present corpus we find Francophone musicians who include English tracks on their albums or whose TV commercials in France feature English lyrics (such as Céline Dion, featured in Chapter 6).

This use of English as a vehicle of global communication to export one's *savoir faire* is also evident in a two-page magazine advertisement for Canon. In the ad, we see a young woman in a library dressed in a white pants suit with English text (from the pages of a book) projected onto her body (as might occur, for example, when using an overhead projector). This illustration, combined with the headline and photo caption, imply that both English and the products depicted in the visual on the facing page (fax machine, video camera, scanner, digital camera, printer, LCD projector, etc.) offer a solution for sharing knowledge and information:

Puis-je échanger mes connaissances?
Partager, conserver, saisir, visualiser. Quelle que soit votre imagination,

avec Canon, bien sûr, vous pouvez!
www.canon.fr

CANON. PARLEZ IMAGE

English translation (mine)

Can I share my knowledge with others?
Share, preserve, capture, visualize. Wherever your imagination takes you, with Canon, of course you can!
www.canon.fr

CANON. SPEAK IMAGE[S]

The signature line next to the company logo (in English with a French translation provided in the copy) further empowers the reader who wants to communicate as effectively as possible with those around her:

you can*
Canon
**Bien sûr, vous pouvez*

One of the hidden messages behind these campaigns, therefore, is that English may be used to 'advertise' French *savoir faire* (as well as the French language and culture) to audiences around the globe. The 'power' of English in entertainment media and international business, for instance, is such that it has become a viable option for communicating one's talents and ideas internationally. English (whether it is intelligible or not, as is often the case for jingles) contributes to the overall theme and atmosphere of a campaign, setting the mood, so to speak, as a way of attracting and maintaining the audience's attention. Motivations for inserting English in advertising distributed in France, however, reach far beyond these two applications. As the following section will illustrate, it may also contribute to the humor conveyed in illustrations and dialogue, enhance brand recall, and/or indicate a product's country of origin.

Humor, brand recall, and origin

English may be used in French advertising to evoke humor as in the Spontex Diabolic TV commercial presented in Chapter 4, featuring a kitchen sponge and a line-up of lovesick hedgehogs. Similar to the Spontex example, a commercial for Président Coeur de Meule Emmental cheese features the following English-language music soundtrack:

What a day for a day dream,
What a day for a day dreaming boy . . .
What a day for a day dreaming boy . . .[9]

On screen a young woman is having a final check in the mirror before heading out on a romantic date. Ah . . . but something is missing. . . . The viewing audience discovers what that is precisely when she runs to the refrigerator, retrieves a package of Emmental and fashions herself a necklace with freshly cut cubes of cheese. Shortly after she settles into the passenger seat of her boyfriend's car waiting to pick her up, her gentleman caller eyes the 'edible necklace' and passionately devours it piece by piece. An off-camera voice delivers the punchline:

Emmental Coeur de Meule de Président
Emmental Président
Un pouvoir insensé

English translation (mine)
Coeur de Meule Emmental by Président
Président's Emmental
An insane power

Brand name recall may be enhanced through English as well, as seen in a print ad for Lierac Nightpeel skin care. The English borrowing 'peeling' (used by the French to refer to a professional skin peeling treatment or peeling face mask) is repeated several times in the copy (in the headline, descriptive text, and on the product label), reinforcing both the results one achieves by using the product (*l'effet peeling*) and the product name (Lierac Nightpeel).[10] This association between the brand name and the various mentions of 'peeling' throughout the copy (*l'effet peeling . . . basé sur la technologie du peeling dermatologique*) is further enhanced by the abbreviation of the product name (Nightpeel), and subsequent translation, to *Nuit* ('night') followed by the borrowing with its immediately recognizable [-ing] affix (*le peeling tri-actif*). The product name (Nightpeel) reappears soon thereafter, cementing the association:

Nuit: le peeling tri-actif
Nightpeel est un peeling nouvelle génération à la fois très actif et très bien toléré par toutes les peaux. . .

English translation (mine)

Night: triple action peeling
Nightpeel is the latest in skin peeling treatments: highly effective and
extremely gentle on all skin types. . .

Brand origins, on the other hand, can also be expressed through the
use of English, one manifestation of this being the English-language
labels that are often prominently displayed as attention-getters in French
advertising for imported alcohol. In their advertising, for instance, Glenfiddich uses a copyright-protected English logo (Glenfiddich. Single
Malt Scotch Whisky) as an attention-getter, along with English-language
slogans (with accompanying French translations) that reflect stereotypes
regarding Scotland, such as:

The independent spirit*

*l'esprit d'indépendance

Other means of reinforcing the brand origins via English in the consumer's imagination include product names (Kellogg's Country Crisp),
taglines (*Jeep. There's only one*) and music soundtracks (or jingles). The
music soundtrack of a commercial for Nike aired in France featured the
following lyrics:

A little less conversation, a little more action please.
All this aggravation ain't satisfactioning (sic) me.
A little more bite and a little less bark.
Come on baby, I'm tired of talking.
Grab your coat and let's start walking.
Come on, come on . . .[11]

Although soundtracks such as these are inserted to create a certain
atmosphere (and not to be intelligible), advertisers in France are well
aware of the popularity of English-language lyrics and make liberal use
of them in their commercials.

It should also be noted, however, that the 'country-of-origin' highlighted in advertising copy does not necessarily convey the location in
which the product is actually made. The label on Foster's ('Australia's
Famous Beer') sold in the US, for instance, tells us that it is actually
'brewed and bottled' in Toronto, Canada, albeit 'under the supervision
of Carlton and United Breweries, Melbourne, Australia'. (For additional
examples, see Kelly-Holmes, 2005: 34–35.) Nevertheless, brands that

originate in countries perceived as 'Anglophone' very often use English as an 'identity marker' in their advertising for the French market.

Audiences and product categories

Product categories favoring English

Although it may seem all pervasive, in advertising distributed in France, English is more likely to appear in certain product categories. Advertising for luxury goods such as expensive watches, jewelry, eyewear, handbags, and other accessories aimed at the upperly mobile professional, wealthy and well-traveled, for instance, typically feature a chic and elegant one or two-word English slogan describing the product, as in the following examples:

> *Versace. Eyewear*
> *Rolex. Perpetual Spirit*
> *Furla. Handbags*

Business products (such as e-business applications, computers, fax machines, copiers) and computer games are consistently advertised in France through the medium of English as well. Canon, Dell, IBM, Microsoft, Xerox, and many other corporations feature English in their product names, signature lines, and slogans for the French market. Consider the following examples:

Product names

IBM	(laptop)	IBM Thinkpad
Microsoft	(software)	Microsoft Word
Microsoft	(computer game)	XBOX

Signature lines

BSA	(software)	Business software alliance
Colt	(telecom)	We make business straight forward
Dell	(computers)	Enterprise Storage. Easy as Dell
Devoteam Siticom	(e-business)	Connecting business & technology
Nortel Networks	(software)	Metro & Enterprise Networks

		Optical Long Haul Networks
		Wireless Networks
Xerox	(copiers)	The Document Company

Slogans (French translations provided in the copy)

Brother	(copiers)	Brother. At your side*
		*A vos côtés
Ricoh	(copiers)	We're in your corner*
		*Nous sommes dans votre camp
XBOX	(computer game)	Play More*
		*Jouez plus

Banks, insurance companies, and telecommunications firms also liberally exploit English for special effect, including French companies marketing their products and services to consumers in France. In one commercial, a French insurance company (MAAF assurances), for instance, is offering an auto loan/insurance package which they are marketing under the name 'PACK MAAF MOTO'. The English borrowing 'pack' in this case is an abbreviated form of 'package'. 'Moto' (an abbreviation as well, but not an English borrowing) is commonly used to refer to motorcycles in French. Here it is also denoting cars. In a TV commercial for a French bank (Crédit Mutuel), on the other hand, one hears the following music soundtrack:

> *The moment I wake up,*
> *before I put on my makeup,*
> *I say a little prayer for you . . .*
> *Together, together, that's how it must be. . .* [12]

With its catchy rhythm, and the fact that the lyrics (although probably unintelligible to French audiences) have nothing whatsoever to do with the banking industry, this music soundtrack is operating as a mood enhancer. English-language lyrics are also featured in a TV commercial for SFR Pro cell phone services. The spot features French soccer star Marcel Desailly engaged in various activities throughout the day, each of which involves some form of telecommunication (speaking on a cell phone in a locker room, checking messages on his cell phone after signing autographs, reading incoming e-mails using a PDA connected to a cell phone while holding a 'meeting' in a hot tub with his team-

mates, surfing the Web on his wireless laptop while relaxing outdoors, and so on). Superimposed on these images in an on-screen narration (presented in writing) that includes two English borrowings: 'e-mail' and 'Internet':

> Written text on screen:
>
> *Depuis que M. Desailly est chef d'entreprise, il ne quitte plus son bureau mobile. Il reçoit ses e-mails même en réunion et navigue sur Internet sur tous les terrains. Avec SFR Pro, M. Desailly a tout compris. Ses collègues aussi d'ailleurs.*
>
> Written text and voice-off:
>
> *Avec SFR Pro, vous serez toujours plus qu'un simple numéro.*

English translation (mine)

> *Written text on screen:*
>
> Ever since Mr. Desailly became a CEO, he never goes anywhere without his mobile office. He has access to e-mail during meetings and surfs the Internet on every playing field imaginable. With SFR Pro, Mr. Desailly is on top of things. His colleagues too by the way.
>
> *Written text and voice-off:*
>
> With SFR Pro, you will always be more than a number.

The insertion of both 'Internet' and 'e-mail' here closely resembles their use in spoken French in daily interactions. (A more detailed discussion of the use of e-mail in France appears in Chapter 6.) The music soundtrack also features English, which, although it may be unintelligible to French audiences, contributes to the overall atmosphere of the commercial.

> *He said 'Captain'. I said 'What?'*
> *He said 'Captain'. I said 'What?'*
> *He said 'Captain'. I said 'What?'*
> *He said 'Captain'. I said 'What?'*
> *He said 'Captain'. I said 'What?'*

Other product categories that use English rather extensively include cosmetics, perfume, clothing, products for personal hygiene (deodorant, shaving cream, shampoo, toothpaste, and so on), household appliances (such as vacuum cleaners, refrigerators, clothes irons), electronic equip-

ment (digital cameras, DVD players, LCD television sets, and so on), and automobiles. English is commonly used in this latter category to highlight product features, many of which appear in the form of acronyms. One notices a similar use of English-inspired acronyms in French advertising for computer products. Often acronyms of this nature are simply a disguised form of English used for special socio-psychological effect, the meaning of which totally escapes French consumers. To the trained eye, however, they are unmistakably derived from rather technical English-language expressions, as in the following examples, all of which appear in the present corpus:

Acronyms in recent French ads for automobiles[13]

ABS	Anti-lock Braking System
CDI	Compact Diesel Injection
CVT	Continuously Variable Transmission
DOHC	Dual Overhead CamShaft
EBD	Electronic Brake-force Distribution
EHPS	Electrohydraulic Power Steering
ESP	Electronic Stability Program
ETC	Electronic Throttle Control
GPS	Global Positioning System
GSM	Global System for Mobile-Communications
JTS	Jet Thrust Stoichiometric
SBC	Sensotronic Brake Control
VTEC	Valve Timing Electronic Control
VVT-i	Variable Valve Timing with intelligence

Acronyms in recent French ads for computers[14]

ADSL	Asymmetric Digital Subscriber Line
PIN	Personal Identification Number
CD-ROM	Compact Disk – Read Only Memory
DDR-RAM	Double Data Rate – Random Access Memory
DVD	Digital Video Disk
GPRS	General Packet Radio Service
IP	Internet Protocol
LAN	Local Area Network
LCD	Liquid Crystal Display
SCSI	Small Computer Systems Interface
SMS	Short Message Service
USB	Universal Serial Bus
VPN	Virtual Private Network

WiFi	Wireless Fidelity
XP	Extreme Performance
WAP	Wireless Application Protocol

English is also prevalent in product naming and music soundtracks in advertising for food products, although these are typically limited to items such as bottled water, coffee, candy, and fast food restaurants. The corpus does, however, include several advertisements for cheese (such as Caprice des Dieux, plus the Emmental de Président example mentioned earlier) and other French specialities. Labeyrie, for example, uses the following English-language jingle in their television commercials for *foie gras*:

> *You are so sweet, honey . . .*
> *Come close to me . . .*

The music soundtrack used in French television commercials for Carte Noire coffee is likely to be just as familiar:

> *Try to remember,*
> *when life was so tender,*
> *and follow . . .*[15]

As was noted earlier, however, the English in music soundtracks is primarily inserted as a mood enhancer, or to create a certain atmosphere, and is in most cases unintelligible to television viewing audiences. Later, however, we will explore several examples of English language lyrics that appear to be directly related to the product being advertised, indicating at least a desire on the part of ad agencies designing the campaigns to create some level of association between the music and the brand. As was also noted earlier, if the commercial with English is used in multiple markets, there is the possibility as well that the English lyrics will be more intelligible to some audiences (in the UK, for instance) than others.

Gender-specific English

Whereas many of the aforementioned product categories are of interest to both men and women, the English appearing in advertising for products such as cosmetics, face and body creams, hair coloring, perfume and women's clothing is primarily directed at female audiences. English-inspired product names are particularly common. Many of these involve

code-mixing, such as Garnier Belle Color (hair color), or Phytomer Body Déclic (body firming cream), while others (regardless of their brand origins) appear entirely in English: Nivea Beauty Double Design (eye make-up) and Colour Pleasure (lipstick), Club Med Happy Body My Ocean (perfume), Lierac Body Lift 10 (body firming cream), Helena Rubinstein Visionary Beauty (make-up), Estée Lauder Advanced Night Repair (face cream), and so on.

In examining French advertisements aimed at women, several product-specific connotations associated with English may also be observed. Indeed, although in a general sense English associates these products with such positive concepts as elegance, sophistication, modernity, and international appeal, several other layers of meaning emerge. The main selling point for women's clothing advertised through the medium of English in France, for instance, appears to be comfort, as seen in the following slogans for three different brands (each of which describe the low-heeled comfortable-looking shoes in the illustration):

Aerosoles. Let yourself go
The casual footwear by Fairmont
Valleverde. Chic & Comfort Shoes

In ads for face creams, on the other hand, English may be used to encourage the pursuit of ageless beauty, as if one could simply halt the passage of time. Sometimes English-inspired product names even go so far as to promise effects similar to those achieved by medical procedures such as collagen injections, laser treatments, or face lifts: Garnier Synergie Stop, L'Oréal Plénitude Age Perfect, Helena Rubinstein Collagenist, Guerlain Issima SuccessLaser, Lierac Aqua Lift, and so on. In product names for cosmetics, however, we find the promise of instant, magical transformation (Covermark Face Magic, Estée Lauder Illusionist), references to glamour and sophistication (L'Oréal New Jet Set, Gemey & Maybelline Water Shine Diamonds) and/or positive associations relative to color and lasting freshness (Estée Lauder Pure Color Crystal, Nivea Beauté Colour Shine, Gemey & Maybelline Mati-teint Fresh).

English product names for perfumes, on the other hand, tend to exude a certain exclusivity (Calvin Klein One, Van Cleef & Arpels First), lustful passion (Christian Dior Addict, Gucci Envy, Trussardi Skin), and/or evoke images of timeless love, innocence, elegance, and simple pleasures: Anna Sui – Sui Love, Calvin Klein Eternity, Calvin Klein Truth, Estée Lauder Pleasure, Kenzo Flower, Thierry Mugler Angel. Whereas

products such as these often feature French labels and brand names when advertised in the US, for instance, companies from around the world (including France, which is known for its perfume industry) are exploiting the positive associations with English (modernity, elitism, and so on) in addressing the French market.

Diet products, also typically aimed at female consumers (through the discourse and imagery of their advertising, and placement in women's magazines), are heavily influenced by English as well (Dietline, Diet Century Plaisia, Weight Watchers, and so on). There is, however, one diet plan in the corpus (Weight Watchers MP5™) that has been designed specifically for men. The symbol™ inserted after the product name in the logo (MP5™) identifies this expression as being a protected trademark of Weight Watchers while differentiating it from the MP3 technology that enables one to download music sound files from the Internet. This technology-driven product name indexes the Weight Watchers website one uses to participate in the program (www.wwmp5.com.fr) and is an ingenious way of attracting the male market by addressing their significant others, who will hopefully convince them that the product is worthwhile. The illustration depicts a woman watching her 'man' admiring his physique in a mirror. The image that is reflected back to him exclusively (a tall handsome 'stud' with well-developed chest muscles and a perfectly flat stomach), however, does not correspond in the least with reality (a much shorter, pudgier gentleman whose waistline far exceeds his chest measurements). The copy is addressed to women readers who might be interested in recruiting their mates into the Weight Watchers program (a diet plan that normally involves weekly attendance to Weight Watchers support group meetings):[16]

> *S'est-il regardé d'un oeil critique, récemment? S'il a quelques kilos en trop et s'il ne peut pas se rendre à une réunion, il est temps de penser à MP5. C'est nouveau, ça marche, et c'est juste pour les hommes.*

English translation (mine)

> Has he taken a good honest look at himself lately? If he's a little overweight and cannot come to meetings, it's time to think about MP5. It's new, it works, and it's just for men.

Elsewhere in the copy we find concepts that are likely to appeal to men, giving their female companions additional arguments to use when discussing with them this Weight Watchers product:

Repas . . . adaptés à son appétit d'homme. . .
Monsieur aura le total contrôle de son amaigrissement . . .
Un kit prêt à l'emploi qui mêle efficacité et fonctionnalité.

English translation (mine)

Meals . . . designed for a man's appetite . . .
He will have total control of his weight loss . . .
A ready-to-use kit which is both functional and efficient.

By positioning the product in such a way as to appeal to both sexes (women wanting a slimmer, sexier partner, men desiring a personally customized plan that delivers results without taking time out of their busy work schedules), and providing a 'packaged discourse' for women to use with their male counterparts, Weight Watchers is able to reach both audiences.

Occasionally, one will notice that other products, such as fragrances, are advertised in English using a slightly different choice of words depending on the audience's gender. With the advent of the 'metrosexual man' in the new millenium, advertising for products such as creams and perfumes are being directed at men as well as their female counterparts. One does notice a slight difference in the linguistic approach however. Consider, for instance, the following slogan featured in print advertising for Paco Rabane cologne for men (Ultraviolet Man):

The new perfume system*
(*nouveau système parfum*)

Although the word 'perfume' has a definite feminine quality, describing this perfume as part of a 'system' gives it a more technical feel that is likely to appeal to male audiences. The word 'Man' appearing in the text also positions the product as something masculine. In Paco Rabane's advertising for women appearing in the same campaign, where the product name is simply referred to as Ultraviolet, on the other hand, we find that the expression 'perfume system' has been replaced by 'fragrance', a much more feminine-sounding word:

The fragrance of a new era

These examples illustrate how certain English borrowings are often directed at specific audiences in France. Although the English expressions

inserted are often linked to the product category (clothing, cosmetics, and so on), the choice of lexicon may also be highly nuanced according to gender in advertising for the same product line, as seen, for instance, in Paco Rabane's 'Ultraviolet' campaign. This phenomenon is one of many exhibited in code-mixed advertising, indicating an increasingly sophisticated use of English in non-Anglophone marketing discourse.

Youth Frenglish

The English borrowings one finds in advertising geared towards teenagers, another favored audience for language-mixing, on the other hand, is even more distinctive. Indeed, much of the English used to address this con- sumer group is very seldom found in advertising for other audiences in France. As in the examples seen above, the types of borrowings one encounters in this advertising discourse are usually directly influenced by the product categories that most interest members of this age group. In advertisements for music recordings and concert announcements, for instance, English is commonly used to refer to musical genres (*hiphop, R'nB, le rap, Rap Groove, le jazz, hits house, le mix trance*) and may be employed to describe a track on an album (*un titre 'groovie' à découvrir absolument*) or a radio station (*1ère radio groove & dance*), many of which (if targeting this audience) use English for their station identification (for example, Fun Radio, Skyrock). English appears in the record labels one sees in advertising for these products (Columbia Music, Sony Music, Universal Music) as well as television channels mentioned in the copy broadcasting music videos in France and other forms of entertainment for younger audiences (Fun TV, Pub TV). It is an advertising landscape where *popstars, hit music, remixes,* and *singles* are nothing out of the ordi- nary. The following excerpts from voice-off commentary heard during French television commercials are rather typical (underlining added):[17]

> . . . *album des <u>singles</u> solo*
> . . . *son nouveau <u>single</u> est enfin disponible*
> . . . *DJ Makina <u>mixé</u> par Bolo et Uri*
> . . . *album <u>pop</u> de l'année*
> . . . *<u>stars</u> tubes!*
> . . . *l'essentiel des <u>clubs</u>*
> . . . *<u>Trance</u> Connexion 5, le <u>mix trance</u> à l'état pur avec Contact FM*[18]

Another English borrowing, 'best of' (appearing also in advertising for NOOS as discussed in Chapter 3), is rather prevalent in this product

category. The voice-off heard during a television commercial for a CD entitled *The Best of Texas* (featuring Barry White and Bob Marley among others) is a prime example (underlining added). As was described in the NOOS example, readers will notice that this particular borrowing is used as both an adjective and noun indiscriminately (meaning 'the very best' or 'top hits'):

> *RTL2 présente Texas, le <u>Best Of</u> évènement. Texas. Vous reconnaîtrez facilement ce <u>Best Of</u> à prix exceptionnel comme les 75 autres de la collection grâce à cette présentation luxueuse. Le <u>Best of</u> Texas, c'est un évènement Universal Music.*

English translation (mine)

> RTL2 presents Texas. The 'Best of' event. You will easily recognize this 'Best of' because of its exceptional price, just like the 75 others in this collection thanks to this luxurious presentation. *The Best of Texas*, a Universal Music event.

As it uses some of the jargon adopted by the recording industry, the jingle featured in a commercial for Nivea Body (skin moisturizer) is also likely to appeal to this audience:

> *Get down,*
> *get down,*
> *get funk down . . .*
> *now I'm telling you . . .*
> *my girl . . .*

Another product category that appeals to this segment of the population and that employs 'Youth Frenglish' rather extensively is that of cell phone accessories. Typically, these advertisements appear in magazines aimed at teenagers (for example, *Star Club*) and propose products and services such as downloadable cell rings, logos for the LCD screen inspired by pop culture, and pre-paid phone cards for additional 'minutes'. Here, again, the choice of English is influenced by the entertainment industry including (in addition to pop recording artists heard on French radio) television shows and movies.[19] One notices in the magazine advertisements addressing this audience linguistic creativity at several different levels. The slogans, for instance (addressing the consumer using '*tu*', the informal version of 'you', to express solidarity and establish a casual rapport), are typically code-mixed, incorporating

such highly assimilated borrowings as 'fun,' 'look,' or 'power,' and are characteristically displayed with one or more exclamation points (a punctuation mark avoided in advertising aimed at older audiences):

Relooker ton mobile
New look pour ton phone!
Mets du fun dans ton mobile!!!
Power up your mobile. Découvre 'the last generation' de logos et sonneries!!!

English translation (mine)

Change the look of your mobile [phone]
New look for your phone!
Put some fun in your mobile [phone]!!!
Power up your mobile [phone]! Discover the last generation of logos and cell rings!!!

The downloadable tunes are typically displayed in the copy under certain category headings (also code-mixed) such as:

French Tops
Rap Groove
Tops du Moments
Hits Dance
Tubes Rap
TV et Films

Under the '*TV et Films*' cell phone ring category listed in one magazine ad, we find a song title inspired by an American television show, Ally McBeal:[20]

Ally McBip

In this catchy invention there are two elements that are particularly appealing to this audience: the association with the television program *Ally McBeal*, very popular among this age group at the time of data collection, and the orthographical transformation of the last name of the show's main character.[21] The latter involves a number of 'steps' as diagrammed below:

McBeal → Beal → ('beep' sound) → Bip → **McBip**

The '*Bip*' equivalent of the English word 'beep', therefore, is actually a form of onomatopoeia for the French who have simply created (using their own phonological rules) a word that imitates the sound one hears before leaving a voice mail: *bip!* The 'Mc' affix (found in the character's original name as well) is also familiar to this audience due to its frequent use in advertising for McDonald's and evokes (through association with the fast food chain no doubt, but also possibly their knowledge of Irish or Scottish culture) a certain 'foreignness', making it all the more appealing. This same word with its onomatopoeic value ('*bip*' to imitate a beeping sound) can be found in a corporate logo in the same product category:

MOBIP
le top pour ton mobile!
www.mobip.com

In this case, the logo (MOBIP) consists of a hybrid combining the French words 'mobile' (meaning 'cell phone') and the onomatopoeic '*bip*'.

[Mobile → MO] + [beep → BIP] = MOBIP

The same principle applies for one additional corporate logo included in this product category which, in this case, displays the English borrowing 'fun':

[Mobile → MOBI] + [FUN] = MOBIFUN

Appearing in another cell phone accessories advertisement for teenagers is an additional example of 'Youth Frenglish'. Here, the first word 'Ze' is an orthographical innovation reflecting the French pronunciation of the English borrowing 'The'.[22]

Ze big love c pour quand

English translation (mine)

[So] the big love [of your life],
when is that going to happen?

The single letter 'C' (commonly seen in text messaging, a form of communication popular among consumers in this age group) is used in this context to denote the French phrase *C'est* (pronounced identically).

Advertising for tourists

The only other consumer group in France that is consistently addressed through the medium of English are international tourists. Any adver-

tising for this audience typically appears in the form of posters (displayed in the Paris subway system and other public spaces). As might be expected, the product categories are limited to department stores, amusement parks, cyber cafés for checking and sending e-mail, and other services of interest to people visiting France on holiday. In one poster advertisement displayed in the Paris metro, for instance, we find an English-language headline with a French translation appearing in slightly smaller print directly below:

Need to e-mail home?
Besoin d'envoyer un e-mail?

To avoid giving complicated directions to the Internet café, the illustration simply shows an enormous arrow pointing in the direction of the stairway exit one should take to find it, accompanied by a very short text indicating its proximity to a popular bookstore just above the metro station: *50 m derrière Gibert Jeune*. At the bottom of the poster we find additional English-language text, followed by a French translation in tiny print and the Internet café's precise location:

easyEverything™
the world's largest internet cafés*
*Les plus grands Cyber-Cafés du monde
6 rue de la Harpe, Saint-Michel

To make the English even more visible and attract the attention of tourists who might otherwise ignore poster advertising as they race to their next tourist attraction, all of the English phrases (and the arrow) appear in white on a bright red backgroud. The French text appears in less visible black.

If the message is directed at local consumers, however, the language-mixing exhibited in French advertising across media, audience, and product categories often involves a certain level of nativization whereby the English inserted in the copy is adapted (or appropriated) in such a way as to be more meaningful and natural-sounding for the intended French-speaking audience. This practice has taken on a life of its own, so to speak, no longer reflecting any particular culture or population on the planet, although there are a few exceptions as in the association of English with the brand origins as discussed at the beginning of this chapter, or certain personalities, television shows,

and so on. I have attempted in my examples to share a few of the strategies involved as well as some insights as to why and for whom the English is inserted. However, there is much more to mixing in advertising discourse than meets the eye. The following section explores in more detail the various means by which English is 'appropriated' by the French who encounter it in their daily diet of advertising discourse.

Bilingual creativity

Linguistic innovations

One of the most common phenomena that can be observed in French–English mixing in this context is the orthographical, morpho-syntactic, and lexico-grammatical innovations encountered in product names, slogans, signature lines, and descriptive copy. Both product names and slogans, for example, very often exhibit some form of bilingual hybridization, whereby a word in one language is fused with one from another to form a single word or phrase. In Braun's product name for a lady's razor (Silk-épil EverSoft), for instance, we find three English elements ('silk', 'ever', and 'soft') mixed with a truncated French word (*'épil'* from *'épilation'*, meaning 'hair removal'). Thus constructed, the product name speaks for itself: 'Shaving your legs with this razor will result in silky, everlasting, softer skin'. An automobile by Renault (the Renault Avantime) is another example of a bilingual hybrid. Here, a French element (*avant*, meaning 'before') combined with English ('time') produces a meaning with a very positive connotation indeed: 'Before its time'. Occasionally, the English element contained within the hybridized product name will reappear in the slogan, creating a sort of pun (for example, NoBacter. No problem).

One also sees spelling transformations, such as [-ic] replacing [-ique] to produce an English-looking word, as in the following examples:[23]

Clarins Huile 'Tonic'	(body firm cream)
Delta Peche Nautic	(boats)
Garnier Grafic	(hairstyling gel)
Ricqles Auto-Tonic	(mint breath freshener)
Therm-Tonic	(sauna kit)

Furthermore, a spelling modification can (quite intentionally) some-times produce an entirely different meaning. A magazine advertise-

ment for Fiat, for example, features the slogan *Six Appeal* (*le bien-être à six*) modeled on the English expression 'Sex Appeal'. The descriptive copy delivers the main selling point (that the Fiat Multipla has six seats):

Plaisir de voyager et joie de recevoir: voici la Multipla Fiat et ses 6 places (dont 3 à l'avant), son espace habitable où il fait si bon vivre . . .

English translation (mine)

The pleasure of traveling and the joy of entertaining. Introducing the Fiat Multipla with seating for 6 (3 of which are in the front), a livable space which one can really enjoy.

The illustration blends the notion of roominess, travel and 'the joy of entertaining' by depicting the automobile (on its chassis, minus the sides and roof) carrying the driver and five happy passengers enjoying each other's company. The car appears in a living room setting (further evoking the notion of entertaining guests) with the automobile's forward movement connoted by the blurry landscape flowing past the window in the background. One also notices that the car model name featured in the ad (Multipla) involves clipping, as the last syllable (-pla) could be interpreted as a truncated version of 'places' as in 'multiple places to sit'. Similar clipping is evident in a product feature mentioned in an advertisement for the Opel Corsa Fashion: the 'Pack Alu' (package → 'pack' + aluminium → 'alu').

Spelling modifications may also be incorporated to reflect the grammatical structure of the French language. Many English borrowings, for instance, are transformed into French verbs by adding the requisite verb endings. One example of this technique can be found in a poster advertisement displayed in the Paris subway featuring a basketball theme and the slogan *Je dunkerai for you* (literally, 'I will [land a slam] dunk for you').[24] Here, the borrowing 'dunk' has been first transformed into a French infinitive (*dunker*) before receiving its future tense marker for the first person singular (-*ai*) to produce a meaning approximating 'I will dunk' (*Je dunkerai*):

dunk → dunker → dunkerai → **je dunkerai for you**

We encounter similar phenomena in a television commercial for a French bank, Caisse d'Epargne. The institution, in this case, is offering a combination package including an auto loan and insurance which they call *IZIAUTO*. This product name involves a spelling transforma-

tion of the English borrowing 'easy' to the nonsensical 'izi', a process which is guaranteed to produce a pronunciation in French that is close to the English original:

$$Easy \rightarrow IZI + Automobile \rightarrow AUTO = IZIAUTO$$

The spot opens with two animated elephant characters who have just 'tied the knot' and are heading off on their honeymoon as friends and family shower them with rice. One of the well-wishers in the crowd is a squirrel (the bank's logo) who seems delighted to see the happy couple drive off in their brand new red convertible (fully insured, of course). The spot concludes with a close-up of the car's vanity license plate which reads:

Just acheted

The inspiration for this rather unusual code-mixed expression (created specifically for the advertising campaign) is, of course, 'just married', an English expression one does occasionally see in the background visuals of print ads in France and is therefore familiar to this audience. In this case, however, the English word 'married' has been converted into a 'Frenglish' equivalent whereby the verb stem is French (*acheter*, 'to purchase') and the verb ending (the past tense marker [-ed]) is English (contrary to the earlier '*Je dunkerai for you*' example which presents the opposite scenario):

English verb stem (*dunk*) + French verb ending [-ai] = *dunkerai*
French verb stem (*acheter*) + English verb ending [-ed] = *acheted*

The word 'just', on the other hand (*just acheted*), is a direct borrowing from English that is immediately recognizable to the French as they have a similar word ('*juste*') that could be used in the same context:[25]

Ils viennent tout juste de se marier.
They've just gotten married.

Because the French equivalent '*juste*' requires a more complicated sentence construction (as seen above), however, it is not surprising that the English borrowing 'just' (from 'just married') was adopted along with the past tense marker [-ed].[26] This Caisse d'Epargne commercial also features an English-language music soundtrack with a rather funky beat

(creating a sharp contrast between the traditionally conservative reputation of banking institutions and the rather whimsically comical atmosphere of the commercial):

I like it . . . I like it . . .

Occurring in both the TV and print data are a number of other orthographical and morphosyntactic variations, most of which involve highly assimilated English borrowings. A classic example seen in advertisements for face creams and body firming creams is the English borrowing 'lift' which appears in all sorts of manifestations in French advertising copy, such as (underlining added):

> *pour lifter*
> *lifting gel*
> *la peau est liftée en 8 semaines*
> *rafermit intensément, lifte visiblement*
> *crème haute performance lift*
> *offrent à votre visage une performance liftante*

Deriving it from the English expression 'face lift', the French have created several 'Frenglish' innovations with this particular borrowing, switching from one grammatical category to another as it suits their communicative needs. In advertising copy, we see it used both as a verb (*lifter, lifte, liftée*) and an adjective (*lifting gel, crème haute performance lift, une performance liftante*). The same applies to other borrowings (note the *mixé, mix, remixes* examples cited earlier). The English word 'stress', for example, appears in the corpus as both a noun (*anti-stress, le stress*) and an adjective (*stressé*), as in the following examples (underlining added):

Jean d'Avèze Paris Crème anti-pollution et anti-stress[27]
(anti-pollution and anti-stress cream) (bilingual label)

c'est le désordre à l'intérieur. A mon âge, ça doit être le stress des exams . . . (dialogue excerpt from TV commercial for Bio de Danone yoghurt)

jeudi dernier une cliente est entrée en se plaignant qu'elle était stressée . . . elle avait le cuir chevelu sec qui la démangeait et elle avait peur d'avoir des pellicules . . . (dialogue excerpt from TV commercial for Head & Shoulders dandruff shampoo)

English translation (mine)

Jean d'Avèze Paris Crème anti-pollution and <u>anti-stress</u> cream . . . (bilingual label)

my stomach is upset. At my age, it must be <u>the stress</u> of exams . . . (dialogue excerpt from TV commercial for Bio de Danone yoghurt)

last Thursday, a [hair salon] client came in complaining that she was <u>stressed out</u> . . . her dry scalp was itchy and she was afraid she had dandruff . . . (dialogue excerpt from TV commercial for Head & Shoulders dandruff shampoo)

This switching of grammatical categories is also evident in a code-mixed slogan for Gemey–Maybelline lipstick and nail polish (probably directed at younger audiences because of the choice of borrowings and exclamation point):

Pretty Cool. Cool, la vie pour ce printemps pretty!

English translation (mine)

Pretty Cool. Cool, [the best in] life for this lovely Spring!

Here, the English borrowing 'pretty' is being used as both an adverb describing 'cool' (*Pretty cool*, as in 'really cool', or 'wonderful') and, post-positionally, as an adjective (*printemps pretty*, 'lovely Spring'). The other borrowing ('cool') also switches grammatical categories, appearing first as an adjective (*Pretty Cool*) and then as a noun (*Cool*).

Word order and punctuation

Occasionally, the appropriation of English within the context of French advertising discourse will simply involve direct borrowings placed in a word order that is familiar to audiences in France. This is a particularly common practice in product naming and signature lines. Thus, in the following English-language example (a product name for a shampoo), the adjective follows the noun as it would in French (*système profession-nel*): *Wella System Professional*. Whereas the word order would appear ungrammatical to fluent English speakers, it closely mirrors the structure of the French language and therefore makes the English more intelligible in this context without diminishing any of its positive connotations (elitism, sophistication, and so on).

Elsewhere, the word order reversal will strongly imply the presence of English, whether or not a borrowing is involved. The following

signature line contains a word ('attitude') that exists in both languages thereby ensuring its intelligibility. The other word, *contemporaine*, is French. However, the word order definitely gives the expression an 'English feel' (the customary French word order in this case being *attitude contemporaine*): *Jean Roche. Contemporaine Attitude* (sofa). In advertising copy, accent marks may also be removed from otherwise 'French' text to produce chunks of language that resemble English (*crème* → creme, or *système* → systeme). L'Oréal, for example, has adopted this strategy in naming one of their products: *Excellence Creme de l'Oréal*. Fiat, on the hand, advertised one of the product features of its Stilo in France as *Systeme Connect NAV*, combining both an English borrowing ('connect') with a French word denuded of accents (*systeme*).

The ubiquitous apostrophe seen in many English-language product names in France is another innovation worth noting. Decathlon's bicycle model called *B'Tween* communicates the idea that the bicycle is suitable for both nature trails and inner city streets. It is, therefore, a bicycle that is 'in between' a mountain bike and a standard model. To ensure that this message is clearly received, however, they describe these advantages in French in their advertising:

Vélo de villes, vélo des champs. Décathlon invente B'Tween. Aussi à l'aise partout que partout . . . (Voice-off excerpt from TV spot)

English translation (mine)

City bike, trail bike. Introducing B'Tween by Décathlon. It works here, there and everywhere . . . (*Voice-off excerpt from TV spot*)

In a TV commercial for C'Clean (another product name involving an apostrophe), on the other hand, we notice that the French pronunciation of the [C + apostrophe] combination, plus the alternative meaning (*c'est*, as in 'it is') available to the reader once it is pronounced, are reinforced in both the dialogue and the voice-off commentary where two commonly used expressions in France involving an English borrowing (*c'est cool* and *c'est clean*) are interwoven with the product name. To produce the play on words, the creators of this advertisement are counting on the audience's double interpretration of the product name repeatedly pronounced throughout the dialogue: *C'Clean* (product name) and *C'est clean* (used in this context to describe 'clear skin', as in 'completely clear of acne'). The commercial opens with two teenage boys discussing an upcoming party (underlining added):

TV commercial for C'Clean

1st teenage boy	*On se voit à la soirée de samedi?*
2nd teenage boy	*Non mais t'as vu ma peau? J'ose plus sortir. J'ai tout essayé et j'ai la peau toute irritée.*
1st teenage boy	*Et ben moi <u>c'est clean</u>. Tous les jours j'utilise le gel <u>C'Clean</u> et <u>c'est clean</u> et il laisse ma peau toute douce.*
Voice-off	*Le gel <u>C'Clean</u> élimine les bactéries de peaux jeunes à problèmes.*

English translation (mine)

1st teenage boy	Are you coming to the party Saturday?
2nd teenage boy	Are you kidding? Have you seen my skin? I wouldn't dare go out. I've tried everything and my skin is all irritated.
1st teenage boy	Well . . . <u>my skin is all cleared up</u> [thanks to C'Clean]. Every day I use <u>C'Clean</u> and <u>my skin looks great</u>. And it leaves my skin really soft.
Voice-off	<u>C'Clean</u> gel eliminates acne-causing bacteria from youthful skin.

Then along comes a pretty girl who gives the first boy (who already uses the product) a big hug, noticing his beautiful, clear complexion:

Teenage girl	*Hmm . . . <u>C'est cool</u>, <u>c'est clean!</u>*
Voice-off	*<u>C'est cool</u>, <u>C'Clean!</u>*

English translation (mine)

Teenage girl	Wow, that's cool! Your skin is so clear!
Voice-off	It's really cool, *C'Clean!*

With its acne theme, extensive language-mixing, and use of the English borrowing 'cool!' in particular, this commercial is clearly aimed at French teenagers.

Other innovations involving punctuation and English borrowings include the use of computer keystrokes as an attention-getter, as in the following product name for a face cream:

Christian Dior No_Age Essentiel

This product naming technique also produces a 'modern' effect as the underscore (_) is sometimes used in composing website addresses. A product name for a women's razor may also be inspired by the 'dot com' industry, with the 'dot com' in this case being replaced by 'dot ice':

Philips Beauty Satin.ice Total Care 2-en-1

This added Internet-inspired punctuation gives the product a more modern, sophisticated image, appealing, for instance, to the upwardly mobile professional.

Phonological cues and pronunciation

Pronunciation also plays an important role in bilingual creativity. As seen in earlier examples, it may be used to accentuate the 'foreignness' of a celebrity delivering a product endorsement (Andie MacDowell in French television commercials for L'Oréal) or to associate the product with a world that is appealing to the intended audience (Ally McBip in print advertising for cell phone accessories). Sometimes an English-like pronunciation is required to produce the brand name correctly. A men's cologne by Dunhill sold under the name *X-centric*, for instance, requires that the initial 'X' be represented as the English letter 'X' (as opposed to the French pronunciation of this letter of the alphabet) in the audience's imagination for the brand name to be recalled as its creator(s) intended. It is also possible, however, that the [X-] prefix seen on so many product names today (for example, Mennen X-treme deodorant for men, Wilkinson Sword Xtreme razor for men, X-tra Blue Power laundry detergent) is understood as an abbreviation for 'ex', automatically producing the desired pronunciation in France because of French words such as *excentrique*, *extrême*, and *extraordinaire*. Whatever the case may be, the latter (*extraordinaire*) is commonly abbreviated as 'extra' in French, creating a significant difference in meaning between the French (*extra* → 'super wonderful') and English (extra → additional) versions. This semantic nuance was obviously not lost on those who decided to market a cereal by Kellogg's (with chocolate chips and nuts) as *EXTRA* in the French market.

Other types of pronunciation-inspired orthographical modifications may also be motivated by the desire for accurate brand name recall. Removing the final [-e] on the first syllable of the English borrowing 'make-up', for instance, was sure to facilitate the pronunciation among French consumers of *Demak-up* by *Supersoft* (with the [De-] prefix added to indicate the intended use of the product, which is make-up removal,

not application). Similarly, the punctuation in a product name for urinary protection pads (Poïse) is likely to aid French consumers in their pronunciation of the brand, possible French equivalents for this English borrowing being *grâce*, *équilibre*, and so on. As the English word 'poise' is not familiar to the general French population, the added marking on the 'i' vowel [ï] draws the reader away from the [pwa] pronunciation (as in *petits pois*, or 'peas') they would otherwise likely produce in seeing the [oi] vowel combination in this particular product name: Poïse.

Semantics

In other borrowings, a semantic shift may indicate an increased exposure to English by the general population.[28] The word 'light', for example, was originally borrowed to replace 'diet' in food and beverage products (for instance, *Coca Light* for 'Diet Coke'), as the word 'diet' had negative associations in certain markets outside the United States. These data reveal, however, that in recent years additional meanings for the English word 'light' have crept into French advertising discourse. Consider the following examples (Martin, 2005):

Brand name	Product type	Meaning of the word 'light' or 'lite'
Dolce & Gabbana Light Blue	Perfume	'softer shade of color'
IBM ThinkLight	Lamp you clip onto laptop	'lamp'
Intersport McKinley Minto Ultra Lite	Sleeping bag	'lightweight'

In French advertising slogans we also find English words that have been borrowed with additional meanings as compared to several years ago (as reported, for example, in Martin, 1998a), indicating their wider acceptance and intelligibility among the targeted population. Appearing in a recent Skil Power Tools ad, for instance, is the word 'smart' (Martin, 2005) – a borrowing originally adopted by the French to refer to someone who is 'handsomely dressed'. Here, however, it is used to denote 'intelligence', a meaning that is very rare indeed for this borrowing in colloquial French discourse. Advising consumers to purchase Skil Power Tools (complete with tool box), the slogan reads: *Soyez smart!* (Be intelligent!). Closer examination of the copy and illustration reveals that this literal (denoted) meaning (that buying Skil Power Tools in a boxed kit with accessories included is an intelligent decision) is accompanied by an

additional (connoted) interpretation: A man who purchases this kit will no longer be 'trapped' in his routine of keeping an odd collection of drill bits and screws in jars normally used for jams and preserves. Indeed, he will have everything at his fingertips (*'tout pour réussir'*). The detailed list of parts included (hammer drill, screws, plugs, and so on) is directed at male readers who want to have all their tools within easy reach (*'tout immédiatement sous la main'*). This solution is very attractive indeed when one considers the frustrated individual depicted in the visual, imprisoned in a recycled glass jar with his various useless odds and ends. The English in the slogan also draws the reader's attention to the product name (*SmartSet*) appearing on the box label. Appearing at the bottom of the page is also the word *'extra's'*. At first glance, one might assume that this is a truncated version of 'extraordinaire' in French (as seen in the Kellogg's example earlier) with the simple affixation of the English possessive marker [apostrophe + s]: + 16 EXTRA'S. However, the context in which it occurs (where the phrase *'+16 extra's'* actually refers to additional items one receives with the tool kit) clearly indicates that the meaning 'additional' has also been borrowed, and that the possessive marker, through the creative process of lexical borrowing, now indicates plurality (as in *16 extra's*, or '16 extra items') [29]

One also notices in French advertising copy a wider range of meaning for the English borrowing 'cool'. As seen in the *Pretty Cool* (lipstick/nail polish) and *C'Clean* (facial cleanser) examples earlier, this word is typically used in colloquial French to mean 'great' or 'wonderful'. In a print ad for Opel automobiles, however, the 'cool temperature' signification of the word in English has also been borrowed as a way to refer to one of the product features (air conditioning). The young man wearing mittens in the illustration further encourages this interpretation. The headline (*Les Journées Cool du 15 mars au 13 avril*) is polysemous, offering both 'wonderful' and 'lower temperatures' as possible readings (my translation):

March 15 through April 13 are cool days
[at your local Opel dealership]

1. *cool days* = wonderful days
2. *cool days* = days where deals on air-conditioning are available

Later in the copy the word 'cool' resurfaces, evoking this time the originally adopted meaning of 'wonderful' (*With Opel, play the coolest games!*) while inviting the reader to 'scratch and sniff' a small square surface on the page 'to experience the airy feeling of an air conditioned Opel':

*Avec Opel, jouez au plus **cool** des jeux! Frottez et sentez, pour connaître la sensation dégagée par une Opel climatisée.*

English translation (mine)

With Opel, play the coolest games! Scratch and sniff to experience the sensation of an air-conditioned Opel.

Bilingual puns

Bilingual puns are another prominent feature of French advertising discourse. Consider, for example, the following slogan for Lavazza coffee (Figure 5.1: Martin, 2005): *Espress yourself** (*Exprimez-vous). Whereas at first glance, this might appear to be a straightforward English-language slogan (with an accompanying French translation), a closer look reveals that the English word 'express' has been orthographically modified to reflect the product being advertised (Italian espresso):

Espresso (coffee)

}   *Espress[o] yourself*

Express yourself

The substitution of 's' for 'x' in this context also mirrors the pronunciation of the first syllable (specifically the [ks] cluster converted to [s]) by certain French speakers and therefore represents a conscious effort on the part of copywriters to imitate the speech patterns of consumers. Whatever the motivation may be, this altered version ('espress yourself', with 's' inserted in place of 'x') phonetically and orthographically links the slogan with the product being advertised (espresso) and thus encourages the following double interpretation by those who notice the pun:

Espress yourself → Drink espresso

or

Espress yourself → Express yourself ('Be who you want to be')

Both the French translation (*Exprimez-vous*) and the rather creative Lavazza-inspired outfits worn by the models in the visuals reinforce this message. By embedding the product (*espresso*) in a meaningful chunk of discourse (*Espress yourself*), the linguistic message guides the reader towards an interpretation of this image as one that symbolizes someone 'expressing' herself through coffee, and who appreciates the experience to such an extent that she literally wraps herself in the product from head to toe. Closer inspection, however, reveals another layer of

Figure 5.1 Lavazza advertisement

meaning. Interspersed with the images of the corporate logo stuck to the model's skin (and scattered on the floor at her feet) are voluptuous lips and cups of espresso of various colors, shapes and sizes. One possible connotation of this mixture of text and images is that the woman and the coffee are inseparable 'lovers' with the various representations of the Italian product (lips, logo, coffee cups filled with espresso) passionately embracing her to the point of entering her very being. The combination of colors (blue, white, and red), plus the pristine white sandy beach and bright blue sky seen through the windows in the background, are all elements that will appeal to the French, evoking not only their nationality (colors of the French flag) but also fond vacation memories of exotic sunny locations. Through these various devices, those who designed this advertisement are encouraging readers to interpret this image as a celebration of lust, desire, and self-expression (with the avant-garde world of fashion as an enticing cultural reference), creating multiple layers of meaning. Thus, any negative connotations (women portrayed as sex objects for commercial gain, branding as a form of mind control, and so forth) are suppressed in favor of a more positive symbolic interpretation: Drink Lavazza espresso coffee, and be unique!

In a print ad for Givenchy, we find another code-mixed pun involving English. In this case, the product name for the perfume featured in the ad (*HOT Couture*) offers a double meaning for the English borrowing 'hot':

1. hot = the latest trend, as in *c'est vraiment hot ça*
2. hot = 'high' as in 'high fashion', or *haute couture*

These interpretations are encouraged by both the French pronunciation of 'hot' (which closely resembles that of the French word *haute*) and the fashion model theme of the illustration. Striking a sexy pose with a sultry gaze directed into the camera, a young fashion model is wearing an elegant dress that has been pinned to the contours of her body with straight pins as if she is being fitted for the garment in preparation for a fashion show. The slogan contributes to the fashion (*haute couture*) reading of the illustration:

> *L'autre façon de porter HOT Couture*
> The other way to wear HOT Couture (my translation)

As it is presented in a larger font as compared to 'Couture', and in capital letters, the English element in the product name ('HOT') also serves as an attention-getter.

Another bilingual pun appears in print advertising for Hépar mineral water. A woman (dressed in black) smiles at the camera looking very relaxed and content. Across her chest in bold white lettering is written the following slogan:

n'eau fatigue
n'eau stress

As the French word for 'water', *eau*, is pronounced as 'oh', the *n'eau* combination quite naturally produces the English word 'no' (or at least its phonetic equivalent) in the reader's imagination. Choosing a French pronoun commonly used in negation (*n'*) to create this slogan strengthens the association [French *n'eau* → English 'no'] one must make to understand the play on words. Whereas in French this element (*n'*) would never occur before a noun, this is irrelevant given the poetic licence of copywriters and only adds to the enjoyment of the reader who will experience this as a novelty. The English borrowing 'stress', as noted earlier, presents no difficulties in terms of intelligibility. Thus, the slogan's interpretation as 'no fatigue, no stress' is more or less guaranteed. The small print at the top left-hand corner of the page gives some 'self-help' suggestions for relaxation, including, of course, use of the product (my translation):

A few good ways to relax:
– laugh
– take breaks during the day
– breathe
– listen to soft music
the best:
– drink Hépar
(1 liter of Hépar = 110 mg of magnesium)
www.hepar.fr

The signature line at the bottom of the page reintroduces the magnesium benefit:

HEPAR. LE MAGNESIUM A SA SOURCE
HEPAR. YOUR SOURCE FOR MAGNESIUM (my translation)

Using puns that capitalize on cultural and linguistic perceptions, these advertisements reveal how advertisers imbue their messages and illustra-

tions with multiple layers of meaning, creating a discourse that speaks directly to their intended audience.

Multimodal mixing

The examples discussed above also demonstrate that bilingual creativity in French advertising may be expressed through several modes or channels. Indeed, the interpretation of language-mixing appearing in product names, slogans, descriptive copy, and elsewhere is reinforced through visual imagery, body language, and music soundtracks. In many cases, one finds evidence of mixing in several modes simultaneously. In a print ad for a men's razor by BaByliss, for example, the English borrowing 'top' (understood as 'top notch', or 'the very best' by French speakers) appears in both the slogan (*Au top de la technologie*, or 'The very best technology has to offer') and on the body of the young man depicted in the visual. Here, however, the individual is seen from directly above (an unusual camera angle for advertising copy) with his head completely shaved except for a small amount of remaining hair that spells out the word 'TOP' in capital letters. It is a striking illustration that serves as both an attention-getter and a source of humor (the idea of someone using a razor to create 'head poetry'). There is also the possibility of an extended semantic range for this borrowing as in the previously cited examples ('light', 'smart', 'extra', 'cool') as the visual, in this case, implies that 'top' can also refer to 'the top of one's head'.[30]

English appears in both the product name and voice-off commentary in a television commercial for a men's razor by Gillette. The off-camera voice describes the product (aptly named the Mach 3 Cool Blue) as offering a closer shave in less time with little or no skin irritation, and as having a 'very cool look' (underlining added):

> *Découvrez Mach 3 <u>Cool Blue</u>, Trois lames pour les plus précis des rasages en moins de passage pour moins d'irritation. Et maintenant avec un nouveau <u>look</u> vraiment très <u>cool</u>. Nouveau Mach 3 <u>Cool Blue</u> de Gillette: La perfection au masculin.*

English translation (mine)

> Discover Mach 3 <u>Cool Blue</u>. Three blades for a quicker, more precise shave, causing less skin irritation. Now available in a <u>look</u> that's really very <u>cool</u>. New Mach 3 <u>Cool Blue</u> by Gillette. Masculine perfection.

French advertising for a breath mint (Menthos Cool Chews), on the other hand, uses the same English borrowing ('cool') in the product name and jingle:

> *Be cool,*
> *Be sharp,*
> *Yeah . . .*
> *Mentos Cool Chew*
> *Gets you up and ready to go . . .*

This 'multimodal mixing' is illustrated in yet another way in a television commercial for Whiskas Délichoc Sac Fraîcheur (cat food sold in reclosable pouches). On the product appears the code-mixed expression '*Zip fraîcheur*' ('zipper-insured freshness'). However, nowhere in the visuals, spoken dialogue, voice-off or music soundtrack does this English borrowing ('zip') resurface.[31] Rather, to call the audience's attention to the 'zip' feature of the packaging, a 'zipping' sound effect is inserted repeatedly in the female voice-off:

> *Il y a encore du nouveau chez Whiskas (zip sound): un sac fraîcheur qui s'ouvre aussi facilement (zip sound) qu'il se referme (zip sound) pour garder intacte la saveur et le croquant de ces savoureuses croquettes fourrées (zip sound) qui font les délices de votre chat (zip sound). Whiskas Délichoc. C'est délicieux (zip sound), il fait le reste (zip sound).*

English translation (mine)

> There's something new again at Whiskas (zip sound): a zipper bag which opens just as easily (zip sound) as it recloses (zip sound) to keep in the flavor and crunchiness of these deliciously filled morsels (zip sound) that your cat will find irresistible (zip sound). Whiskas Délichoc. It's delicious (zip sound) and [the packaging] does the rest (zip sound).

Obviously, the possibilities for delivering meaning in advertising are endless due to the visual elements, different (written, spoken, sung) verbal modes, the mood-enhancing properties of music soundtracks, the use of sound effects, and other elements. It is a rich environment indeed for the use of English borrowings that, as demonstrated through the examples contained within these pages, have, in many cases, been refashioned or 'nativized' for optimal effect. Through the various devices described herein, 'Frenglish' (or *franglais*) is becoming the 'language of

advertising' *par excellence* in France for many product categories and audiences, producing multiple meanings and bilingual puns, many of which reflect a level of complexity (and coercion) that extends far beyond the processes of borrowing and mixing one finds in other genres. It is a discourse unlike any other, skillfully crafted by copywriters, creative directors, art directors, and others who basically have *carte blanche* in terms of creativity and choice of expression. The bottom line, however, remains company sales. And in order to entice a consumer to purchase an item or service being advertised, the copy must be capable of relaying the message of the campaign, a situation that can sometimes be problematic when language-mixing is involved. Let us turn our attention then, to the many techniques used to translate English elements inserted in French advertising copy.

Translations

The translation of advertising copy differs from that of other areas of discourse in that 'literal' translations are interspersed with translations introduced for special effect. Indeed, the translation of foreign language elements in advertising copy distributed in France (required by the 1994 Toubon Law, which will be discussed in detail in Chapter 6) may involve a number of different strategies depending on various factors. These include (i) the media in which the advertisement appears; (ii) the degree to which the word or expression has been assimilated into French (*week-end* requiring no translation, for instance); (iii) whether or not the material is protected by copyright (as is the case with product names and jingles); (iv) the position in which the English occurs (slogans, descriptive text, dialogue, and so on) and hence its overall visibility; and (v) the extent to which a French translation will alter the original message of the campaign. If a translation is provided elsewhere in the copy, this is normally indicated by an asterisk (or, in the case of television advertising, as subtitles preceded by an asterisk).

Direct translations

In many cases, the French translation remains very close to the original English text, as in the following slogans found in the print data:

Hugo Boss Woman	(perfume)	Expect Everything* *Attendez-vous à tout*
Mont Blanc	(watch)	Is that you?* *Est-ce bien toi?*

Nivea for Men	(facial cream)	Play hard – look young* *Vivez intensément – restez jeune*
Sector	(watch)	Personality is not a limit* *La personnalité n'est pas une limite*
Tissot T Touch	(watch)	T Touch. The touch screen watch* *montre à écran tactile*
Wella System Professional	(shampoo)	Beautiful hair needs an expert* *La beauté des cheveux naît de l'expertise*

Translations of this nature also appear in television commercials. Consider, for example, a TV spot for a mascara (Nouveau Mascara de Bourjois) featuring the English word 'stretching'. In the commercial, a woman enters the living room of her Paris apartment, inserting a fitness DVD in her DVD player for a 'stretching session'. The voice-off, however, reveals that the exercise has nothing whatsoever to do with muscles, but rather the movement one makes with a mascara brush to 'stretch' one's eyelashes as far as possible:

Allez, on démarre par une séance de stretching. Et un, j'étire vers le haut. Allez encore plus haut! Et deux, j'intensifie mon mouvement. Bravo les filles, vous êtes étirées jusqu'au bout des cils. Nouveau Mascara ultra-allongeant de Bourjois: la séance de stretching des cils. (Voice-off excerpt from TV spot for Bourjois)

English translation (mine)

OK, everybody ready? Off we go! We're going to start with some stretching exercises. One . . . I'm stretching upwards. Come on, you can go higher than that! Two . . . I'm stretching just a little bit further. Good job, girls! You've stretched all the way to the end of your eyelashes. New ultra-lengthening Mascara by Bourjois. The stretching session for your eyelashes. (Voice-off excerpt from TV spot for Bourjois)

The commercial concludes with the following written code-mixed text appearing on the screen: *le stretching des cils** (subtitled as **gymnastique d'étirement*). In a TV ad for Timotei Gel Extreme (hair styling gel), sub-

titles are provided for English appearing on the product label: Timotei Natural Style* (**le coiffage naturel*).

Even English appearing on items in the background visual will sometimes be subtitled in French television commercials. A spot for Opel, for instance, features two families unloading their various accessories from their respective automobiles before spending a relaxing day at the beach. One of the families sets up a gigantic inflatable toy for their children bearing the logo 'HAPPY CLOWN'. Due to its high visibility on-screen, this bit of English text is subtitled simply as *joyeux. (The second word, 'clown', requires no glossing as it is identical in French). The voice-off commentary addresses members of the viewing audience who 'think big':

> *Vous rêvez de voir la vie en grand?*
> *Nous construisons votre voiture.*
> *L'Opel Combo Tour.*

English translation (mine)

> Do you want to live large?
> Then we have just the car for you.
> Introducing the Opel Combo Tour.

Slightly modified translations

Occasionally, ad agencies in France receive copy with English text which is difficult to translate and/or would sound much less appealing in French. To adapt the advertisement to the French market, they resort to a slightly changed version designed to achieve a similar effect. Consider the following examples (Martin, 2005):

Devoteam Siticom	(e-business)	Team up* *Ensemble
Fairmount	(shoes)	The casual footwear by Fairmount* **élégance décontractée*
IBM	(computers)	Découvrez e-business on demand. The next utility* **e-business à la demande, le nouveau service essentiel*

The Devoteam Siticom slogan uses a more succinct French translation (*ensemble*, meaning 'together') to replace the original English colloquialism ('team up') as any direct translation (such as '*Faites équipe!*') would have been less appealing. The French translation appearing in the Fair-

mount ad (*élégance décontractée*, or 'casual elegance') is also well chosen as it adds a certain flair to the original version. This ploy was, in fact, rather ingenious given that French consumers typically value refinement in everything related to fashion. Thus, the notion of 'chic' is introduced in place of 'footwear', used in the original English text. As for the word 'utility' in IBM's slogan, it probably would have thoroughly stumped French audiences (who might have mistaken it for *utilité*, or 'usefulness'), hence 'the latest service you cannot live without' in the French version (**e-business à la demande, le nouveau service essentiel*).[32]

In the IBM example, one also notices that the expression 'e-business' has been carried over into the translation. A highly assimilated borrowing, this lexical item does not require any glossing for the French public. Inspired by the widespread use of this borrowing in business (and advertising), however, France Telecom established a new level of creativity in a print ad for its multiple business solutions, extending the 'e-business' borrowing to rename various departments within the company depicted in the visual. In the illustration appears a pizza delivery man in the lobby of an office building. Holding a stack of pizza boxes reaching all the way to his chin, he ponders the directory of departments (each on a different floor) displayed on the lobby wall:

> *e-direction générale*
> *e-marketing*
> *e-service études*
> *e-ressources humaines*
> *e-service achats*
> *e-service clients*
> *e-accueil*

English translation (mine)

> e-management
> e-marketing
> e-research department
> e-human resources
> e-purchasing department
> e-customer service
> e-reception desk

Another e-business-inspired neologism (*e-applications*) appears in the descriptive copy informing the reader that 'France Télécom . . . enables you to discover and implement new e-applications every day' (My

translation. Original text: '*France Télécom . . . vous permet de découvrir et d'exploiter chaque jour de nouvelles e-applications*').

Slightly modified translations for English-language slogans also occur in television commercials, in which case they appear as subtitles. Examples in the corpus include:

Mentos Cool Chew	(breath mints)	The Freshmaker*
		le déclic fraîcheur
Nissan X-trail	(automobile)	See the change*
		Vous changez, nous aussi
Lipton Ice Tea	(ice tea)	Be Alive*
		plein de vie
Club Med	(fragrances)	Happy Body*
		un corps en pleine forme

The approximate English equivalents for each of the altered French translations would be as follows (English translation mine):

le déclic fraîcheur	→ Triggers freshness
Vous changez, nous aussi	→ You change, so do we
plein de vie	→ Full of life
un corps en pleine forme	→ A healthy body

In each of these cases, a literal translation would have sounded far less appealing, producing phrases such as '*fabricant de fraîcheur*', '*voyez le changement*', '*soyez vivant*', and '*corps heureux*', none of which has positive connotations in French. The French translation for Mazda's slogan (*Zoom, zoom*) is even further removed from the original, and (as *zoom, zoom* exists in French as well) was purely added for special effect (English translation mine):

On n'arrête pas le plaisir	→ There's no stopping pleasure

In a print advertisement for Givenchy make-up, on the other hand, we find what, at first glance, appears to be an English translation for French text, highly unusual indeed given the fact that this is advertising in France where one would expect quite the opposite (French text with no translation, or fine-print French translations for English-language slogans used as attention-getters). The English-language slogan appears, in smaller print, immediately below its French equivalent:

EMOI DE SOIE

EMOTION IS MINE

Closer examination reveals that this French text is, in fact, a pun suggesting another French expression (*émoi de joie*) meaning 'excitement'. To arrive at this orthographical representation, the copywriter(s) added the letter [e] to the word *soi* ('oneself'), producing a double layer of meaning (derived from a mental connection between *soi* and *joie*):

1. émoi de soi   → one's own emotions (literally, 'emotion of oneself')
2. émoi de joie   → excitement

The catchy English equivalent displayed in the copy (EMOTION IS MINE) is simple and direct, and thus better suited for advertising than other possible translations (such as the interpretations suggested above). It also has the added advantage of featuring a repeated consonant sound (/m/) making it all the more memorable (E*M*OTION IS *M*INE). Given the fact that the English is not likely to contribute to the intelligibility of a play on words presented in French (*EMOI DE SOIE*) read by French consumers, it was undoubtedly inserted to evoke certain positive associations with the product (that it is modern, chic, has international appeal, and so on). As for the positioning of the English in smaller print after the French slogan (as opposed to larger print before the French, as is usually the case), this essentially encourages a deeper analysis of the French text containing the carefully crafted pun necessary to make the connection between 'self' and 'excitement'. The focus on 'self' evident in both the French and English versions of the slogan is further reinforced by the Givenchy logo imprinted directly on the pupil of the young female model in the illustration. The reader's attention is thus automatically drawn to parts of the copy where meaning is most intensified (slogan, product, logo).[33]

In a television commercial for Perrier sparkling water, on the other hand, we have two slightly modified French translations for an English voice-off commentary. Replacing the traditional automobile crash test with a more 'water-inspired' theme, the spot depicts a pair of crashtest dummies manoeuvering (using a bicycle-pedaling motion) their two-seater boat into a brick wall. The voice-off, delivered in English with a thick French accent, gives the vehicle (that is, product packaging) a perfect safety rating: *Perrier. Unbreakable.* The French translation written

on the screen alludes to the portability benefit as well: *In-cas-sable. Trans-por-table.* The word *incassable* ('unbreakable') then reappears in the subtitles: **bouteille incassable* ('unbreakable bottle'). Thus, two separate and slightly modified French translations (one as a slogan, the other as subtitles) are provided for a single spoken English borrowing ('unbreakable'):

1. *In-cas-sable. Trans-por-table*
2. **bouteille incassable*

Whereas it might appear a bit cryptic to consumers in other markets, this fanciful combination of images and languages is very appealing to the French who not only enjoy (and expect) symbolism and humor in their advertising, but also find decoding advertising messages much more satisfying than a direct, hard-sell approach (Zandpour, Chang, and Catalano, 1992).

Code-mixed translations

Translations for English-language elements in French advertising copy may also involve code-mixing, as seen in earlier examples of print advertisements (for example, IBM's *e-business à la demande . . .*). One encounters the same phenomenon in television commercials in France. A TV spot for a Nestlé candy bar (Kit Kat Chunky), for instance, features the following voice-off commentary (underlining added):

> <u>Have a break</u>. *Nouveau Kit Kat Chunky. Kit Kat Chunky. Plus gros. Plus gourmand. Signé Nestlé.* (voice-off)
>
> **Faites un <u>break</u>* (subtitles)

English translation (mine)

> <u>Have a break</u>. [Discover the] new Kit Kat Chunky. Kit Kat Chunky. Bigger. Better. By Nestlé. (voice-off)
>
> **Take a <u>break</u>* (subtitles)

As can be observed in the French version, the subtitles provided for the borrowed expression used here ('Have a break') also contain English: **Faites un break*. This language-mixing in television commercial subtitles (as well as code-mixed translations seen in print advertising) only occurs when the borrowing involved is highly assimilated, and thus easily recognizable. A French radio station (NRJ, pronounced as *énergie*, or

'energy'), for instance, uses the following slogan and accompanying translation in their television advertising (Martin, 2005):

NRJ, hit music only*
Que du hit sur NRJ

The English word repeated here ('hit') is, in fact, quite popular in French advertising aimed at younger audiences, so much so that it has become standard fare in voice-off commentary, descriptive text, slogans, and product names for certain product categories that interest this segment of the population.

Occasionally, a code-mixed translation is inserted as a means of creating a bilingual pun. A slogan used in a TV commercial for Fanta (soda) is one such example (Martin, 2005):

Made in Fun*
Fun de folie

The translation provided (*Fun de folie*) contains elements from both English ('fun') and French (*de folie*, meaning 'like crazy'), a bilingual combination that phonetically resembles a French colloquialism (*vent de folie*, meaning 'crazy passion'). The all-English slogan (Made in Fun) also has several layers of meaning, as one might associate it with the mention 'made in USA' seen, for instance, on product labels and packaging. Although the brand does indeed originate in the US (Fanta is a trademark of the Coca-Cola Company), 'Made in Fun' was a wiser choice as (i) it uses an unusual combination of words and thus operates as an attention-getter; (ii) it involves a borrowing ('fun') used often by members of this audience group (French teenagers); and (iii) it is more in line with the 'fun' atmosphere of Fanta's advertising campaigns, all of which makes 'Made in Fun' much more likely to appeal to the intended audience. One of the television commercials for Fanta in the corpus features this very same code-mixed translation along with spoken English in the dialogue and imagery from Scotland. The spot opens with a group of young co-eds relaxing in a rowboat in the middle of a lake, identified (in writing) on screen as *Lac Loch Ness Ecosse* ('Loch Ness, Scotland'). One of the girls is enjoying a can of Fanta when a guy tickles her, making her accidentally drop her Fanta into the lake. A few moments later, Nessie (the notorious 'Loch Ness monster'), who never directly shows up in front of anyone, pokes her head above water and greets them in English

(*Hello!*), prompting a burst of laughter from the boat's passengers. A voice-off delivers the slogan (with subtitles matching those described earlier):

Fanta Madness: Made in Fun*
Fun de folie

To conclude, the use of English in advertising distributed in France is a complex phenomenon that is best examined in terms of motivational factors, intended audience, product category, and bilingual creativity. The print advertisements and television commercials described throughout these pages clearly demonstrate that English, for the purpose of marketing products and services to consumers in France, is being refashioned in myriad ways, through its orthographical modification, its insertion into the grammatical structure of the French language (and vice versa), as well as its phonological and semantic reshaping, and has become an integral part of the advertising landscape of France. Thus, in advertising, we are often dealing with a specialized variety of English, created specifically for the purposes of a particular campaign and tailored to the linguistic behavior and expectations, mentality, and worldview of the intended audience.[34]

The use of English in French advertising examined throughout this chapter is better appreciated, however, if one considers the 'World Englishes' paradigm introduced by Braj Kachru (1982; 1986a and b). Kachru (1996: 138) eloquently describes how English is linguistically and culturally assimilated in certain contexts through such processes as 'Englishization', 'nativization' and 'acculturation':

> across languages and literatures, the impact of World Englishes is Janus-like, with two faces. One face is that of ENGLISHIZATION, the process of change that English has initiated in the other languages of the world. The second face is that of the NATIVIZATION and ACCULTURATION of the English language itself, the processes of change that localized varieties of English have undergone by acquiring new linguistic and cultural identities.

This 'acculturation' of English is evident throughout the present corpus where English expressions are continually embedded in the French grammatical system (for example, *je dunkerai for you; une performance liftante*) or otherwise altered to accommodate French speakers (as in the product name, *Poïse*). Indeed, as many of these examples illustrate,

English as it appears in this context is very often transformed into a Frenglish variety specifically designed for advertising campaigns where product names and slogans defy grammatical categorization (such as the slogan, *n'eau fatique, n'eau stress* for Hépar mineral water) and produce multiple meanings that tie together the product, brand, copy, and overall message of the campaign (for example, Braun's Silk-épil EverSoft razor; Givenchy's HOT couture). In this manner, English contributes to the artistry exhibited in many of the advertisements featured in these pages, producing a blend of cultural references, humor and symbolism that is very likely to appeal to this audience.

English also has a certain connotative value depending on its context of use (Kachru, 1996: 142), serving in some cases as a cultural mirror or symbol of modernization, for instance, and in others as an access code or a reflection of superior technology. In examining the use of English in French advertising across media, we also notice that English is operating (as described by Halliday, 2003) as both a global language for world audiences (as seen in the poster advertisement for the easyEverything™ internet café in Paris aimed at tourists, for instance, or the TV commercial for swiss cheese featuring the English-language endline 'SWITZER-LAND'), and a more appropriated, locally adapted international language for local markets (for example, *Que du hit sur NRJ; le best of évènement; fun de folie; ze big love c pour quand*). Although some may argue that this omnipresence of English is more of a 'cultural and linguistic invasion' than a rich display of linguistic creativity and whimsical expression, these data suggest that the English described herein has been carefully selected and often refashioned as a simple form of entertainment, and that the French cultural identity remains very much intact despite the high concentration of both English and American images in entertainment media. The influence of English on the French language, however, continues to be the focus of intense debate in France, a topic that will be explored in detail in the following chapter.

6
French Resistance to English

This chapter will highlight various efforts on the part of the French government to limit the public's exposure to English in the media and will examine the advertising industry's reactions to such intervention. This discussion will include a brief historical overview of language planning in France, noting, for example, the establishment of various official organizations mandated to 'protect the French language' as well as government-appointed terminology commissions responsible for coining new 'recommended' French equivalents for Anglicisms frequently used in the media and advertising industries, as well as other professional domains. Following this discussion will be a description of the 1994 Toubon Law, the most comprehensive legislation to date in France designed to curb the use of English in the media. Specific areas of the legislation that pertain to advertising will be discussed in detail (such as the required equally 'legible, audible and intelligible' French translations for foreign languages used in slogans and dialogue), along with the general public's attitudes towards English. Reactions from members of the French advertising industry to this legislation as reported during ad agency interviews in Paris, the role that English plays in their inter- (and intra-) agency communication, and the mission of several organizations regulating the advertising industry will then be addressed. Through additional analyses of advertising copy, it will also be demonstrated precisely how those who design advertising for the French market are continuing to exploit English as a creative means of expression despite the legal restrictions imposed on them.

Language planning in France

Language planning in France is a centuries-old tradition, beginning with the Edict of Villers-Cotterêts imposing French as the official written

212

language of the court and government (replacing Latin) in 1539. In 1635, the *Académie Française* was formed as an organization whose mission was to codify the language, striving to maintain its purity and eloquence to the greatest extent possible, particularly in regards to the arts and sciences.[1] To this day, the Academy's official recommendations on language use appear in the form of a regularly revised dictionary (*Dictionnaire de l'Académie Française*) and its members continue to be consulted on issues related to language use. Although the influence of English on French had long been a topic of discussion, it was during the years following World War II, when America emerged as an economic and military superpower, that France began to experience the effects of Americanization and a growing consumer culture. Etiemble (1964) parodies the impact of English on French in this post-war era, presenting *franglais* (or Frenglish) as a form of linguistic and cultural invasion from the US, setting the stage for many 'language purists' who have since spoken out in defense of the French language in their writings (for example, Le Cornec, 1981; Saint Robert, 1986; Dutourd, 1999, among others). During this same time period, French president Charles de Gaulle proposed various language protectionist measures, establishing, with his successor Georges Pompidou, the High Committee for the Defense and Expansion of the French Language (*Haut comité pour la défense et l'expansion de la langue française*) in 1966.[2] To assist this language organization in carrying out its mission of promoting and protecting the French language, Georges Pompidou later assigned various terminology committees (the first of which were created in 1970) the task of formulating new French words and phrases to replace 'undesirable borrowings' used in specific domains such as foreign affairs, computer science, the military, sports, telecommunications, agriculture, economics, law, medicine, transportation, and so on.[3] The lists of recommended terms published in the *Journal Officiel* by the terminology committee for broadcast media and advertising (created in 1980) includes such items as *aguiche* for 'teaser' (designating an advertisement that 'teases' the public by shrouding the product in mystery until a second advertisement appears) and *accroche* for 'catching'.[4] This latter item, one may observe, is not actually a direct borrowing from English, but rather a lexical item refashioned by the French from the terms 'catchline' and 'catchphrase'. These expressions are used in the advertising industry to refer to a word or phrase appearing under the company's logo (also called 'endline' or 'hookline') (Duvillier, 1990: 151).[5] Since 1996, however, the *Académie Française* has veto power over the decisions made by the terminology committees.

In 1975, the first consumer-protection language law (the Bas–Lauriol Law) was passed, officially rendering the 'non-use of French' in certain public domains (including advertising) in France illegal.[6] Shortly thereafter (in 1976) was founded a linguistic watchdog association known as the General Association of French Users (*Association Générale des Usagers de la Langue Française* or AGULF) which was charged with bringing 'language offenders' to justice. One of the first to be cited by AGULF for the 'non-use of French' was the Paris Opera whose 5-page program for a play entitled 'Bubbling Brown Sugar' caught their attention. The program in question was presented entirely in English accompanied only by a short French summary. The court ruled in favor of AGULF stating that the French version appearing in the playbill did not contain essential information (including some of the play's central characters). The fine imposed amounted to 3,460 francs (500 US dollars at the time).[7] Several years later, the Paris Metropolitan Transit Authority (RATP) met a similar fate for having used a poster advertisement for bus and subway tickets written exclusively in English. The advertisement, presumably aimed at foreign tourists navigating the public transport system, read: *All of Paris for Just One Ticket, Paris Sesame, A2, 4 or 7 days. Ticket for Unlimited Travels on Metro-Buses and RER Lines A and B (B South of Gare du Nord)*. The fine in this case was 4,000 francs (800 US dollars).[8]

The 1980s ushered in another round of protectionist measures, including a 40 per cent quota for French-language programs and cinematic productions on television and a similar quota requiring that 40 per cent of music sung on French radio be in French.[9] Films imported from the US to France have also met with some resistance by the French government who first set an annual quota of 150 American films entering the French market with the Henriot Law of 1928. The 1948 Blum–Byrnes agreement replaced the quota system with a 4 per cent tax on all American films shown in French theaters (money that was subsequently used to promote French cinema). Today the tax on films imported from the US stands at 11 per cent (Abrate, 2004: 29). In 1989, two additional language associations were created, the Superior Council for the French Language (*Conseil Supérieur de la Langue Française*) and the General Language Delegation (*Délégation Générale à la Langue Française*, now known as the *Délégation Générale à la Langue Française et aux Langues de France* or DGLFLF), both of which continue to play an active role in promoting and protecting the French language today.[10] The loopholes in the 1975 Bas–Lauriol Law were such, however, that the legal system's determination to police the 'non-use of French' (and

the use of English in particular) eventually subsided. Writes Loretta Nelms-Reyes (1996: 288–9) in her article detailing France's legal 'crusade' against English:

> Overall, the 1975 language statute, perhaps because it was camouflaged as a consumer-protection law, had little impact on the increasing number of Anglo-American terms being used in everyday French . . . Poor drafting, which required broad judicial interpretation to redefine the statute, coupled with inconsequential fines, made the statute largely unsuccessful in limiting the use of English, especially by the advertising industry. Thus, although thousands of companies and individuals were investigated under the 1975 law, the language ban was routinely defied or circumvented.

The Toubon Law

In 1994, the French government adopted a new language statute (commonly referred to as the Toubon Law after France's Minister of Culture at the time, Jacques Toubon), replacing the Bas–Lauriol legislation.[11] Articles 2 and 12 of the Toubon Law pertain to the advertising industry most specifically:[12]

Article 2

The use of French shall be mandatory for the designation, offer, presentation, instructions for use, and description of the scope and conditions of a warranty of goods, products and services, as well as bills and receipts. The same provisions apply to any written, spoken, radio and television advertisement. The provisions of the present article shall not apply to the names of typical products and specialties of foreign origin known by the general public. Legislation relative to brands shall not prevent the application of . . . the present Article to the remarks and messages recorded with the brand.

Article 12

The use of French is compulsory in all the programmes and advertising messages of radio and television broadcasting organisations and services, whatever their mode of dissemination or distribution, with the exception of motion picture and radio and television productions in their original language version. [This] shall not apply to musical works which contain text written wholly or partly in a foreign language . . . Where the broadcasts or advertising messages . . . are

accompanied by translations in a foreign language, the presentation in French must be as legible, audible and intelligible as the presentation in the foreign language.

Thus, in regards to advertising, the Toubon law stipulates that (i) French is required in all print, radio, and television advertising distributed in France, and that (ii) if English is used anywhere in the copy, it must appear with an equally 'legible, audible and intelligible' French translation (which, as will be discussed in the following pages, is not often the case).[13] According to this legislation, the only contexts in which English (or any other foreign language) unaccompanied by a French translation is deemed 'legal' in French advertising copy are the following:

- Music soundtracks in television and radio commercials
- Corporate and brand names
- Foreign product names and specialties familiar to the general public (for example, chorizo, cookie, couscous, gin, gorgonzola, hot dog, jeans, paella, pizza, sandwich, scotch whisky).

The application of this law to all radio and television advertising distributed in France is ensured by the French Television and Radio Supervisory Council (*Conseil supérieur de l'audiovisuel* or CSA) which is charged with imposing fines and other legal sanctions in cases of infringement. This agency is also authorized to discontinue the broadcasting of a television or radio advertisement at any time if it is deemed to contain illegal or offensive material. The television station Euronews was recently contacted by the CSA after broadcasting several commercials in English with no translation, displaying French subtitles that were too difficult to read, and featuring program sponsor announcements containing untranslated English. Eurosport was also reprimanded for providing French subtitles of insufficient size for English-language commercials.[14] Another organization known as the BVP (*Bureau de vérification de la publicité* or Advertising Control Bureau), on the other hand, plays more of an advisory role, informing ad agencies in France ahead of time about words (including English words) which should be avoided in advertising copy as well as offering additional recommendations regarding both verbal and visual content. Before being broadcast on French television, all commercials, however, must be screened by the BVP who can suggest that certain changes be made to the film and/or prevent the spot from airing (Koehl, 2002: 49). Out of the 850 television commercials for which the BVP recommended changes between May 1, 2003 and April

30, 2004, 219 (26 per cent) were in violation of the Toubon Law. BVP statistics published for 2002/2003 reflect similar findings (that is, 196 out of 752 requests for modifications to television commercials were directly related to the use of English, also 26 per cent).[15]

Around the time the Toubon Law went into effect, another watchdog agency appeared on the horizon known as the *Avenir de la langue française* (ALF).[16] Created in 1993, the ALF's mission is to 'contribute to the defense and expansion of the French language so seriously threatened both nationally and internationally.' According to their website, the members of this organization are reaching out to 'all those who refuse to submit themselves to the total domination of the "language of the dollar" and who wish to continue **living in French** (sic) in France, in Francophone countries, in a multilingual Europe, in a world rich with all of its languages and cultures.'[17] The ALF also publishes its own interpretive manual (*Le Guide de l'Usager*) for the Toubon Law, explaining in precise terms what is legal and illegal, and discerns an annual prize (*la Carpette anglaise*, which literally means 'person acting as a doormat through their use of English') to leading political figures, corporations and their CEOs, members of the European parliament and others whose use (or endorsement) of English they find offensive.[18] Past *lauréats* include the French cosmetics company Christian Dior for using English-inspired product names (Higher, Maxim'eyes, No Age Crème, Hydra-Move, and so on) and a Danish toy maker (Lego) for advertising its newest line exclusively in English using expressions such as 'explore together' and 'explore imagination'. Also nominated for the award (among others) was the French Rugby team who used an English-language music soundtrack 'Standing Ovation' as their anthem. If the data presented throughout this book is any indication of how very popular English has become as an advertising tool (including for companies based in France), those who sit on the *Carpette anglaise* committee have their work cut out for them. This purging of English in advertising has also reached cyberspace. In 1996, Georgia Tech Lorraine (a French branch of the Georgia Institute of Technology in Atlanta) was cited for violation of the Toubon Law for having advertised all of its course information in English on their website (Ager, 1999: 138).

French public's attitudes towards English

As for the general public's attitudes towards English, it is difficult to ascertain whether or not the language policy implemented by the gov-

ernment reflects the views of average French citizens on this matter. Six years before the Toubon Law took effect, a small-scale study by Flaitz (1988: 198), however, found that French attitudes in regards to English were 'generally positive' and that 'these attitudes diverge very clearly from those of the French power elite'.[19] Ager (1999: 109–11) reports that a more extensive opinion survey sponsored by the French Ministry of Culture was conducted around the time the Toubon Law was adopted (SOFRES, 1994).[20] The findings indicated that the French in general were not particularly concerned about the contact of French with English, with an approximately equal number of respondents labeling the use of English borrowings in French as 'good' (42 per cent) or 'bad' (44 per cent). The words most often chosen by respondents to describe the use of English in daily interactions were 'modern' (41 per cent), 'useful' (30 per cent), and 'amusing' (19 per cent) (as compared to 'snobbish' at 16 per cent, 'annoying' at 14 per cent, and 'stupid' at 6 per cent). Whereas 60 per cent of those responding to the survey claimed to be 'strongly attached' to the French language, just as many (59 per cent) felt that the French educational system should be responsible for 'defending' French (as opposed to only 15 per cent selecting the media and 10 per cent the government to assume this protectionist role). Ager (1999: 111) concludes:

> These results show that the French general public does not feel particularly insecure in its language, and that perhaps those policy-makers intent on protecting the language were over-zealous.

As for choosing between English and French terminology when discussing certain topics, linguists have demonstrated in their writings that language evolves through time, use and language contact, and that variation (based on geographical region, functional domain, interlocutors, and so on) is inevitable. This variation can be seen in France, for instance, in the multiple manifestations of the word 'e-mail' which, depending on various contextual variables, may be produced in French discourse as *courrier électronique*, *message électronique*, *courriel*, *e-mail*, or *mail*. In an effort to discourage the use of the two English borrowings at the end of this list, the French terminology commission charged with coining computer-related terms recommended *courriel* in 2003, with *courrier électronique* and *message électronique* (introduced in 1997) as possible synonyms. An additional item (*mél*, derived from *messagerie électronique*) was proposed as a 'symbol' to be used solely in written form on letterhead and business cards as a visual complement to the

abbreviation *tél* used for *téléphone*. Despite these recommendations, however, the alternation between English and French in discussing e-mail correspondence (as in so many other topical domains) persists.

In advertising copy as well, we notice a similar rotation between English and French terminology. The English borrowing 'spray', for instance, appears in product names (Nivea Spray Color Enfants), descriptive copy (*Rexona Men Ionic deoderant . . . en spray et stick*), and slogans:

> *Renversant, le Spray qui autobronze partout sans laisser de traces* (Garnier Ambré Solaire)

English translation (mine)

> Renversant, the self-tanning spray that tans your entire body without leaving any marks (Garnier Ambré Solaire)

Highly assimilated, this borrowing does not require any glossing, although occasionally its meaning is referenced in the descriptive copy in the form of paraphrasing. Such is the case in a print advertisement for Topicrem® Spray (by Charlieu). The illustration (depicting a woman's forefinger pressing down on the spray mechanism) also foregrounds the spray function of the bottle:

> *D'un geste, d'une pression, Topicrem® Spray submerge la peau avec ses actifs et de ses bienfaits.*

English translation (mine)

> With a single gesture, one push with the finger, Topicrem® Spray saturates the skin with its active ingredients and beneficial effects.

The borrowing 'spray', however, is sometimes replaced in advertising copy by a term used in French to imitate the sound a spray bottle (or can) makes when dispensed: *Pschittt*. This particular form of onomatopoeia (featuring a rather unusual triple 't' spelling) can be found in both print and television advertising in France, serving as either an adjective (*Pschittt Gel*) or a verb (*Pschitttez*), and can appear in both the product name and copy simultaneously. Consider the following excerpt from a television commercial for Garnier Fructis Style Pschittt Gel (Underlining added. Asterisk indicates English-like pronunciation):

> *Fini les coiffures coincées. Garnier Fructis Style* crée <u>Pschittt</u> Gel*. Le premier gel qui va secouer votre style. <u>Pschittt</u> Gel*: <u>Pschitttez</u>, agitez, ça*

décoiffe très fort. Pschitttez. Ça décoiffe aussi les cheveux longs. Nouveau Fructis Style* Pschitt Gel*. Ça va secouer votre style.

English translation (mine)

No more boring hair styles. Garnier Fructis Style presents Pschitt Gel. The first gel to shake up your style. Pschittt Gel: Spray it on and shake your head for a totally windblown look. Spray it on long hair as well for a similar effect. New Fructis Style Pschittt Gel. It's going to shake up your (life) style.

As for the public's exposure to English, Truchot (1990: 173) reports that the media are a major source of English penetration in France:

> *Les médias écrits, électroniques et informatiques, les produits médiatiques comme le disque, le cinéma, les programmes télévisés, jouent un rôle fondamental dans la diffusion de l'anglais . . . Pour un enfant ou un adolescent, le temps passé devant l'ordinateur ou à écouter de la musique anglo–américaine est bien plus long que celui passé dans la classe d'anglais.*

English translation (mine)

The written, electronic and web media, and media products such as music recordings, cinema, and television programs, play a fundamental role in the diffusion of English . . . A child or teenager [in France] spends far more time on his computer or listening to American music than in English class.

This influx of Anglo–American English and culture has also resulted in a certain prestige status in France for Francophone artists who successfully market their craft in the US. The following comment made by Quebecer Denise Bombardier (2000: 62), therefore, comes as no surprise:

> *Ma compatriote Céline Dion, déjà superstar au Québec, ne reçut qu'un accueil mitigé lorsqu'elle tenta une première offensive chez vous. Ceux-là mêmes qui l'avaient écoutée distraitement ne jurèrent plus que par elle quand elle débarqua de nouveau via les USA où elle faisait un malheur. Désormais, Céline chantait en anglais. La France pouvait donc lui ouvrir les bras.*

English translation (mine)

My fellow Canadian Céline Dion, already a superstar in Quebec, received a rather lukewarm reception when she first tried to market

herself in France. The very same people who listened to her with so little enthusiasm thought she walked on water when she came back after becoming a hit in the US. Thereafter, Céline sang in English. France, from that point on, could welcome her with open arms.

In an interview on French television for the launching of her album 'A New Day Has Come' (TF1, March 2002), Céline Dion was asked by news anchor Patrick Poivre d'Arvor why, with her French–Canadian background, she sang in English (*'Pourquoi chanter en anglais? Vous n'avez pas ce français qui coule dans vos veines?'*). In her response, she began by highlighting her Quebecois origins ('I am a little like a maple tree with my roots in Quebec ... Of course, French is still flowing through my veins'). Later in the interview, however, she did describe English as her way of 'traveling across time, across languages, and around the world', noting that she 'would like to have an international career' and that 'English is the language of international communication'. (This interview was conducted entirely in French. English translation mine.)

For those who may be frustrated by English in advertising, on the other hand, there is always graffiti. On a poster advertisement for a radio station aimed at younger audiences (Fun 101.9 FM) displayed in the Paris subway, for instance, a passerby changed the English word 'dance' appearing in the slogan (*Fun Radio. 1ère Radio Groove & Dance*) to its French spelling (*danse*) using a ball point pen. Although one cannot be sure of the motivation behind this 'cosmetic makeover', it is quite possible that attitudes towards English in advertising (or in general) had something to do with it. Another possibility, of course, is that this subway commuter couldn't resist correcting what was perceived as a spelling error, having been raised on dictations in the French educational system and followed Bernard Pivot's annual spelling competitions, *Les Dicos d'Or*, on television (discussed in Chapter 4).[21]

The advertising industry's reaction

When interviewed regarding their reactions to the Toubon legislation, members of the advertising industry working in leading agencies in Paris expressed a certain level of frustration.[22] Noted one individual:

La legislation française devient telle que les créatifs sont coupés dans tous les sens.

English translation (mine)

French legislation has reached a point where advertising copywriters feel like they have their hands tied behind their backs.

Describing this latest language statute as 'the straw that broke the camel's back', another commented that translating slogans such as Nike's *Just do it* into French (*juste fais-le*) was both superfluous and laborious:

> *Ça a été vraiment la goutte qui a fait déborder le vase par rapport à toutes les choses qu'on n'a pas le droit de faire. Donc, ça en plus, ça devient encore un contrainte supplémentaire . . . C'est pénible quoi de devoir traduire . . . Je trouve ça un peu ridicule. 'Just do it', c'est 'Just do it' et puis voilà.*

English translation (mine)

It was really the straw that broke the camel's back given all the things we're not allowed to do. So that, on top of everything else, becomes one more restriction . . . It's a pain, really, to have to translate . . . I find it a little ridiculous. 'Just do it' is 'Just do it'.

Others described the importance of being able to exploit in their advertising the role of English as an international language, noting its usefulness in advertising campaigns conceptualized for a world audience:

> *Aujourd'hui, le plus souvent, quand on s'adresse à une cible, elle est bien souvent plus du tout géographique. C'est des cibles transversales, et donc il faut casser cette logique de frontières, cette logique géographique.*

Today, more often than not, when we target consumers, they are no longer thought of in a geographical sense. They're global targets, and therefore we have to abandon this logic of national borders and geography.

According to some who were interviewed, consumers in France often interpret the use of English in their own advertising as an indication that the product has international appeal and must therefore be superior (or at least desirable to a wide audience). As one respondent noted, however, traditional products (such as French cheese) are more likely to be advertised entirely in French to maintain their cultural authenticity:

Je sais que ça a un effet peut-être rassurant de voir qu'un produit se traduit en anglais. Ça veut dire qu'il voyage, mais ça dépend des produits. Si c'est un produit dans lequel la culture française est très, très prégnante – je pense par exemple au fromage – en tant que consommateur, ça m'ennuierait un peu de voir que l'étiquette comporte une mention en anglais. Par contre, si c'est un produit du type cosmétique, ça peut jouer un rôle de rassurance.

English translation (mine)

I know that it may be reassuring to see a product translated into English. That means that it's a product that travels, but that depends on the product. If it's a product strongly linked to French culture – cheese, for example – as a consumer, it would bother me to see English on the label. On the other hand, if it's a product like cosmetics, [English] can play a reassuring role.

In speaking with copywriters, strategic planners, creative directors, and others involved in designing advertising campaigns for the French market, it became apparent that English is also operating as a link language within the industry itself. The reality of advertising is such that various professionals who work with copy aimed at international audiences invariably deal with English during some stage in the process. If a commercial, for instance, was filmed in the US or Great Britain, it usually contains English-language dialogue that must be either dubbed or subtitled for distribution in France. Sometimes the adaptation of commercials filmed in other countries will also involve replacing certain visual elements so that television viewers in France will identify more easily with the images depicted in the spot, as noted in the following comment:

Il y a un film brésilien là que je suis en train d'adapter pour la France. Le mec, il ne fait pas français du tout, donc on enlève un peu du garçon et on met plus de fille, parce que, une jolie brune, et voilà. . . . On reçoit très souvent des pubs qui viennent de Londres, adaptées aussi donc nous on les recoupe un peu parce qu'il y a des plans qui sont trop anglais où on voit trop le décor et tout ça et on dit, ah, ça fait trop Angleterre, ça ne fait pas français, donc on coupe . . . puis on met des voix françaises dessus.

English translation (mine)

I'm adapting a Brazilian commercial now for France. The guy [in the commercial] doesn't look French at all, so we're taking

some of his shots out and putting in more of the young woman, because, a beautiful brunette, you know, and there you go . . . We often get commercials from London, which we adapt also, and so we edit them a little because there are scenes that look too 'British' where we see too much of the background visual, etc., and we say 'That looks too much like England. It doesn't look French'. So we edit . . . and then we dub it with French voices.

Another respondent described how her own copy (written in French) had to be translated into English before being sent to partner agencies around the world. By the time it came back to her, certain editorial changes had been incorporated, forcing her to revamp her original French version:

Je faisais la création en français, et après elle passait à la moulinette internationale où mes textes étaient traduits en anglais pour tout simplement pouvoir être vendus dans la langue internationale. Pas seulement auprès des pays anglophones, mais auprès de l'Espagne, auprès de l'Italie, auprès de l'Allemagne, auprès du Brésil, du Canada, du Japon. Il fallait bien qu'il y ait une langue internationale pour que tout le monde puisse comprendre le texte et le conception du film. Donc, ça passait par l'anglais . . . Donc, moi, je me voyais parfois écrire mon texte en français, il passait à la moulinette de l'anglais, et souvent il y perdait, parce qu'il n'y avait plus forcément les jeux de mots, c'était pas forcément traduisible de la même façon, vendu à l'international, revenir découpé dans tous les sens, modifié en anglais, et je devais le réadapter encore en français.

English translation (mine)

I created [the advertising copy] in French, and then it went through the international 'mill' where my texts were translated into English, so that they could be sold in the international language . . . not only to Anglophone countries, but also Spain, Italy, Germany, Brazil, Canada, Japan . . . It was clearly necessary to use an international language so that everyone could understand the text and the concept of the spot. Therefore, English was used . . . So sometimes I wrote my text in French, it went through the English 'mill' (and often lost its original meaning because the word games weren't necessarily there anymore, and you couldn't necessarily translate it in the same way), then it was sold internationally and finally came back to me completely refashioned, translated into English, and I had to write it all over again in French.

A certain amount of mixing with English also occurs in conversations among those working within an agency who, as a result of using English as a link language with colleagues from other countries, have developed their own lingo:

> *Quand j'ai un truc à faire ici, on me dit 'on vient te briefer'. 'Briefer', c'est 'briefing'. Ils ont mis un [-er]. On parle comme ça. 'Briefer'. Normalement, c'est 'je viendrai te donner un 'brief' à la rigueur, mais non, 'je viens te briefer.'*

English translation (mine)

> When I have something to do here, they tell me 'We're here to brief you ['*On vient te briefer*']. '*Briefer*' means '*briefing*'. They stuck an [-er] on the end. That's how we talk. '*Briefer*'. Eventually they could say 'I'll come and give you a brief' ['*Je viendrai te donner un 'brief*'], but no, they say 'I'll come and brief you' [*je viens te briefer*].

In another example, the English-language phrase 'eating enjoyment' is directly borrowed and implanted in a French sentence:

> *On travaille avec des boîtes [américaines], et eux, c'est encore plus fou! Eux, ils parlent du 'eating enjoyment' au milieu d'une phrase. Ils vont dire 'Ah, le eating enjoyment n'était pas super.'*

English translation (mine)

> We work with [American] companies, and with them it's even crazier! They talk about 'eating enjoyment' right in the middle of a [French] sentence. They say 'Ah, the eating enjoyment wasn't so great.' ['*Ah, le eating enjoyment n'était pas super*'.]

Sometimes, English nouns or verbs that are borrowed into French become adjectives:

> *[J'y] vais tous les jours et la bonne femme là hier, elle m'a dit 'C'est très take-off, ça'* . . . *'Take-off', c'est quand on mange une céréale le matin et, ouais, on part comme ça!* (making a rocket launching gesture). *Wow! C'est une énergie 'take-off'!*

English translation (mine)

> I go over [there] every day and the woman there yesterday said to me, 'It's very take-off' [*C'est très take-off, ça*.] 'Take-off', that's when

you eat a breakfast cereal in the morning and, wow, you take off like a rocket! (making a rocket launching gesture). Wow! It's 'take-off' energy! [*une énergie 'take-off'!*]

To meet the demand for English-language skills in the industry – particularly those who must be able to sell their agency's ideas and creations to a wider audience (company clients, most specifically) – the Association of French Advertising Agencies (*Association des agences conseil en communication* or AACC) offers specialized training seminars to art directors, copywriters, account directors, creative directors, and so on. Detailed descriptions and registration forms for these workshops are posted on the AACC website (www.aacc.fr).[23] The fact that English is the official language of the European Association of Advertising Agencies (Crystal, 1996: 85) also suggests that English is often required for communicating with other agencies within Europe.

As for whether or not an English word or phrase requires a French translation in advertising copy used in France, the degree to which the English is assimilated seems to be the determining factor. In an effort to address this very issue, the BVP provides a list of Anglicisms (Appendix 1) that they are willing to accept in advertising copy, with their use indicated (with certain specifications) as either 'discouraged' or 'authorized'.[24] To assist advertising agencies, the CSA also provides an online database of French equivalents for English words commonly used in advertising.[25]

Circumvention of the legislation

Print size of French translations

In examining advertising across media, however, one does notice that certain requirements stipulated by the Toubon Law have met with some resistance, the most obvious of which is the print size issue. Whereas Article 12 states that 'the presentation in French must be as legible, audible and intelligible as the presentation in the foreign language', advertising contained within the present corpus indicates that French translations for English-language slogans are typically much less noticeable than their English equivalents.[26] In magazine advertisements, for instance, more often than not, the French text appears in tiny print in less conspicuous positions such as along an outside vertical edge or in the crease of the magazine, so as not to detract from the English-language attention-getter. In poster advertising as well,

when English words or phrases are featured as headlines, the French text is invariably smaller and at times barely visible at all. English appearing in television commercials, however, is systematically subtitled (including, in some cases, English appearing on items in the background visual, as was illustrated in the previous chapter). This level of consistency in broadcast media is not surprising given the requirement that all commercials be screened by the BVP before they are aired on French television. Although they are regulated to a certain extent as well, print advertisements are not subjected to this same level of advance scrutiny.[27]

Music soundtracks

In those areas of the copy exempted from the Toubon Law, such as music soundtracks, English is used quite liberally for everything from shower gel and razors, to computers and automobiles. Companies based in France are no exception. French banks (Caisse d'Epargne, Crédit Mutuel), telecommunication companies (France Télécom), automobiles (Citroën, Peugeot, Renault), vacation packages (Club Med), mineral water (Evian), cosmetics (Christian Dior, Garnier, Yves Rocher), and, yes, even cheese (Caprice des Dieux, Emmental de Président), all have commercials in the corpus featuring English-language jingles.[28] An English-language music soundtrack is also featured in a spot sponsored by the League Against Cancer (*La Ligue contre le cancer*) announcing Cancer Awareness Week:

> *Day after day*
> *Night after night*
> *When everything fades*
> *And nothing seems right*
> *There still comes a time*
> *When I'm by your side*
> *Somebody's there . . .*

As the music unfolds, one by one, we see men who are completely bald slowly raising their bowed heads to face the camera, only then revealing their celebrity status (all are famous soccer players). The last man to raise his bald head and gaze (quite somberly) into the camera, however, is a cancer patient. The subtitles read (*supporters* used in this context to mean 'fans'):

> *Fabien Barthes, Manchester United*
> *60 millions de supporters*
>
> *Frank LeBoeuf, O.M.*
> *60 millions de supporters*
>
> *Nicolas Anelka, Liverpool FC*
> *60 millions de supporters*
>
> *Jacques, malade de cancer*
> *Et lui, combien pour le soutenir?*
> (Jacques, cancer patient. And how about him? How many fans does he have?) (translation mine)

Primarily, English-language music soundtracks operate in French television commercials as a mood enhancer, or to create a certain atmosphere. They may, for instance, evoke sensuality and lust, as in a spot for a perfume by Christian Dior (*J'adore*):

> *oh . . . oh baby. . . . oh baby*
> *Come on baby . . .*
> *Mmm . . . mmm . . . mmm . . .*

Or, as in a commercial for men's razors (Gillette Venus), they may have a more stimulating and energizing beat (recalling, in this case, the product name as well):

> *I'm your Venus*
> *I'm your fire*
> *At your desire . . .*

The music soundtrack for Labeyrie's *foie gras* (considered a delicacy for special occasions in France), on the other hand, has a smooth, jazzy feel – quite appropriate for a food item often associated with sophisticated tastes and the pleasures of fine dining:

> *You are so sweet honey . . .*
> *Come close to me . . .*

Music may also be used as a signature, reappearing in the commercials for a specific brand over an extended period of time, and may be used in multiple markets. The following 'signature' for the Eastman Kodak

Company appears in both the music soundtrack of their commercials in France and as slogans in print advertisements:

Share Moments. Share Life.®

In other cases, particularly since the lyrics are not likely to be understood by the general public, the theme of the music may have nothing whatsoever to do with the product or service. In a commercial promoting the *autoroute* system in France, for instance, the music soundtrack features the following (rather nonsensical) lyrics:

> *Are you the fishy wine*
> *that will give me a headache in the morning,*
> *or just a dark blue land mine*
> *that'll explode without a decent warning?*
> *Give me all your true hate,*
> *and I'll translate it in our bed*
> *into never seen passion,*
> *never seen passion.*
> *That is why I am so mad about you . . .*
> *Mad about you . . .*
> *Mad about you . . .*
> *Mad . . .*

The images and copy, on the other hand, speak directly to French motorists, assuring them (with messages written in elements of nature such as the sky and grass) that the *autoroute* will bring them closer to their loved ones:

Text featured in spot	English translation (mine)
Je te vois presque déjà.	I can almost see you from here.
Une pause et j'arrive.	A quick rest stop and then I'll be there before you know it.
Je viens t'embrasser.	Save a kiss for me.

The tagline accentuates the relationship theme of the commercial:

> *L'autoroute. Un trait d'union entre nous*
> The autoroute. Keeping us connected. (translation mine)

Product names, labels, and assimilated borrowings

The English in product names, another exemption under the Toubon Law, is also exploited for its socio-psychological effect in French advertising copy. Whereas one might expect to see a product name repeated throughout the descriptive text to enhance recall, careful examination of the data also reveals that English elements are sometimes drawn out of the product name so as to be used in an entirely different context elsewhere in the copy. Thus, in a print advertisement for Aroma Fit by Lancôme, for example, where the body fragrance is positioned as a 'health perfume' enriched with 'the nature essences of oranges, mandarines, carrots and basil' (*parfum de santé aux essences naturelles d'orange, de mandarine, de carotte et de basilic*), we find the following headline:

> *Le corps Fit et l'esprit frais*
> A healthy body and fresh spirit (translation mine)

By capitalizing the English word 'Fit', the copywriters bring it to the reader's attention, further accentuating the notion of fitness and good health. The capitalization in the headline also serves to identify the word as part of the (copyright protected) product name, thus making its use 'legitimate' (according to the specifications of the Toubon Law) without an accompanying French translation. This repetition of the English portion only of the product name in a slogan can also be seen in an advertisement for Garnier's Synergie Stop. The slogan suggests that use of the product (a face cream) will stop the hands of time:

> *Dire stop aux 1ères marques du temps.*
> Say 'stop' to the first signs of aging. (translation mine)

English on product labels is also used for maximal effect throughout the copy. A hairstyling gel (Garnier Fructis Style), for instance, displays the term 'shake effect' on its product packaging, along with the 'pschitt' neologism discussed earlier (*Pschitt gel décoiffant shake effect*). These elements later reappear in the copy (capitalized and in bold lettering) as a means of describing the 'windblown' look one can achieve by applying this product:

> *Fructis Style Nouveau.*
> *Le 1er Pschitt gel décoiffant,*
> *Shake-Effect longue durée.*

English translation (mine)

New Fructis Style
The first spray gel to produce a long-lasting wind-swept look.

English on labels may also be used as an attention-getter in lieu of a slogan by prominently displaying the product label in the illustration.

Whereas the examples just cited contain English borrowings that are, in essence, protected by copyright since they are part of the product name, the use of Anglicisms (some assimilated to a greater degree than others) that are not connected in any way to the brand can also be observed. In this manner, French advertising copy very much resembles French as it is used in everyday discourse. Thus, Sharp, in advertising their Aquos LCD television sets, describes the brand as a *'leader en technologie LCD'* offering a TV set *'au design si novateur'*. Similarly, Nivea's Spray Color sunblock lotion for children is guaranteed to be *'extra-waterproof'* and Waterair sells its swimming pools *'en kit'*. Quantas airlines, on the other hand, offers *'villes relax'* ('relaxing cities') as possible destinations in the Land Down Under:

> *Animaux bizarres. Outback rouge. Villes relax les pieds dans l'eau. L'expérience australienne, c'est mille expériences.*

English translation (mine)

Weird animals. Red Outback. Relaxing cities where you can dip your feet into the water. The Australian experience. It's a thousand experiences rolled into one.

Assimilated borrowings such as these may also appear in slogans, as in a print advertisement for Gemey–Maybelline Durci Pastel Diamant nail polish (Figure 6.1) which features the following (untranslated) headline: *Pétale Power*. The word 'power', as was noted in the section on Youth Frenglish in Chapter 5, is a word often used in advertising aimed at younger audiences (for example, *Power up your mobile . . .*). Here, it is used in a code-mixed expression evoking 'Flower Power', an interpretation further encouraged by the flower petals depicted in the illustration.

English-language product features

Closer inspection also reveals, however, that English borrowings that are not particularly well known to the general public are sprinkled throughout the descriptive copy of advertising in France and (with the

232

Figure 6.1 Gemey–Maybelline Durci Pastel Diamant advertisement

very rare exception) do not usually appear with any form of French translation either. This phenomenon, which one most commonly encounters in magazine advertisements, includes the use of English to describe specific product features. Thus, a women's deodorant might come with a 'twist-off' bottle cap (*Adidas Deo Performance Sensitive*), a bagless vacuum cleaner may operate with top efficiency thanks to its 'Air force system' (*aspirateur sans sac de Rowenta*), or a dog food might offer 'High Digestive Security' (*Vet Size de Royal Canin*). Similarly, an automobile (such as the *Alfa Romeo Sportwagon*) may feature 'Common Rail', a scooter (such as *Peugeot's ElyStar*) may offer a 'Powered Braking System', and a microwave oven may come with an additional 'Power Steam' function (*Samsung EasyLogic*).

Advertisements for computer products are particularly prone to mixing of this sort in the descriptive copy with Canon's BubbleJet Printer's 'MicroFine Droplet Technology', Dell's 'Touchpad & Stickpoint', and the Apple iMac's 'SuperDrive' being only a few examples. Even banks (despite their conservative reputation) are using English in this manner. Note, for instance, the 'Cash Management' available at both Société Générale and CIC Banques, and the 'Asset Management' at Crédit Lyonnais. In most cases, these English-language product features inserted in otherwise French copy are either capitalized or placed in quotation marks, suggesting a desire to accentuate their connotative value (well-engineered, convenient, efficient, highly tested, and so forth) by making them more visible. Corporations will also copyright terms such as these in hopes of avoiding legal battles with competing firms using similar terminology (or, in this case, the French 'language police'). (The use of copyright will be discussed in more detail in a subsequent section.)

Occasionally, these English-inspired product features are tied in with visual elements as well, thus further ensuring their intelligibility. This strategy is particularly popular in French advertising for cosmetics which tends to exploit dream-like images evoking timeless beauty, elegance and glamour. Helena Rubinstein's ad for lipstick (marketed as *The Stellars*), for instance, uses an English-language feature ('the Sparkling Reflectors') combined with both astronomy-inspired imagery and vocabulary to anchor the product name in the consumer's imagination. The illustration features a pair of lips modeling the product (which produces a sparkling effect on the skin). A 'sparkling' star appears on the edge of the bottom lip, associating the lips (and product) with the galaxy image appearing elsewhere on the page. Superimposed on these images is the headline '*Croqueuse d'étoiles*'. This rather picturesque

expression (literally meaning 'a woman who sinks her teeth into stars') resembles an equally symbolic colloquial expression in French: *croqueuse de diamants* ('gold digger' or 'woman who sinks her teeth into diamonds'). In addition to the sparkle of stars and diamonds thus evoked by the phrase '*Croqueuse d'étoiles*', there is also an association to be made between '*Croqueuse d'étoiles*' and the glamour of Hollywood (*étoile* meaning 'star'), as evidenced by the color name for the lipstick featured in the illustration (85 Movie Star).[29] This play on words combined with multilayered, multimodal symbolism (Voloshinov, 1929; Bakhtin, 1986) adds an additional level of intrigue, making the ad all the more appealing to French audiences. The rest of the copy is sprinkled with references to shiny brilliance and sparkling light produced by the special crystal particles referred to in the ad as the famous 'Sparkling Reflectors':

> *The Stellars. Scintillement extrême, brillance ultime. Stellars repousse les limites de la brillance pour faire scintiller les lèvres de mille éclats. Les Sparkling Reflectors, fines particules cristallines enrobées d'argent, subliment la couleur pour une brillance étincelante toute en transparence.*

English translation (mine)

> The Stellars. Sparkling to the extreme, the ultimate shine. Stellars pushes the limit of shine to make your lips sparkle with a thousand points of light. The Sparkling Reflectors, fine crystal particles coated in silver, create sublime color for a sparkling transparent shine.

When they are used in magazine advertisements, product features described in English in this manner are very seldom translated into French. For television commercials to receive the BVP's approval, however, they would typically need to provide a French translation for these items, as we see in a television spot for Ariel Poudre laundry detergent. The commercial features a white dress and its owner, Leila, both of whom owe their lasting beauty to Ariel and its exclusive 'Pure White' formula (*Ariel Tablets et sa formule exclusive Pure White*). This fortunate set of circumstances is narrated by the dress itself, (as a female voice-off) seen in a shop window as the commercial opens:

> *Je suis 'ze' robe* (*la robe). Quand Leila m'a vue, ça a été le coup de foudre. Sexy, blanche . . . Qu'est-ce que je ferais sans nouvel Ariel Tablets et sa formule exclusive Pure White* (*blanc pur). C'est mon secret pour m'aider à garder mon joli blanc d'origine. Avec Leila, on se dit que le nouvel Ariel, c'est trop top, qu'on est trop belle. . . .*

English translation (mine)

I am the dress* (**la robe*) you absolutely must have. When Leila saw me, it was love at first sight: sexy, white . . . What would I ever do without new Ariel Tablets and its exclusive Pure White* (**blanc pur*) formula? That's my secret for maintaining my pretty original whiteness. Leila and I are always telling ourselves how wonderful the new Ariel is, and how great we look.

Thus, in this commercial, two 'Frenglish' elements are subtitled for the television viewing audience:[30]

English heard during spot:	Subtitles:	English translation (mine):
'ze' robe	* la robe	[Your dream] dress
Pure White	* blanc pur	(Pure White)

The words 'sexy' (*Sexy, blanche . . .*) and 'top' (*c'est trop top*), however, are not, providing further indication that the line between assimilated ('legal') and non-assimilated ('illegal') English is being drawn by copywriters (and those who review their campaigns before diffusion).

Use of copyright

Following the initial (Bas–Lauriol) consumer-protection language law of 1975, some companies chose to copyright certain product features in hopes of using them in French advertising copy without a French translation. The term 'airbag' is one such example. This English borrowing is commonly preferred over its more lengthy French equivalent (*coussin gonflable de protection*) in advertising copy, leading many automobile manufacturers to copyright it for use in their campaigns (for example, airbag Fiat®, airbag Ford®, airbag Lancia®, and so on, all of which appear in the present corpus). One does notice, however, that the word 'airbag' seems to have taken on a life of its own in other product categories (as is the case with so many other borrowings). In a magazine advertisement for home improvement products, for instance, we find the following phrase (with no indication of copyright) to describe a shower curtain that can be inflated for special effect: *Rideau de douche gonflable Airbag Azur* ('Airbag Azur inflatable shower curtain'). This practice of registering English-language features as trademarks extends to other product categories as well, whether it be the Stability Web® and N-durance® of a running shoe (New Balance), the PowerSHAPE® and Brushing® devices used to perfect one's eyelashes (Lancôme Flextencils

mascara), or the Odour Control® of a urinary protection pad (Tena Discreet).

As for advertising slogans, the 1996 Circular of Application issued two years after the Toubon Law went into effect specifically states that registering such texts as company trademarks does not exempt them from the French translation requirement:[31]

> the remarks and messages attached to the brand in a foreign language must, when used in France, include a translation in French which is as legible, audible or intelligible as the presentation in the foreign language. This rule shall apply even when the remarks and messages have been registered as part of a brand in compliance with copyright law.

Thus, slogans such as Sony's *Go Create* must presumably appear with their French equivalent (Koehl, 2002: 39). In this regard, all of the advertising professionals interviewed for this study agreed that they were taking the necessary steps to meet the requirements of the law (by providing French subtitles and translations). The following signature lines (each with its accompanying French translation as it appeared in the advertisement) are a sampling of those present in the corpus:

(computers)	Fujitsu Siemens Computers. People moving on, move to Fujitsu Siemens Computers* *Suivez le mouvement, suivez Fujitsu Siemens*
(digital video cam recorder)	Hitachi. Inspire the Next* *Inspirer l'avenir*
(automobile)	Honda. The Power of Dreams* *Donnez vie à vos rêves*
(washing machine)	Indesit. We work, you play* *Nous travaillons, vous vivez*
(automobile)	MG. Life's too short not to* *La vie est trop courte pour se priver*
(cell phone)	Motorola. Intelligence everywhere* *Toujours de l'intelligence*
(automobile)	Nissan. SHIFT_expectations* *DEPASSER_les attentes*

(cell phone)	Nokia. Connecting People* *Pour Relier les Hommes
(autmobile)	Rover. A class of its own* *une classe à part
(LCD television)	Sharp Aquos. Bringing LCD to life* *entrez dans l'ère LCD
(airline club)	SkyTeam. Caring more about you* *Vous d'abord
(shower)	Teuco. Aqua by teuco* *L'eau par Teuco

In the years following the Toubon Law, the government did grapple somewhat with the issue of 'legal' versus 'illegal' English, making some attempts to meet the industry's demands by permitting the use of certain phrases commonly used in advertising copy such as 'on/off', 'made in', and 'copyright'.[32] This policy shift was underscored as well during the advertising agency interviews. One respondent commented on how the phrase 'made in' in particular had become a useful advertising tool for French companies marketing their products abroad:

'Made-in', on a décidé de le garder principalement pour que les Français qui exportent puissent écrire sur leur packaging (sic) 'made in France' . . . La plupart des sociétés françaises, en fait, gardent le 'made in' parce que c'est rentré dans les usages commerciaux.

English translation (mine)

[The government] decided to keep 'made in' so that the French who export can write 'made in France' on their packaging . . . Most French companies, in fact, have kept using 'made in' because it's become customary business practice.

As seen in earlier examples (such as the Made in Fun* *Fun de Folie slogan used in television commercials for Fanta), however, the use of this expression in France stretches far beyond the label inscription (the intended use prescribed by the government) indicating that even insipid phrases such as these carry symbolic meaning.[33] Club Med, for instance, uses it as a slogan in their advertising: Made in Club Med. As for the use of 'on/off' mentioned in the Circular of Application, this was referring to the buttons one might see directly on the product (such as a video camera recorder, or DVD player). As with the term 'made in', however,

copywriters have also taken English-language control buttons such as these and inserted them as slogans in advertisements. In examining a magazine advertisement promoting tourism in Mauritius, for instance, we have the impression of looking through a video camera lens at scenery one might encounter on the island. Displayed in large lettering at the center of the page as an attention-getter (as if one were looking through a viewfinder) is the word 'replay', insinuating that a vacation spent in Mauritius only makes one want to return again and again (that is, 'replay' the experience, at least in one's imagination).

Referencing legislation in advertising copy

It may also be observed that those who work in advertising exercise their creativity and freedom of expression in myriad other ways, providing, for example, copy that, while informative, directly pokes fun at the government's restrictions. In 2000, for instance, spoofing a text required in all French advertising for alcoholic beverages (*L'abus d'alcool est dangereux pour la santé. Consommez avec modération*, 'Alcohol abuse is dangerous for your health. Consume with moderation.'), a print advertisement for Schweppes (Indian Tonic Light) featured the following slogan:[34] *A consommer sans modération*. Placed along the bottom edge of the page as would normally be the case for the afore-mentioned alcohol warning, the text is presented at a slight angle, displaying the word 'without' (*sans*) in a larger font so as to better attract the reader's attention and ensure its intended interpretation ('Consume without moderation', or 'Drink all you want!'). Because of its irreverence and humor (that is, slogan disguised as a circumvention of government legislation), this advertisement is perfectly designed for French audiences.

Following the Toubon Law and its required French translations (com-monly indicated by an asterisk), other advertisements began to appear where the 'translation asterisk' was used to draw the reader's attention to something else entirely. The present corpus, for instance, includes a print advertisement for Ford (Figure 6.2) that displays the asterisk (in very large font) all alone as an attention-getter directly above an image of the sun-roofed-equipped automobile featured in the ad (the Ford Ka). The over-sized asterisk directs the reader to a (French) text below the illustration that reads: *Avant de sauter de joie, ouvrez le toit* ('Before jumping for joy, be sure to open the roof'). This humor is further rein-forced later in the copy with the mention *attention à la tête* ('watch your head'). This is a beautiful example of a government-imposed practice in advertising (the French translation marked by an asterisk) turned into a source of creativity and entertainment.

Figure 6.2 Ford Ka advertisement

Advertising for Kriter champagne uses a similar strategy. One advertisement in the corpus shows a rather small dog admiring an enormous bone (presumably from a dinosaur) in a museum-like setting. The 'headline' in this case consists of a bottle of Kriter champagne with its cork flying presented in 'balloon form' to indicate it as something the dog is thinking. Included next to the celebratory bottle of bubbly is the 'translation asterisk' in parentheses directing the reader's eye to a slogan at the bottom of the page:

(*) KRITER, toujours là quand ça pétille depuis 1955.

English translation (mine):

(*) Since 1955, KRITER has always been there when it's time to celebrate [when the bubbly flows].

In another Kriter advertisement appearing around the same time, we see a camel pondering the arrival of electric fans parachuting from the sky. What better reason to break out the bubbly than the prospect of cool air delivered directly to you in your hot, desert environment (lack of electricity notwithstanding)? As in the other example, the camel's thoughts are focused on a bottle of Kriter champagne duly uncorked to celebrate this joyous event (same asterisk, same slogan). These examples indicate a desire on the part of the advertising industry to maintain the greatest level of creativity and seduction possible in their advertising copy (as well as their freedom of expression) despite restrictions placed on them by the French government. Copywriters have also found ingenious ways to reference these restrictions directly in their advertising copy, introducing them, through creative manipulation, as attention-getters and elements of humor.

As the examples described above illustrate, English continues to flourish as a communicative tool in France despite the government's efforts to curb its influence on the French language and restrict the public's exposure to English in the media. With its long history of language policies and the watchful eye of defense language associations who bring 'non-users of the French language' to justice, France is a country where the general public and language purists seem to be operating on two separate planes. Whereas considerable time, energy, and ink have been devoted to the 'defense and expansion of the French language', the examples discussed throughout this chapter illustrate how the language of advertising continues to evolve, an evolution that includes the use of English in specific ways that circumvent the current legislation.

Whether it be English in music soundtracks, on background visuals, in product names and package labels, or borrowings embedded directly in the descriptive copy, those who design advertising copy are (rather ingeniously) incorporating English in their messages despite the Toubon Law, and, as the print-size issue demonstrates, are clearly aware of the positive impact its presence in advertising has on consumers' reaction to a product. At every turn, it is sung, capitalized, put in quotation marks, enlarged, reinforced by visuals, or otherwise accentuated so as to be as visible and audible as possible, suggesting that its connotative value is very positive indeed in this environment.

The language of advertising remains, for all practical purposes, a discourse of free expression, where 'anything goes', and even (visual and verbal) puns directed at the government may serve to evoke humor and draw attention to the product's qualities or features (sun roof on an automobile, refreshing beverage, and so on). In this regard, those who design advertising campaigns for the French market have become 'creators of meanings' rather than merely remaining 'consumers of the meanings of others' (Halliday, 2003: 417). Language, as it turns out, cannot be fully controlled in a media environment. And, as the data presented in these pages illustrate, the French advertising industry has no intention of relinquishing English as a communication strategy. As one advertising executive interviewed in Paris put it:

> *Ce qui est amusant en France, c'est qu'ils n'arrêtent pas de faire des lois et . . . on n'arrêtent pas de les contourner.*

English translation (mine)

> The funny thing about France is that they keep making [language] laws and . . . [the French] never stop finding ways to get around them.

Conclusion

Through an analysis of advertising practices, social trends, consumer perceptions of global brands, American imagery, and both the advertising industry's and French government's reactions to the spread of English, this book examines French advertising from a variety of perspectives, providing a comprehensive overview of advertising in France with respect to English and global imagery. Presenting this discourse within its sociolinguistic and sociocultural context, this book also explores in detail the specific concepts that appeal to French audiences and the adaptation of international campaigns for local markets from the advertising industry's perspective.

The examples presented throughout this book underscore the myriad ways in which local and global identities are formulated through advertising discourse, demonstrating how imagery and language combine to create a 'glocal' cultural reality. To achieve this effect, the verbal and textual images seen in advertising escort audiences through a kaleidoscopical landscape of foreign imagery while encouraging them to interpret these messages through their own cultural lens. Through their skillful adaptation, these advertisements address French consumers in a language they understand, emphasizing their needs and desires within their own personal frame of reference. Thus, with the interpretative guidance of carefully crafted advertising slogans, images from Tokyo may be used to communicate the advantages of using the latest technologies in one's office in Paris (Microsoft), or scenes from Beijing, with its street signs printed in Chinese characters, may assure the reader that their (Bouygues) cell phone purchased in France will function overseas.

English emerges from this sociolinguistic profile as a marker of globalization and modernity symbolizing technology, global intercon-

nectivity, and professional mobility, along with a host of other concepts depending on the context in which it appears. In this respect, it is operating very much as described by Kachru (1996) who labels the 'power' of English according to certain functional domains. It may, for instance, be used as an access code for reaching international audiences or as a link language for communication among members of the advertising industry. It may also serve as a 'cultural mirror' highlighting the country origin of the brand, or connote the scientific research behind a product's performance, whether it be the laboratory testing of a face cream or the engineering of an automobile. Through English, a product may be associated with the glamour of Hollywood or the art of 'chic' in the fashion industry (for example, cosmetics, perfume). Specific English borrowings may also appeal more to certain segments of the population, as illustrated by the examples of advertisements aimed at French teenagers (for instance, *dance & groove, mix trance*).

Furthermore, a word in one context can mean something entirely different in another. This is particularly evident when comparing audience and product categories. Thus, an English borrowing such as 'top', for instance, can refer (as a noun) to hit music in advertisements directed at younger audiences (*French tops*) or (as an adjective) to describe the extraordinary whitening power of a laundry detergent (*c'est trop top*). This 'multivoicedness of meaning' (Bakhtin, 1981), however, must be viewed from another perspective as well when examining English borrowings in non-Anglophone advertising. Consider, for example, the word 'lift' borrowed into French to refer to a 'face lift' (*un lifting*), a borrowing that has been integrated into the grammatical structure of the French language (for example, *liftée, liftante*) and is highly assimilated, as are so many others. Inserted in advertising, however, this word acquires the additional meaning of 'rejuvenating properties' and is specifically used to describe face and body creams (*un gel lifting*).

The examples discussed throughout this book suggest that English as it appears in the language of French advertising is operating both as a global and international language (Halliday, 2003) whereby audiences are being addressed as both global and local consumers. English functions not only as a global link language in international campaigns distributed to multiple markets (for instance, *EVIAN, made in French alps*), but may also be a locally brewed variety where English has been completely refashioned by both the general public (for example, *relooker, surfez, brunche, stressée*) and copywriters whose repertoire includes code-mixed slogans, puns, and other linguistic devices used for special effect (for example, *Six appeal* for Fiat, *n'eau fatigue n'eau stress* for Hépar,

Espress yourself for Lavazza). The same processes are evident in brand naming (for instance, Givenchy *HOT Couture*, Braun *Silk-épil EverSoft*). Furthermore, the multiple meanings of these discoursal elements are often derived through an analysis of several (written, spoken, visual) modes simultaneously, whereby a product name or slogan can produce several different interpretations by 'anchoring' (Barthes, 1977) preferred readings of the illustration. In this regard, the advertising landscape of France (as elsewhere) is an intricate universe of 'myths' (Barthes, 1972) that are constructed by advertisers around certain products and services.

Although ideological processes are certainly evident in the corpus chosen for this analysis, the verbal and visual discourses found in many of these advertising texts very much reflect the French culture and world-view. Not only is English quite often (seamlessly and with French culture-specific humor) incorporated into the language of French advertising rather than being inserted arbitrarily ('pre-packaged', in its unaltered 'native' form, so to speak) in many of the examples presented in this book, but also the images have been 'adapted' in such a way as to appeal to the target audience's sensibilities. Whether it be the French–German pun appearing in print ads for Nivea, the metric system prominently displayed in print ads for Ford, or the soccer theme featured in Coca Cola commercials, there is mounting evidence that the advertising industry is becoming more skilled at speaking to audiences in different markets and is using themes that resonate with local consumers (for additional examples, see Biswas, Olsen, and Carlet, 1992; Zandpour, Chang and Catalano, 1992; Zandpour *et al.*, 1994; Mueller, 1996; Taylor, Hoy, and Haley, 1996).

American brands are not the only ones making this effort to 'speak directly' to French consumers. One only has to see the French TV commercial for the Toyota Yaris to appreciate the types of strategies used by multinational corporations to appeal to local audiences. As was discussed in Chapter 4, in this particular instance, the product in question is blatantly presented (through music, text and imagery) as 'the French voiture' (*voiture* meaning 'automobile'), thereby avoiding any associations one might be tempted to make between the product and its Japanese brand origins. It is also a clever way of highlighting the fact that the Toyota Yaris model is 'homegrown' (that is, manufactured at a Toyota production facility in France). These and other examples provide evidence that although English and global imagery play an important 'symbolic' role in French advertising, the current trend toward 'localization' is difficult to ignore.

There is also evidence that advertisers are mastering the art of blending languages and cultures into a single concept as a way of appealing to global consumers, as was seen in the OMO campaign featuring code-mixing chimpanzees and the nomads ordering up Hollywood movies (using their VISA credit card) on their wireless computer-equipped sunglasses while watching the sun set outside their tent in the middle of the desert. Indeed, advertising is a world where ad agencies have *carte blanche* in terms of their communication strategies, and where cultures and languages collide in an imaginary universe of dreams, illusions, and entertainment.

The extent to which English is incorporated in product names, slogans, jingles, and dialogue, along with commentary provided by advertising specialists working in ad agencies in Paris, also suggests that the Toubon Law and similar initiatives have done little to curb the use of English in French advertising. Whereas language is difficult to control in any environment, advertising with its infinite variety of creative strategies and unconventional use of language is even more elusive, and copywriters are clearly striving to maintain their freedom of expression, multilingual or otherwise. In examining this situation, one is reminded of Kachru's (1996: 150) description of the world's love–hate relationship with English:

What is viewed as deficit by one group of English users indicates pragmatic success to other users. What causes linguistic agony to one group is the cause of ecstasy for the other.

Whereas I would not describe advertisers' use, nor French consumers reactions to English in this context as a form of ecstasy, this comment does underscore the opposing views of English in certain countries, and France is certainly a prime example.

At the same time, one senses that advertising agencies in France are making every attempt to avoid 'illegal' English (as defined by the Toubon Law) and have made a concerted effort to include in their copy French translations for English slogans and other material (with a creative flair, of course). Although those who design advertising for the French market are eager to push the limits of creativity and expression for the sake of entertainment (and other factors, including brand recall), they are more than willing to 'play by the rules' and have found ingenious ways of doing so through powerful manipulation of visuals, text, and music. With their originality of thought and keen sense of consumers' cultural and linguistic perceptions, creative teams in France are keeping their

finger on the pulse of society and speaking directly to their audience with drama, intelligence, humor, and symbolism, treating advertising as an art form. Although the bottom line will always be company sales (and attracting company clients to the agency), ad makers are a special breed who would not be able to accomplish what they do without talent, training, and perceptive analysis of society. Those who lack imagination, humor, superior language skills, intercultural awareness, and above all, creativity, need not apply.

Appendix 1: Sample List of Authorized Anglicisms Issued by the BVP

Termes étrangers	Déconseillés	Authorisés
Airbag	X *(terme générique)*	X *(lorsque faisant partie de la marque déposée)*
Beatnik		X
Bella		X
Blues man		X
Box office	X	
Brushing		X
Bunker		X
Cartooner (verbe)		X
Cash	X	
Challenge	X	Chalenge *(écrit ou prononcé à la française)*
Ciao		X
Clip		X
Clipper (verbe)		X
Cookies		X
Cool		X
Cow boy		X
Crash	X	
Crooner		X
Design		X
DJ *(prononcé à l'anglaise)*	X	
Escalator		X
Fan club		X
Ferry		X
Fiesta		X
Flash *(appareil photographique)*		X
Flashant *(dans le sens de l'effet dû à l'absorption de drogue)*	X	

Termes étrangers	Déconseillés	Authorisés
Footing		X
Garden party		X
Hamburger		X
Hello		X
Jazz man		X
Job		X
Jumping		X
Kit	X	
KO		X
Leader	X	
Listing	X	
Live	X	
Look		X
Looping		X
Magnet	X	
Meeting aérien		X
Miles (*contexte maritime*)		X
Milkshake		X
Non stop	X	
OK		X
Pack	X (*en matière de sport*)	X (*pour les paquets*)
Poster		X
Pressing		X
Punch		X
Quizz		X
Remix		X
Rock star		X
Scoop	X	
Show	X	
Skate	X	
Smash		X
Snack		X
Speed	X	
Sponsor	X (*terme générique*)	X (*si marque déposée*)
Spray		X
Star		X
Stick		X
Swing		X
Thriller	X	
Top	X	
Week-end		X
Yeah		X

Appendix 2: Web Resource Directory

Advertising agencies

BDDP & Fils
www.bddpetfils.fr

EURO RSCG Worldwide
www.eurorscg.com

J. Walter Thompson
www.jwt.com

LM Young & Rubicam
www.lmyr.com

McCann-Erickson
www.mccann.com

Ogilvy & Mather
www.ogilvy.com

Publicis Conseil
www.publicis.fr

Saatchi & Saatchi Paris
www.saatchi.fr

TBWA France
www.tbwa-france.com

Professional organizations

Association des Agences Conseils en Communication (AACC)
www.aacc.fr

Bureau de Vérification de la Publicité (BVP)
www.bvp.org

Conseil Supérieur de l'Audiovisuel (CSA)
www.csa.fr

Union des Annonceurs (UDA)
www.uda.fr

Advertising databases

Ad Forum
www.adforum.com

La Nuit des Publivores
http://www.publivore.com/

Musée de la Publicité
www.ucad.fr

Advertising awards and festivals

Cannes Lions International Advertising Festival
www.canneslions.com

Clio Awards
www.clioawards.com/html/main.isx

Epica Awards
www.epica-awards.com

Mondial de la Publicité Francophone
www.aacc.fr/mondial/

Prix Effie
www.effie.fr

Advertising trade magazines

Advertising Age
www.adage.com

CBNews
www.toutsurlacom.com

Stratégies
www.strategies-online.com

Market and advertising research

Institut Français d'Opinion Publique (IFOP)
www.ifop.com

Institut Public de Sondages d'Opinions et de Statistiques (IPSOS)
www.ipsos.com

Institut de Recherches et d'Etudes Publicitaires (IREP)
www.irep.asso.fr

Société d'Etudes Consommation-Distribution-Publicité (SECODIP)
www.secodip.fr

Société Française d'Etudes par Sondages (SOFRES)
www.sofres.com

Audience ratings and readership figures

Audiences, Etudes sur la Presse Magazine (AEPM)
www.pressemagazine.com

Centre d'Etudes des Supports de Publicité (CESP)
www.cesp.org/

Diffusion Contrôle (formally OJD)
www.diffusion-controle.com/fr

Médiamétrie
www.mediametrie.fr

French language and culture

The French Ministry of Culture and Communication
www.culture.gouv.fr

- Délégation générale à la langue française et aux langues de France
- Le Conseil supérieur de la langue française
- La commission générale de terminologie
- 1994 Toubon Law (available online in English, French and German): *La loi du 4 août 1994 et ses textes d'application*

La Documentation Française
www.ladocumentationfrancaise.fr/

Académie Française
www.academie-francaise.fr

Avenir de la langue française (ALF)
www.avenirlanguefrancaise.org

Notes

1 Linguistic Analyses of Advertising

1. The circulation figures presented in italics were provided by the magazine publisher, as indicated by the *Association pour le Contrôle de la Diffusion des Médias* (www.diffusion-controle.com/fr). Information regarding advertising expenditures and audience statistics is distributed by several other organizations in France. The *Institut de Recherches et d'Etudes Publicitaires* (IREP), for instance, publishes an annual report on the French advertising market stipulating the amount spent on advertising by various companies and their representation in different media. The *Société d'Etudes Consommation–Distribution–Publicité* (SECODIP) studies examples of advertising being distributed and summarizes advertising investments in terms of product categories, companies and media. The *Centre d'Etudes des Supports de Publicité* (CESP) publishes audience and readership figures (Leteinturier, 1991). See Annex for additional resources.

2. One additional one-hour interview involved a journalist from an advertising trade magazine in France who was closely involved with the Epica Awards (annual European advertising award ceremony).

3. See also Flusty (2004).

4. See also Danesi (1999).

5. Saussure's lecture notes (taken between 1906 and 1911) were published posthumously by his students in the form of a book entitled *Course in General Linguistics* (1916).

6. Many scholars contend that the author of Voloshinov's book entitled *Marxism and the Philosophy of Language* (published in Russian in 1929) was actually Voloshinov's friend and colleague Mikhail Bakhtin. More details regarding this debate over the book's authorship appear in the translators' preface (Voloshinov, 1929: ix–xi).

7. For further discussion on English in France, see Kibbee (1993) and Calvet (1993: 142–69).

8. See also Dyer (1982).

9. Fairclough credits this distinction between *strategic* and *communicative* discourse to Habermas (1984), noting that strategic discourse is 'oriented to instrumental goals' whereas communicative discourse is 'oriented to reaching understanding between participants' (Fairclough, 1989: 198).

10. Cook (1992: 29) describes ads as 'parasitic' noting that advertisements 'typically occur together with, or embedded in, other discourses, to which they make no direct reference'.

11. The anthropologist Claude Lévi-Strauss (1969) first introduced this notion of 'cooking' whereby culture-specific, symbolic meanings are attached to 'raw' concepts. Although its original essence may be significantly transformed in advertising discourse, the strongest association possible is maintained between the concept in its purest form and its 'cooked' version. Based on this argument, Lévi-Strauss describes advertising as a 'bricolage' of socially

prescribed myths, and the symbolic systems of meaning created and circulated through advertising as 'ideological castles'.

12. Williamson (1978: 174) makes a similar observation, noting that 'ads which can incorporate criticisms of themselves have a much higher credibility than those which don't'.

13. For an earlier discussion of gender bias in advertising, see Goffman (1979). Bhatia (2000: 239–65) also provides a well-illustrated analysis of female imagery in rural advertising in India.

14. Riou (1999: 34) reports that the first French Omo Micro campaign using chimpanzees speaking Poldomoldave appeared in 1991. The commercial described here was recorded in 2002. For further linguistic analysis of this code-mixed language of Omo commercials, see Adam and Bonhomme, 1997: 162–3.

15. *Le Petit Robert* dictionary lists the word 'clean' as having been first borrowed from English into French in the early 1980s.

16. Goddard (2002: 60–61) lists several companies that specialize in finding appropriate names for products (e.g. Interbrand, The Brandnaming Company) and describes the process by which they eliminate unsuitable candidates. She notes, for instance, that once shortlisted, names have to meet several criteria such as being 'pronounceable in all the world's major languages' and having 'the right connotations'. Bessis and Bessis (2001) describe in fine detail the creation (and connotations) of product names for the French market.

17. This renaming of Coca-Cola for the Chinese market is also discussed in some detail in Smet and Criso (2004).

18. Bhatia (2000: 208) provides several examples of English product names being misinterpreted by audiences in India. The product name *Fresh-n-Juicy*, for instance, was understood as meaning 'Fresh but NOT juicy' by most educated English-speaking consumers in that market.

19. For studies on code-mixed advertising in Europe, see Bhatia (1987, 1992), Larson (1990), Vesterhus (1991), Cheshire and Moser (1994), Checri (1995), Gerritsen (1995), Griffin (1997), Martin (1998a, 1998b, 2002a, 2002b, 2005), Hermerén (1999), Gerritsen *et al.* (2000); Kelly-Holmes (2000); Piller (2001), Hilgendorf and Martin (2001); Pavlou (2002); Smet (2004); Einbeck (2004), and Meurs *et al.* (2004); among others. Dumont (1998) examines English in Senegalese advertising. English in Mexican advertising is explored in Baumgardner (1997, 2000, 2005) and Baumgardner and Montemayor (2004). Thonus (1991) and Ovesdotter Alm (2003) treat code-mixed advertising in South America. For studies on Asian advertising, see Masavisut, Sukwiwat, and Wongmontha, 1986; Takashi, 1990; Jung, 2001; and Hsu, 2002. See also Meraj (1993) for English in advertising in Pakistan and Bhatia (2000, 2001) for language-mixing in Indian advertising.

20. Although web advertising has become a very popular area of research in recent years (for example, Ju-Pak, 1999; Tsao and Chang, 2002; Pashupati and Lee, 2003; among others), linguists have yet to explore in any meaningful way language-mixing in banner ads and other types of advertising distributed via the Internet. (See, however, Kelly-Holmes, 2005.) Some research has been published on other types of media discourse, however, including the mixing of languages in Bollywood films (e.g., Vaid, 1980) and the infusion of English in Japanese and Korean pop music recordings (e.g., Moody and Matsumoto, 2003; Lee, 2004).

21. For ethnocultural stereotypes and qualities associated with European languages in Japanese advertising, see Haarmann (1984).
22. Notes Myers (1994: 97): 'The most prestigious accent, spoken by only a tiny percentage of the population, is popularly called BBC English or Oxbridge English, but is given by linguists the more neutral name of "Received Pronunciation" or RP. The simplest uses of accent, those you might expect knowing British prejudices, equate RP with wealth and power, and any other accent with provinciality and stupidity.'

2 The Global Consumer

1. Levitt (1983), Vardar (1992), Mueller (1996), Kanso and Nelson (2002), and Frith (2003), among others, provide a discussion of standardization vs. localization in international advertising. For a sampling of cross-national research on advertising messages, see Biswas, Olsen, and Carlet (1992), Zandpour, Chang, and Catalano (1992), Zandpour et al. (1994), Cutler and Javalgi (1992), Cheng and Schweitzer (1996), Caillat and Mueller (1996), Taylor, Hoy, and Haley (1996), and Albers-Miller and Gelb (1996). Multicultural marketing and the 'hybrid identities' of today's consumers are discussed in McMains (2003).
2. For a detailed discussion on globalization in British and American advertising, see Myers (1999: 55–71).
3. A more detailed discussion on the legal restrictions on advertising in France is provided in Chapter 6.
4. Ironically, many American celebrities who agree to participate in such advertising would never promote these products at home and sign contracts stipulating that the commercials never be aired in the US. For a sampling of Japanese TV commercials featuring famous Europeans and Americans, visit Gaijin a Go-Go Café online at www.gaijinagogo.com. See also Kilbourne (1999: 60–1) and Ogilvy (1985: 109).
5. See also Giddens (1990), Lash and Urry (1994), Barber (1996), Hall (1996), Appadurai (1996, 1999, 2003), Tomlinson (1999), Berardi (2001), Bolívar (2001), Frith (2003), Heller (2003), Halliday (2003), Hasan (2003), Hetsroni and Tukachinski (2003), and Kraidy (2003), among others.
6. Retrieved from www.lexpansion.com. This article, dated January 15, 2004, appeared shortly before the first Starbucks store opened in Paris. Quite ironically, around the same time Starbucks was using images that Americans typically associate with French cafés in their web advertising (www.starbucks.com). Under their Hear Music link, for example, they were selling a CD compilation of French music sung by various artists. The album, entitled Rendez-vous à Paris, featured the Eiffel Tower on its cover accompanied by this rather nostalgic description of the typical French café: 'A philosophy of life. French cafés became a nexus for the exchange of ideas and philosophies, life-as-art encapsulated by the plethora of music that floated throughout.' (Retrieved April 16, 2004)
7. This town, located in the Aveyron region, is approximately 100 km from Montpellier. The demonstration in question (which involved some 300 people) took place on August 12, 1999, just several months prior to the (November 30, 1999) anti-globalization protests held during the WTO summit in Seattle (Bové and Dufour, 2002: 15).

8. A son of academics who spent some of his formative years in the US, José Bové is no ordinary farmer. A veteran activist, he is also an advocate of locally and organically grown produce, campaigning internationally against the genetic modification of crops.

9. The fact that McDonald's and other fast food chains advertise their products in schools across the US (Klein, 2000: 90–1) has not escaped their attention either. The broadcasting of *Channel One* in high schools throughout the US in exchange for corporate funding of school programs has also sparked considerable debate in France, and is the driving force behind the annual anti-advertising protest known in France as 'Back-to-School without Advertising' or *La rentrée sans marques* (www.casseursdepub.org). The McDonald's corporation has also had to contend with a film documentary *Super Size Me* which highlights the inner workings of the fast food industry (www.bbc.co.uk/films/2004). See also Schlosser (2002) and www.mcspotlight.org.

10. Another ad in this editorial series was entitled '*McDo vu par les nutritionnistes*' ('Nutritionists talks about McDonalds') *Santé Magazine*, mai 2002, p. 197.

11. Nutritional information for McDonald's appears on other country-specific websites as well (see, for example, www.mcdonalds.ca or www.mcdonalds.com.br). McDonald's also offers customized menus for local markets (Smet 2002).

12. Although many of their activities specifically target advertising practices (such as the use of sexual female imagery), some of their rhetoric is also aimed at global brands.

13. See also Amalou (2001), Losson (2002), and stopub.org.

14. Nguyen (2004) notes that the flag first appeared around the time of the 1999 World Trade Organization protests in Seattle.

15. US Congress opts for 'freedom fries'. Retrieved from http://news.bbc.co.uk on July 13, 2004.

16. Similar incidents of 'French-bashing' by the American press are discussed in Verdaguer (1996) who unravels the many (negative and positive) American-held stereotypes regarding the French.

17. The acronym SNCF stands for *Société Nationale des Chemins de Fer*. An example of imitation *verlan* used in advertising for SNCF appears in Chapter 4.

18. With its use of the comparative word *comme*, this slogan also evokes a colloquial expression in French: *C'est simple comme bonjour!* ('It's easy as pie').

19. For a sampling of 'smileys' online, visit www.netlingo.com/smiley.cfm.

20. *Notre Temps*, mars 2002, p. 134.

21. Typically, however, seniors are not treated as mainstream consumers in advertising. Similar to the 'women as sex objects' imagery reported in Chapter 1, the visual representation of the elderly in advertising can also be rather unrealistic. In the present corpus, for instance, we find young bodies (which appear to belong to individuals in their 20s or 30s perhaps) modeling diapers designed for seniors suffering from incontinence (*Poïse* ad in *Notre Temps*, mars 2002, p. 139). Even younger models appear in *Evian* ads aimed at similar audiences (*Notre Temps*, mai 2002, pp. 7–8). In this case, in order to market their bottled water to seniors, *Evian* touts their product as relieving muscle and joint stiffness, a problem that is not likely to plague the teenagers depicted in the visual: '*une eau pure et équilibrée en minéraux contribue à la souplesse de vos muscles et de vos articulations*'.

22. See, for example, *Le Phenomène SMS ne fait que commencer*, *Le Figaro* Magazine, 25 mai 2002, p. 127, or *Do you speak SMS? Stratégies*, 29 mars 2002, p. 71.

23. Due to the widespread use of cell phones, text messaging itself is now being used to transmit advertising messages to younger consumers (Van der Pool, 2003). TV-style commercials are also being sent to private cell phone users. For examples of the latter, visit www.cellular-news.com/tv_commercials.

24. The English borrowing 'people', when it is mixed with French and pronounced with a French accent, has several possible interpretations, including 'the rich and famous' (such as Hollywood movie stars and top models) and 'ethnic group' (as in 'my people'). The orthographical modifications (4 for 'four', LUV for 'love', U for 'you'), on the other hand, are used in exactly the same manner in both languages (and are especially appealing to teenagers).

25. One could argue that the choice of expression '*les pieds*' in the first line of this original French version involves a play on words in that the singular form ('*le pied*' as in '*c'est le pied*') means 'it's fabulous' in French slang.

26. Reality shows have also made their way across the Atlantic and are quite popular on French television (Musnik, 2002; Van Son, 2004).

27. Hetsroni and Tukachinsky (2003) examined the themes of questions asked during *Who wants to be a millionnaire?* as broadcast in America, Russia and Saudi Arabia. The authors found that the quiz show accommodates cultural differences in terms of question selection, as well as 'using local tongue, employing local emcees [and] introducing local contestants' (*ibid.*: 176).

28. A more detailed discussion regarding this particular campaign appears in Martin (2002a).

29. In his analysis of 'the imagery and rhetoric of globalization' Greg Myers (1999) refers to multiracial groupings such as these used in advertising as 'The Family of Man', drawing his inspiration from Edward Steichen's (1957/1983) photographs taken during his world travels.

30. For more discussion of market research on minority groups in France, see Arrighi (2005).

31. The reader may recall an earlier TV commercial for IBM (subtitled in English) featuring Tibetan monks on a Himalyan slope discussing computers.

32. The English-language slogans used in the Roche Bobois campaign which feature décors inspired by various world regions are discussed in greater detail in Chapter 5.

33. For an inside look at the use of stock images by advertising agencies, see Kattleman (2003).

34. Listed in French, these cities would have appeared as Paris, Londres, Bruxelles, New York, Beverly Hills, Hong Kong and Tokyo, respectively. The use of New York City specifically (both in the visual and the copy) is treated in the chapter devoted to American imagery in French advertising (Chapter 3).

35. An earlier study (Martin, 2002a) provided similar examples, such as a young punk eyeing a (British) Rover automobile in an upscale London neighborhood as if he intended to steal it. In this commercial he first spits on the hood (heightening the intrigue) before unexpectedly whipping out a handkerchief to gently polish the car's finish. The tagline: *La nouvelle Rover Série 200: une voiture dont les Anglais ne sont pas peu fiers* ('The brand new Rover 200, a car that the British are extremely proud of').

36. Other examples of 'self-stereotyping' in French advertising appear in Martin (1998a: 146–8).
37. A discography for this British pop singer, who recorded songs in both French and English, is available online at www.petulaclark.net.
38. For additional information on the European Union and the euro, visit http://europa.eu.int.

3 Seducing the French with Americana

1. These particular festivals promote poetry, cinema, the French language and Francophone culture. For more information regarding these and other activities sponsored by the French Ministry of Culture and Communication, visit www.culture.gouv.fr.
2. See also Gordon and Meunier (2002: 88–95).
3. For earlier analyses on the use of American imagery in French advertising, see Fourgeaud-Cornuéjols (1993) and Martin (2002a).
4. The area known as Monument Valley is located on the Arizona–Utah border. The rock formations seen in this ad closely resemble those found in this popular and remote tourist destination. Cacti of this size and shape are not particularly prominent in the area but do evoke images of the American West in the French consumer's imagination (hence their probable inclusion here).
5. To their credit, Renault discontinued this ad upon receiving a complaint from a Native American association.
6. Source: http://de.wikipedia.org/wiki/Made_in_Germany. Special thanks to Andrea Golato for bringing this to my attention.
7. John Denver in 'Let This Be A Voice', part of the *Nature* video series produced for PBS by Thirteen/WNET, New York, a trademark of the Education Broadcasting Corporation.
8. This corpus also features a black panther appearing in a TV commercial for the Wilkinson Protector 3D men's razor.
9. For a discussion on the use of movie stars in advertising, see Lemoyne (1989: 121–32).
10. This poll was conducted in October 2001 with 572 French readers of *Marie Claire* (out of 800 contacted) responding to questionnaires received in the mail. Julia Roberts won top prize in the Anglophone category, followed by Renee Zellweger (second place) and Susan Sarandon (third place).
11. For further discussion of this particular borrowing, see Thody (1995: 201).
12. This actress is particularly well-known for her role in the long-running US series *Buffy the Vampire Slayer* (www.bbc.co.uk/cult/buffy). The fact that other advertisements in the corpus aimed at French teenagers mention the TV show by name (offering, for example, its musical theme as a cell phone ring tone option) suggests that this main character of the TV show is likely to be recognized by younger audiences in France.
13. I would like to gratefully acknowledge Luc Decroix, International Advertising and Consumer Marketing Manager for TAG Heuer headquarters in Switzerland, who kindly drew my attention to this advertisement.
14. Occasionally, one also sees actors of other nationalities featured in French advertising who are described in terms of their Hollywood connections. Salma Hayek (a Mexican actress appearing in Hollywood movies), for instance,

is identified in a Head and Shoulders commercial simply as: Salma Hayek, actrice Hollywoodienne.
15. Britney Spears also appears in several TV commercials in the corpus.
16. The use of the English borrowing 'fun' in these French government-imposed translations is explored in more detail in Chapter 5.
17. A quota requiring that 40 per cent of the music broadcast on French radio be sung in French has been one response on the part of the French government to the spread of English in the media. This 1994 Pelchat amendment to the Carignon Law went into effect on January 1, 1996.
18. 'On l'appelle le "boss"', *France–Amérique*, 26 juillet au 8 août, 2003, p. 12.
19. Article appearing in *Femme Actuelle*, 22 avril 2002, p. 82.
20. Séguéla (1995: 57) reports that the individuals depicted here were all Native American Indians from the 'Great Plains' who traveled to Mexico for the shooting of the commercial.
21. An American business man also appears in a TV commercial for German automobiles (Audi A6). The commercial features a high-powered corporate executive whose manners are less than polished.
22. The asterix indicates a French translation (required by law). This text was translated in fine (black) print at the bottom of the poster as **J'ai besoin de vous*.
23. The double asterix indicates a second translation which, in this case, was ***Venez nous rencontrer*.
24. While it is certainly conceivable that some French consumers would equate these images (particularly the maple leaf and syrup) with Canada, pancakes are most normally discussed in France within the context of the US and are, for the French, yet another example of how Americans overeat. For a French perspective on obesity in the US, see Dumay (2004).
25. The American Academy of Dermatology is also mentioned in a magazine ad for L'Oréal Paris Plénitude Activ-Futur face cream.
26. Another Nokia ad features Anakin Skywalker, another character in the Star Wars film series.
27. Copyright Haribo 2002. BATMAN and all related characters and elements are trademarks and copyright DC Comics.
28. The Walt Disney theme is also featured in a television commercial for Opel.
29. Trademark and copyright Warner Bros. Entertainment Inc. A full description of this Warner Bros. cartoon series, along with commentary from its creator, Chuck Jones, is available online at looneytunes.warnerbros.com/stars_of_the_show/wile_roadrunner/wile_story.html. Another Looney Tunes character, Tweety, appears in a TV commercial for Aquarel mineral water.
30. One also finds instances of Hollywood films being adopted as the theme of a campaign without specific scenes or characters being depicted. In a TV commercial for Karcher power washers for example, a team of 'ghostbusters' look-a-likes come to the rescue of a mother whose kids have left an impressive mess in the kitchen. The music soundtrack also features instrumental music from the 'Ghostbusters' movie. In the corpus we also find a commercial for Air Waves chewing gum inspired by the movie 'Indiana Jones' as well as one for Hollywood chewing gum using a 'Jaws' theme.

31. A different version of the commercial featuring senior citizens performing various water exercises also appears in the corpus. The spot opens with a single line of text, inviting the viewing audiences to closely observe the images on screen: *Observons l'effet d'Evian sur votre corps* ('Observe the effect of Evian on your body'). The music soundtrack that accompanies the ensuing pool scene is entirely in English: 'Wouldn't it be nice if we were older . . . Then we wouldn't have to wait so long. And wouldn't it be nice to live together in a kind of world where we belong.' As in the other version, the spot closes with the claim that Evian helps one to stay young: *Evian. Déclarée source de jeunesse par votre corps.*

32. Although offering subtitled foreign films as well as foreign films dubbed in French is common practice in large metropolitan areas in France such as Paris, movie theaters in the provinces still rely heavily on dubbed versions, making this 'original version' option with French subtitles on cable television particularly appealing to French audiences.

4 Adaptations for the French Market

1. See Biswas, Olsen, and Carlet (1992), Zandpour, Chang, and Catalano (1992), Zandpour *et al.* (1994), Mueller (1996), Taylor, Hoy, and Haley (1996), Mooij (1998), Kanso and Nelson (2002), Frith (2003), and Chen (2003), among others.

2. The interviews described in this section focused on globalization and the representation of America in international advertising adapted for the French market. All interview data were collected in Paris between March and June 2002. Participating advertising agencies included Publicis, McCann–Erickson, Ogilvy & Mather, Optima Media, and Action d'Eclat-Archipel (agency specializing in pharmaceutical products). One additional interview involved a journalist from an advertising trade magazine in France (*Stratégies*) who was closely involved with the Epica Awards (annual European advertising award ceremony). A separate round of interviews (recorded in 1996, two years following the Toubon Law) addressing the use of English in advertising distributed in France (Martin, 1998a) will be featured in the discussion on French resistance to English in Chapter 6.

3. Some insight can also be gained by examining ads that would never be successful in other markets. In a series entitled 'Ten ads we'll never see in the US', *Advertising Age* (December 22, 2003, p. 30) mentioned a Gucci ad created for editions of *Vogue* distributed in Europe which features a model 'displaying her pubic hair shaved into the letter G as a man kneels before her'. Both the full-frontal nudity and 'G-spot' reference in this advertisement would be considered far too offensive for American audiences.

4. This ad appeared in *House Beautiful*, October 1996, p. 8.

5. Particularly attractive to young people, the *Nuit des Publivores* (which can be translated roughly as 'the evening for advertising junkies') experience is very much like that of the Rocky Horror Picture Show in that audience members are encouraged to interact with the action, imagery, and language of each commercial. Local entertainers 'open' the show to warm up the crowd who receive free promotional materials (lollipops, condoms, etc.) from corporate

sponsors as they enter the theater. Video and DVD recordings of the event are available on the *Nuit des Publivores* website: www.nuitdespublivores.com.

6. See also Harp (2001).

7. This practice of inverting syllables to create new words is not a recent phenomenon. According to C. Duneton (cited in Merle, 2000), the eighteenth-century French writer Voltaire (1694–1778), formed his pseudonym through the inversion of the two syllables of the toponym Airvault, the closest city to the village Saint-Loup-sur-le Thouet in the Poitou region where his grandfather was born. For additional information on French slang, see Valdman (2000) and Fagyal (2004). Prévos (2001) provides valuable insight regarding the French rap culture (including the verlanization of the English borrowing 'bitch' into *tchébi*, *chéb*, and *cheub*).

8. One also encounters English obscenities used in advertising aimed at this segment of the population. Although they do not have the same sociopsychological impact as their French equivalents, they are likely to be perceived as a form of rebellion by younger audiences. This phenomenon explains their use, for example, in public service anouncements to increase AIDS awareness (Martin, 1998a: 124). For a similar example in German advertising, see Myers (1994: 95).

9. As is customary among the French, the original term used for 'organic' (*biologique*), was truncated (to *bio*) shortly after organic foods and health food stores became popular in France. For an in-depth discussion on the tendency of the French to abbreviate words in this fashion, see Picone (1996).

10. The canned goods industry in France (identified in their advertising as the *Union Interprofessionnelle pour la promotion des industries de la conserve appertisée*) is facing a similar challenge. Well aware that canned goods do not have a wonderful reputation among French consumers who typically prefer fresh products purchased at local farmers' markets, they are very careful to use imagery in their advertising that will likely appeal to local consumers. Foods that the canning industry makes readily available at a moment's notice, for instance, include *foie gras* (considered a delicacy in France, and quite expensive) and wild mushrooms (another delicacy), both of which are featured in recent ads in *Modes et Travaux* and *Top Santé* (French magazines aimed at women).

11. Information on organic farming in Europe is available (in eleven languages) online at http://europa.eu.int/comm/agriculture/qual/organic/. A description of the AB label is also available (in French) on the French Ministry of Agriculture's website (www.agriculture.gouv.fr).

12. According to the copy, this face cream contains Vitamin F in the form of grape seed extract. Source: *Notre Temps*, May 2002, p. 65.

13. Source: *Modes et Travaux*, May 2002, p. 57.

14. Fans of the *'dictée de Pivot'* can also participate via the Internet through one of its sponsors (e.g. French television network France 3: www. http://dicos-dor.france3.fr/).

15. There are other companies targeting French consumers who identify their product and services as European-based, including Fidelity Investments. In the copy of a recent French advertising campaign, they refer to themselves as *Fidelity Europe* and invite their audience to visit a website hosted in France (www.fidelity.fr).

16. A list of English-inspired acronyms used in French advertising for automobiles and computers appears in Chapter 5. For additional acronyms used in French, see Bouscau-Fauré (1995). Barsoux and Lawrence (1997: xi–xii) provide acronyms for use in business contexts.
17. In some countries, bilingual labels are required by law. Reports Mueller (1996: 40), for instance, 'products destined for Canada must carry product information in both English and French, while firms marketing products in Belgium and Finland must incorporate dual language labels'.
18. Toyota's Yaris model was designed at the company's European design center (ED2) in Sophia Antipolis (near Nice) and is manufactured in Valenciennes–Onnaing (located in Northeastern France), Toyota's largest manufacturing plant in continental Europe (Source: www.investinfrance.org). For more information regarding Toyota's operations in France, visit www.toyota.fr.
19. The hybrid used in this slogan is composed of two French words – *écologie* ('ecology') and *économique* ('affordable') – both of which have been truncated and joined to form a single word created specifically for the campaign: *écolonomiques* (which includes an 's' plural ending). Grunig (1990: 59–67) and Picone (1996) describe this process for creating French neologisms in detail.

5 Language Mixing and Translation in French Advertising Copy

1. For the purposes of this discussion, a signature line will refer to any sentence or phrase found in close proximity to the company logo (generally in small print immediately after or below the logotype) that is consistent throughout their advertising (for example, Nokia. Connecting People). In advertising, this may also be referred to as the endline, or hookline (Duvillier, 1990: 216). Slogans (or headlines), on the other hand, will be used to refer to any text printed in large, bold letters that serves as an attention-getter.
2. For a very insightful discussion of the 'commercial value' of English in France, see Miller and Fagyal (2003).
3. Readers may also recall the print ad for Umarex rifles cited in Chapter 3 where the phrase 'made in Germany' appears in English in the descriptive copy.
4. This slogan appears elsewhere in the corpus in all lower case letters with a slightly different translation: black story* (*histoire noire). Three other Roche Bobois slogans also appear without French translations: Flower Mood, Kilim Mood, and Magic Dream.
5. For a discussion of American and British pop culture from a semiotic perspective, see Danesi (1999: 186–90).
6. These lyrics were featured in the musical *Hair*.
7. Artist: Louis Armstrong.
8. *Piano Bar* by Patricia Kaas, RTL & Columbia Music.
9. Band/artist: Lovin' Spoonful. This music soundtrack is also used in a commercial for butter sold under the same brand name (Président).
10. In an article adjacent to an advertisement for Diadermine Lift + Hydratant face cream (appearing in the women's magazine *Prima*), we find another manifestation of this borrowing where the expression *les peel-off* is used to describe peeling face masks. Other code-mixed expressions featured in the text include *mascara hi-tech* and *des cils de star* ('the eyelashes of a movie star').

11. Artist: Elvis Presley.
12. Artist: Dionne Warwick.
13. Source for car acronym English equivalents: www.angelfire.com/hiphop3/ppddaiddddyy/CarAcronyms.html.
14. Source for computer acronym English equivalents: *Babel: Glossary of Computer Oriented Abbreviations and Acronyms*: www.geocities.com/kind_babel/babel/babel.html#A.
15. These lyrics were featured in the 1960s Broadway musical *The Fantasticks*.
16. This advertisement appeared in a women's magazine (*Modes & Travaux*, 2 mai 2002, p. 178).
17. Whereas some of these English expressions do not have French equivalents (the musical genres and record labels, for instance), their insertion in advertising copy for French audiences nevertheless conveys a certain 'hipness' and is therefore an effective strategy for addressing this audience.
18. The word *trance* is used to describe techno music.
19. Some movie and TV show titles appearing in cell phone rings in the corpus include The Adams Family (*la famille Adams*), (The) Simpsons, Friends, Beetlejuice, Superman, Indiana Jones, Rocky, Pretty Woman, Beverly Hills (91210), Dallas, Dawson Creek, and Buffy (The Vampire Slayer). See also the Star Wars theme and discourse used in the print campaign for Nokia mentioned in Chapter 3.
20. Of the 181 cell rings listed in another print ad for this audience, 64 (35 per cent) had full English titles (for example, *All Rise; Uptown Girl; U got it bad; Queen of my heart*) and 4 displayed some form of code-mixing (*I love you, merci; Strip-tease féminin; Harrison Ford, dingue de toi; Hollywood fraîcheur*).
21. Visit www.foxhome.com/ally/index_frames.html for a synopsis of this television program.
22. A magazine advertisement for Buggy Shoes, however, includes a slogan that uses this same spelling (*Ze*) to represent the French word for 'I' (*Je*) as in: *Ze bronze zébré et z'aime ça* ('I get a striped tan and I like that'). The shoes depicted in the illustration feature strips that go across the top of the foot producing the uneven tan alluded to in the slogan.
23. Although both [-*ique*] and [-*ic*] exist as French endings (as in *boutique* and *public*) with the pronunciation being identical in both cases, this orthographical modification seen in French advertising is used for special effect (that is, applied to words that are normally spelled with [-*ique*] in French to imitate English).
24. I am extremely grateful to Laurence Mall who photographed this poster ad during a recent trip to France and brought it to my attention.
25. Readers may recall another phonological pun involving French (*juste*) and German (*schuss*) discussed in Chapter 4.
26. The code-mixed text appearing on the license plate (*just acheted*) in this commercial was, however, subtitled as *juste achetée, presumably as a form of simplification so that the text could be read (and understood) during the few seconds the subtitles were visible on screen.
27. The corpus also includes an advertisement for Kérastase Nutritive Bain Oléo-Relax shampoo that uses the expression '*anti-frizz*' as in: . . . *un système protection anti-frizz longue durée*.

28. See Rifelj (1996) for an earlier analysis of the semantic range of English words and expressions borrowed into French.
29. This affix (borrowed from English) is also tacked on to other English borrowings in French, whether they are singular or plural (for example, *un pin's, des jean's*), a process outlined in detailed by Picone (1996).
30. This highly assimilated borrowing ('top') appears frequently throughout the corpus, including a television commercial dialogue delivered by babies. In a TV spot for Bébé Cash diapers, one of the three babies chatting on-screen remarks '*Tu as vu les nouvelles couches Bébé Cash? Elles sont super! Là, c'est vraiment top, pas une fuite!*' ('Have you seen the new Bébé Cash diapers? They're great! They're really top notch, not a single leak!'). The word 'top' is now being used in French to refer to clothing as well. One of the women's magazines in the corpus (*Prima*, mai 2002, p. 74) includes an article that mentions a sewing pattern for a '*top au look latino*'. This 'Latino-looking top' (my translation) is reproduced in a bright red fabric in the illustration and is described as 'devilishly feminine' ('*féminin en diable, ce top!*') with 'American-style armholes' (*emmanchures américaines*).
31. The French equivalent for 'zip' is *fermeture éclair*®.
32. When referring to utilities such as gas, water or electricity, the French typically refer to each separately (*le gaz, l'eau, l'électricité*) or use the word *charges* if referring to them in a collective sense (as in *charges comprises* 'utilities included').
33. The French slogan *EMOI DE SOIE* also evokes the silkiness of the eyeshadow depicted in the visual (*soie* meaning 'silk'). The English slogan directly beneath it (EMOTION IS MINE), however, directs the reader towards the interpretation of 'self' (as in 'awareness of oneself and one's emotions').
34. Miller and Fagyal (2003) provide examples of English film titles that have been 'translated' into a more user-friendly version of English for the French public. They report, for instance, that *Out Cold* was renamed *Snow, Sex, and Sun*, evoking the title of a song (*Sea, Sex, and Sun*) made popular by French singer Serge Gainsbourg. *Eight-legged Freaks*, by the same token, became the much snappier *Arac Attack*, modeled on the French words *arachnéen* ('arachnidan') and *attaque* ('attack').

6 French Resistance to English

1. For more discussion of the *Académie Française*, see Chansou (2003).
2. The *Haut Comité* was soon followed by the *Conseil International de la Langue Française*, founded in 1967 (Chansou, 2003: 7). Other language agencies of this nature which already existed in France at the time include the *Défense de la Langue Française* founded in 1958, replacing the *Cercle de Presse Richelieu* created in 1952 (Chansou, 2003: 43–4, 47). Another organization known as the *Office de la Langue Française* was created in 1937 but abandoned during World War II. This organization was re-established, however, in 1957 as the *Office du Vocabulaire Français* (Ager, 1999: 147). Organizations founded more recently include the *Commissariat Général de la Langue Française* (replacing the *Haut Conseil* in 1984) and the *Conseil Supérieur de la Langue Française*, created in 1989 (www.culture.gouv.fr). For a complete listing of language defense organizations in France, see Chansou (2003: 205–6).

3. The lists produced by these terminology committees (working in conjunction with the *Académie Française*) are published regularly in the *Journal Officiel de la République Française* and can be accessed online through the CRITER database at www.criter.dglflf.culture.gouv.fr/. They also appear in the Dictionary of Official New Words (*Dictionnaire des néologismes*) and the Dictionary of Official French Terms (*Dictionnaire des termes officiels de la langue française*), published by the DGLF (*Délégation Générale à la Langue Française*).
4. The *Journal Officiel de la République Française* is a bulletin published by the French government that includes detailed information regarding laws and other official announcements.
5. *Journal Officiel de la République Française*, February 18, 1983, Annex 1.
6. Law No. 75-1349 of December 31, 1975.
7. Judgment of December 20, 1983 (AGULF v. *Puaux*), as reported in Nelms-Reyes (1996: 285).
8. Judgment of December 8, 1987 (AGULF v. *Reverdy*), as reported in Nelms-Reyes (1996: 286).
9. Law of No. 86-1067 of September 30, 1986. See also the Pelchat amendment to the 1994 Carignon Law which went into effect on January 1, 1996.
10. Decree No. 89-403 of June 2, 1989.
11. Law No. 94-665 of August 4, 1994. It should be noted that the text of this law was already being circulated in 1991, written up by the association known as *Défense de la Langue Française* mentioned above.
12. The Toubon Law in its entirety is available in French, German, and English on the French Ministry of Culture's website at www.culture.gouv.fr.
13. This Toubon legislation was largely modeled on consumer protection laws already passed in Quebec, such as the *Charte de la Langue Française* adopted in 1977 (otherwise known as Bill 101). For a complete listing of language legislation in Quebec, consult the *Office québécois de la langue française* (www. olf.gouv.qc.ca).
14. *Rapport au Parlement sur l'emploi de la langue française* (2004: 18–19). This annual report is published by the French Ministry of Culture and Communication and the *Délégation générale à la langue française et aux langues de France* and is available online at www.dglf.culture.gouv.fr.
15. *Rapport au Parlement sur l'emploi de la langue française* (2004: 14–15).
16. A list of organizations distributing information regarding the French language and culture is available at the French Ministry of Culture and Communication (*Ministère de la culture et de la communication*) (www.culture.gouv. fr). For a more in-depth discussion of language policy in France, see Chansou (2003), Ager (1990), Marek (1998), Kibbee (1993, 1998, 2003), and Ball (2003) provide additional insight.
17. Excerpt from online mission statement (my translation). For the entire mission statement of the *Avenir de la langue française* (ALF) and a description of their various activities, visit http://perso.wanadoo.fr/avenirlf/.
18. This organization is presided by Philippe de Saint Robert whose (1986) book entitled *Lettre ouverte à ceux qui en perdent leur français* explores this very topic.
19. See also Flaitz (1993).
20. See also Chansou (2003: 160–2).
21. For additional examples of graffiti on ads, see Cook (1992: 30).

22. All English translations are mine. The interview data reported in this section were collected in Paris in 1996, two years after the Toubon Law went into effect to assess ad agencies' reactions to this legislation, and are discussed in detail in Martin (1998a: 307–37). Agencies participating in the 1996 round of interviews included Euro RSCG, Young & Rubicam, J.W. Thompson, BDDP, and Saatchi & Saatchi. The interview data appearing in Chapter 4 were collected in 2002 in the following advertising agencies: Publicis, McCann-Erickson, Ogilvy & Mather, Optima Media, and Action d'Eclat-Archipel (agency specializing in pharmaceutical products). A journalist from an advertising trade magazine in France (Stratégies) also participated in the Paris interviews conducted in 2002.

23. Information retrieved from the AACC website (www.aacc.fr) on December 6, 2004.

24. Compliments of EURO-RSCG, Paris office.

25. Visit www.csa.fr/infos/langue/langue_listemots.php.

26. An earlier study on English in French advertising (Martin, 1998a) produced similar findings in this regard.

27. Two years after the Toubon Law went into effect, the government issued another communication (Circular of 19 March 1996 concerning the application of law No. 94–665 of 4 August 1994 relative to the use of the French language) in which it clarified this section of the legislation, stating that 'a remark, inscription or announcement made in another language must not because of its size, script, colour, sound volume or any other reason be better understood than the French version'. Addressing the occasional slightly modified translations already appearing in advertising at the time, it was also noted in the 1996 circular that 'the translation is not required to be a word for word translation, so long as the meaning and nuances of the original text are successfully conveyed.' These excerpts from the English version were retrieved from www.culture.gouv.fr on November 12, 2004.

28. With as many native regional varieties of cheese in France as there are days of the year, the French understandably take pride in this culinary specialty. Cheese is so intertwined with the French cultural identity, in fact, that it is even cited as a cultural reference by major political figures. President Charles de Gaulle, for instance, once remarked, 'How can you govern a country that makes 365 kinds of cheese?' (Hall and Hall, 1990: 105).

29. When referring to American movie stars, the French typically use this English borrowing, as in '*stars d'Hollywood*'.

30. The reader may recall another example cited in Chapter 5 where 'ze' is used to indicate 'the' in an advertisement for cell phone accessories: *Ze big love c pour quand*.

31. The translation requirement for slogans used in French advertising is also discussed by Koehl (2002: 38–9). Vernette (2000: 125–6) explains the criteria that must be met in terms of originality in order to protect a slogan by copyright.

32. Circular of 19 March 1996 concerning the application of law No. 94–665 of 4 August 1994 (published in the *Journal Officiel* of 20 March 1996).

33. The specifications regarding this expression in the Circular of 19 March 1996 appear under the heading 'Inscriptions on products, on their packing or

packaging'. In this context (that is, labeling), it is noted that 'terms or expressions can be accepted without a translation, if they are terms or expressions that have become part of everyday usage or stem from the application of international conventions (e.g. on/off, made in, copyright).'

34. Law No. 91–32 of 10 January 1991 (also referred to as the Evin Law) published in the *Journal Officiel* of 12 January 1991.

Bibliography

Abrate, Serge (2004). Comment les Etats-Unis sont perçus par les Français, *American Association of Teachers of French*, National Bulletin, November, 30(2), 27–33.

Abrate, Serge (2005). La France vue par les Français, *American Association of Teachers of French*, National Bulletin, January, 30(3), 29–33.

Adam, Jean-Michel and Bonhomme, Marc (1997). *L'Argumentation Publicitaire: Rhétorique de l'Eloge et de la Persuasion*. Paris: Editions Nathan.

Ager, Dennis (1990). *Sociolinguistics and Contemporary French*. Cambridge: Cambridge University Press.

Ager, Dennis (1999). *Identity, Insecurity and Image: France and Language*. Clevedon: Multilingual Matters Ltd.

Albers-Miller, N. and Gelb, B. (1996). Business advertising appeals as a mirror of cultural dimensions: a study of eleven countries, *Journal of Advertising*, 25(4), 57–70.

Al-Olayan, F.S. and Karande, K. (2000). A content analysis of magazine advertisements from the United States and the Arab world, *Journal of Advertising*, 29(3), 69–82.

Amalou, Florence (2001). *Le livre noir de la pub: Quand la communication va trop loin*. Paris: Stock.

Angelini, Eileen M. and Federico, Salvatore (1998). Understanding French culture through advertisements, *Global Business Languages*, 110–20.

Appadurai, Arjun (1996). *Modernity at Large: Cultural Dimensions of Globalization*. Minneapolis: University of Minnesota Press.

Appadurai, Arjun (1999). Disjunction and difference in the global cultural economy. In M. Featherstone (eds), *Global Culture*. London: Sage.

Appadurai, Arjun (ed.) (2003). *Globalization*. Durham: Duke University Press.

Ariès, Paul (1997). *Les Fils de McDo: La McDonalisation du Monde*. Paris: L'Harmattan.

Arrighi, Marie-Dominique (2005). Les minorités, clientèle à saisir, *Libération*, February 17, p. 25.

Asselin, Gilles and Mastron, Ruth (2001). *Au Contraire! Figuring Out The French*. Yarmouth, Maine: Intercultural Press.

Atkinson, Claire (2003). Ogilvy launches trend-tracking unit, *Advertising Age*, October 13, p. 12.

Axtell, Roger (1994). *The Do's and Taboos of International Trade*. New York, NY: John Wiley & Sons, Inc.

Azra, Jean-Luc and Cheneau, Véronique (1994). Language games and phonological theory: Verlan and the syllabic structure of French, *Journal of French Language Studies*, 4(2), 147–70.

Bakhtin, Mikhail (1981). *The Dialogic Imagination: Four Essays by M. M. Bakhtin*. (Michael Holquist ed., trans. by Caryl Emerson and Michael Holquist). Austin: University of Texas Press.

Bakhtin, Mikhail (1984). *Problems of Dostoevsky's Poetics* (Caryl Emerson ed. and trans., introduction by Wayne C. Booth). Minneapolis: University of Minnesota Press.

Bakhtin, Mikhail (1986). *Speech Genres and Other Late Essays* (Caryl Emerson and Michael Holquist eds, trans. by Vern W. McGee). Austin: University of Texas Press.

Ball, Rodney (2003). Language: divisions and debates. In Nicholas Hewitt (ed.), *The Cambridge Companion to Modern French Culture*. Cambridge: Cambridge University Press, 125–44.

Banned: Brad Pitt car ad insult to Asians, says Malaysia (Bernama, AFP), *The Strait Times*, December 18, 2002.

Barber, Benjamin R. (1996). *Jihad vs. McWorld*. New York: Ballantine Books.

Barsoux, Jean-Louis and Lawrence, Peter (1997). *French Management: Elitism in Action*. London: Cassell.

Barthes, Roland (1972). *Mythologies*. Translated by Annette Lavers. New York: Hill and Wang. Originally published by Editions du Seuil, Paris, 1957.

Barthes, Roland (1977). *Image, Music, Text*. Essays selected and translated by Stephen Heath. New York: Hill and Wang.

Baudrillard, Jean (1986/1988). *America*. Translated by Chris Turner. London and New York: Verso. Originally published as *Amérique* by Bernard Grasset, Paris, 1986.

Baumgardner, Robert J. (1997). English in Mexican Spanish, *English Today* 13(4), 27–35.

Baumgardner, Robert J. (2000). The Englishization of Mexican Advertising. Paper presented at the 7th International Conference on World Englishes, Portland State University, December 14–16.

Baumgardner, Robert J. (2005). The Visual Rhetoric of Mexican Signage in English. Paper presented at the Symposium in Rhetoric: Rhetoric and Culture. Texas A&M University-Commerce, February 25.

Baumgardner, Robert J. and Montemayor, María (2004). English in Spanish and Spanish in English: Cultures in Contact in Advertising. Paper presented at the 34th Popular Culture/American Culture Association Annual Meeting, San Antonio, TX, April 7–10.

Beauvoir, Simone de (1952). *America Day by Day*. Translated by Patrick Dudley. London: Duckworth.

Benoist, Jean-Marie (1976). *Pavane pour une Europe défunte*. Paris: Editions Hallier.

Berardi, Leda (2001). Globalization and poverty in Chile, *Discourse and Society*, 12(1), 47–58.

Berns, Margie (1988). The cultural and linguistic context of English in West Germany, *World Englishes* 7(1), 37–49.

Bessis, Muriel, and Bessis, Pierre (2001). *Name Appeal: Créez des noms qui marquent*. Paris: Editions Village Mondial.

Bhatia, Tej K. (1987). English in advertising: Multiple mixing and media, *World Englishes* 6(1), 33–48.

Bhatia, Tej K. (1992). Discourse functions and pragmatics of mixing: Advertising across cultures, *World Englishes* 11(2–3), 195–215.

Bhatia, Tej K. (2000). *Advertising in Rural India: Language, Marketing Communication, and Consumerism*. ILCAA Study of Languages and Cultures of Asia and

Africa Monograph Series, No. 36, Tokyo University of Foreign Studies, Tokyo, Japan.

Bhatia, Tej K. (2001). Language mixing in global advertising. In Edwin Thumboo (ed.), *The Three Circles of English*. Singapore: Singapore University Press, 195–215.

Biswas, Abhijit, Olsen, Janeen E., and Carlet, Valerie (1992). A comparison of print advertisements from the United States and France, *Journal of Advertising*, 21(4), 73–80.

Bolívar, Adriana (2001). Changes in Venezuelan political dialogue: The role of advertising during electoral campaigns, *Discourse and Society*, 12(1), 23–45.

Bombardier, Denise (2000). *Lettre ouverte aux Français qui se croient le nombril du monde*. Paris: Albin Michel.

Boulet-Gercourt, Philippe *et al.* (2004). L'Amérique qu'on aime, *Le Nouvel Observateur*, January 22–28, pp. 12–33.

Bouscau-Fauré, Jean-Pierre (1995). *Dictionnaire Général des Sigles*. Paris: Dalloz.

Bové, José and Dufour, François (2002). *Le monde n'est pas une marchandise*. Paris: Editions La Découverte & Syros.

Caillat, Z. and Mueller, B. (1996). Observations: The influence of culture on American and British advertising: An exploratory comparison of beer advertising, *Journal of Advertising Research*, 36(3):79–87.

Calvet, Louis-Jean (1993). *L'Europe et ses langues*. Paris: Plon.

Camus, Albert (1978). Pluies à New York. In *Essais*. Paris: Gallimard (Pléiade).

Carroll, Raymonde (1988). *Cultural Misunderstandings: The French–American Experience*. Translated by Carol Volk. Chicago and London: University of Chicago Press. Originally published as *Evidences Invisibles* by Editions du Seuil, Paris 1987.

Cateora, Philip (1990). *International Marketing*. Homewood, IL: Irwin.

Caussat, Pascale (2002). McDonald's en fait des tonnes, *Stratégies* no. 1239, May 31, p. 16.

Chansou, Michel (2003). *L'aménagement lexical en France pendant la période contemporaine (1950–1994)*. Paris: Champion.

Checri, Carole (1995). L'Expressivité de l'emprunt en publicité. In *Plurilinguismes: Les Emprunts*, No. 9/10, Paris: Centre d'Etudes et de Recherches en Planification Linguistique (CERPL).

Chen, Lei (2003). Standardize or localize? A selective 10-year review of published research on international advertising, *International Communication Bulletin*, 38(1–2) (Spring), 13–37, 64.

Cheng, H. and Schweitzer, J.C. (1996). Cultural values reflected in Chinese and US television commercials, *Journal of Advertising Research*, 36(3), 27–45.

Cheshire, Jenny and Moser, Lise-Marie (1994). English as a cultural symbol: The case of advertisements in French-speaking Switzerland, *Journal of Multilingual and Multicultural Development*, 15(6), 451–69.

Cook, Guy (1992). *The Discourse of Advertising*. London: Routledge.

Corliss, Richard (2004). The world according to Michael, *Time*, July 12, pp. 62–70.

Crystal, David (1996). *English as a Global Language*. Cambridge: Cambridge University Press.

Cutler, Bob D. and Javalgi, Rajshekhar G. (1992). A cross-cultural analysis of the visual components of print advertising: The United States and the European Community, *Journal of Advertising Research* (January/February), 71–80.

Danesi, Marcel (1999). *Of Cigarettes, High Heels, and Other Interesting Things*. New York: St. Martin's Press.

Dávila, Arlene (2001). *Latinos, Inc.: The Marketing and Making of a People*. Los Angeles: University of California Press.

Delcayre, Alain (2002). McDo à livre ouvert, *Stratégies* no. 1228, March 15, p. 16.

Deneire, Marc and Goethals, M. (eds.) (1997). Special Issue on English in Europe, *World Englishes* 16.

Do you speak SMS?, *Stratégies* no. 1230, March 29, p. 71.

Duhamel, Georges (1931). *America, the Menace: Scenes from the Life of the Future*. Translated by Charles M. Thompson. Boston: Houghton Mifflin.

Dumay, Jean-Michel (2004). L'Amérique XXL, *Le Monde*, October 1, p. 22.

Dumont, Myriam (1998). *Les Enseignes de Dakar: Un Essai de Sociolinguistique Africaine*. Paris: L'Harmattan.

Dutourd, Jean (1999). *A la recherché du français perdu*. Paris: Plon.

Duvillier, Fabienne (1990). *Dictionnaire bilingue de la publicité et de la communication*. Paris: Bordas.

Dyer, Gillian (1982). *Advertising as communication*. London: Methuen.

Einbeck, Kandace (2004). Mixed messages: English in German advertising, *The Journal of Language for International Business*, 15(1), 41–61.

Elliott, Charlene (2001). Consuming Caffeine: The Discourse of Starbucks and Coffee, *Consumptions, Markets and Cultures*, 4(4), 369–82.

Engel, Dean and Peterson, Larry K. (1997). *Business Class USA*. Paris: Les éditions d'organisation. Translated by Florence Paban. Originally published as *Passport USA*, by World Trade Press, San Rafael, California, 1996.

Etiemble, René (1964). *Parlez-vous franglais?* Paris: Gallimard.

Evin, G. (2004). Starbucks s'attaque à la France L'Expansion, January 15. Retrieved January 15, 2004 from www.lexpansion.com.

Fagyal, Zsuzsanna (2004). Action des médias et interactions entre jeunes dans une banlieue ouvrière de Paris: Remarques sur l'innovation lexicale, *Cahier de Sociolinguistique*, 9, 41–60.

Fairclough, Norman (1989). *Language and Power*. London: Longman.

Fairclough, Norman (1992). *Discourse and Social Change*. Cambridge: Polity Press.

Firth, J.R. (1935). The technique of semantics. *Transactions of the Philological Society*. Reprinted in J.R. Firth (1957). *Papers in Linguistics 1934–1951*. London: Oxford University Press, 7–33.

Flaitz, Jeffra (1988). *The Ideology of English: French Perceptions of English as a World Language*. Berlin: Mouton de Gruyter.

Flaitz, Jeffra (1993). French attitudes toward the ideology of English as an international language, *World Englishes*, 12(2), 179–92.

Flusty, Steven (2004). *De-Coca-Colonization: Making the Globe from the Inside Out*. London: Routledge.

Fourgeaud-Cornuéjols, Chantal (1993). C'est l'Amérique: Représentation des Etats-Unis et des Américains dans la publicité française, *Contemporary French Civilization*, 17(1), 102–30.

Friedrich, Patricia (2002). English in advertising and brand naming: sociolinguistic considerations and the case of Brazil, *English Today*, 18(3), 21–8.

Frith, Katherine T. (2003). Advertising and the homogenization of cultures: Perspectives from ASEAN, *Asian Journal of Communication*, 13(1), 37–54.

Frith, Katherine T. and Frith, Michael (1990). Western advertising and Eastern culture: The confrontation in Southeast Asia, *Current Issues and Research in Advertising*, 12(1/2), 63–73. Ann Arbor, MI: University of Michigan.

Garnier, Camille (2000). Halloween au pays d'Astérix, *Contemporary French Civilization*, 24(1), 75–88.

Garnier, Camille (2001). Dicos d'or et Spelling Bee: Français et Américains face à leur langue, *Contemporary French Civilization*, 25(1), 97–120.

Geis, Michael L. (1982). *The Language of Television Advertising*. New York: Academic Press.

Gerritsen, Marniel (1995). 'English' advertisements in the Netherlands, Germany, France, Italy and Spain. In Bozena Machová and Slava Kubátová (eds), *Uniqueness in Unity: The Significance of Cultural Identity in European Cooperation*. Prague: Envirostress, 324–41.

Gerritsen, Marniel, Korzilius, Hubert, Meurs, Frank van, and Gijsbers, Inge (2000). English in Dutch commercials: Not understood and not appreciated, *Journal of Advertising Research*, 40(4), 17–31.

Giddens, A. (1990). *The Consequences of Modernity*. Cambridge: Polity.

Gill, Saran Kaur (2000). *International Communication: English Language Challenges for Malaysia*. Selangor Darul Ehsan: Universiti Putra Malaysia Press.

Girard, Laurence (2004). Selon les publicitaires, l'argument écologique n'est pas le plus vendeur, *Le Monde*, octobre 1, p. 17.

Giroux, H.A. (1994). Consuming social change: The United Colors of Benetton, *Cultural Critique*, Winter, 5–32.

Goddard, Angela (2002). *The Language of Advertising*, 2nd ed. London: Routledge.

Goffman, E. (1979). *Gender Advertisements*. London: Macmillan.

Gordon, Philip H. and Meunier, Sophie (2002). *Le Nouveau Défi français: La France face à la mondialisation*. Translated by Sylvette Gleize and Sylvie Kleiman-Laton. Paris: Editions Odile Jacob. Originally published as *The French Challenge: Adapting to Globalization* by The Brookings Institution Press, Washington, DC, 2001.

Goudailler, J.-P. (1997). *Comment tu tchatches! Dictionnaire du français contemporain des cités*, 1st ed. Paris: Maisonneuve-Larose.

Gould, Stephen J, Gupta, Pola B., and Grabner-Kräuter, Sonja (2000). Product placements in movies: A cross-cultural analysis of Austrian, French and American consumer's attitudes toward this emerging, international promotional medium, *Journal of Advertising*, Volume XXIX, Number 4, Winter, 41–58.

Graby, Françoise (2001). *Humour et comique en publicité: Parlez-moi d'humour*. Colombelles, France: Editions EMS/Management & Société.

Grice, H.P. (1975). Logic and conversation. In P. Cole and J.L. Morgan (eds.), *Syntax and Semantics III: Speech Acts*. New York: Academic Press, 41–58.

Griffin, J. (1997). Global English invades Poland. An analysis of the use of English in Polish magazine advertisements, *English Today*, 13(2), 34–41.

Grunig, Blanche (1990). *Les Mots de la Publicité: L'Architecture du Slogan*. Paris: Centre National de Recherche Scientifique (CNRS).

Haarmann, Harold (1984). The role of ethnocultural stereotypes and foreign languages in Japanese commercials, *International Journal of the Sociology of Language*, 50, 101–2.

Habermas, Jürgen (1984). *Theory of Communicative Action Vol. 1: Reason and the Rationalization of Society* (trans. by T. McCarthy). London: Heinemann.

Hall, Edward T. and Hall, Mildred Reed (1990). *Understanding Cultural Differences: Germans, French and Americans.* Yarmouth, Maine: Intercultural Press.

Hall, Stuart (1996). The question of cultural identities. In S. Hall *et al.* (eds), *Modernity: An Introduction to Modern Societies.* Cambridge: Blackwell Publishers, 595–629.

Hall, Stuart (1997). The local and the global: Globalization and ethnicity. In Anthony D. King (ed.), *Culture and Globalization and the World-System.* Minneapolis: University of Minnesota Press, 38–9.

Halliday, Michael A.K. (1973). *Explorations in the Functions of Language.* London: Edward Arnold.

Halliday, Michael A.K. (1978). *Language as Social Semiotic: The Social Interpretation of Language and Meaning.* London: Edward Arnold.

Halliday, Michael A.K. (2003). Written language, standard language, global language, *World Englishes,* 22(4), 405–18.

Halliday, Michael A.K. and Ruqaiya Hasan (1985). *Language, Context and Text: Aspects of Language in a Social-Semiotic Perspective.* Oxford: Oxford University Press.

Harp, Stephen L. (2001). *Marketing Michelin: Advertising and Cultural Identity in Twentieth-Century France.* Baltimore and London: The Johns Hopkins University Press.

Hasan, Ruqaiya (2003). Globalization, literacy and ideology, *World Englishes,* 22(4), 433–48.

Hausmann, Franz Josef (1986). The influence of the English language on French. In Wolfgang Viereck and Wolf-Dietrich Bald (eds.), *English in Contact with Other Languages.* Budapest: Akademiai Kiado, 79–105.

Heller, Monica (2003). Globalization, the new economy, the new commodification of language and identity, *Journal of Sociolinguistics,* 7(4), 473–92.

Hermerén, Lars (1999). *English for Sale: A Study of the Language of Advertising.* Lund, Sweden: Lund University Press.

Hetsroni, Amir and Tukachinski, Riva H. (2003). 'Who wants to be a Millionnaire' in America, Russia and Saudi Arabia: A celebration of differences or a unified global culture? *The Communication Review,* 6, 165–78.

Hilgendorf, Suzanne (1996). The impact of English in Germany, *English Today,* 12(3), 3–14.

Hilgendorf, Suzanne and Martin, Elizabeth (2001). English in Advertising: Update from France and Germany. In Edwin Thumboo (ed.), *The Three Circles of English.* Singapore: University of Singapore Press, 217–40.

Hoeschmann, M. (1997). Benetton culture: Marketing difference to the new global consumer. In S. Riggins (ed.), *The Language and Politics of Exclusion: Others in Discourse.* London: Sage, 183–202.

Hsu Jia-Ling (2002). English Mixing in Advertising in Taiwan: A Study of Readers' Attitudes. Paper presented at the 13th World Congress of Applied Linguistics, Singapore, December 16–21.

Hunter, Sandy (2003). C.O.D.: Hitting the road big time for Volkswagen, *Creativity,* September, p. 59.

Hymes, Dell (1972). Models of the interaction of langauge and social setting. In John J. Gumperz and Dell Hymes (eds.), *Directions in Sociolinguistics.* New York: Holt, Rinehart and Winston, 35–71.

Johnson, Michael (1996). *French Resistance: Individuals versus the Company in French Corporate Life*. London: Cassell.

Johnston, Steve and Beaton, Harold (1998). *Foundations of International Marketing*. London: International Thomson Business Press.

Jung, Kyutae (2001). The Genre of Advertising in Korean: Strategies and 'Mixing'. In Edwin Thumboo (ed.), *The Three Circles of English*. Singapore: Singapore University Press, 257–75.

Ju-Pak, Kuen-Hee (1999). Content dimensions of Web advertising: A cross-national comparison, *International Journal of Advertising*, 18(2), 207–31.

Kachru, Braj (1982). *The Other Tongue: English across Cultures*. Chicago: University of Illinois Press.

Kachru, Braj (1986a). The power and politics of English, *World Englishes*, 5(2/3), 121–40.

Kachru, Braj (1986b). *The Alchemy of English: The Spread, Functions, and Models of Non-native Englishes*. Chicago: University of Illinois Press.

Kachru, Braj (1996). World Englishes: Agony and Ecstasy, *Journal of Aesthetic Education*, 30(2), 135–55.

Kahane, Henry and Kahane, Renée (1992). Franglais: A case of lexical bilingualism, *World Englishes*, 11(2/3), 151–4.

Kanso, Ali (1991). The use of advertising agencies for foreign markets: Decentralized decisions and localized approaches, *International Journal of Advertising*, 10(2), 129–36.

Kanso, Ali and Nelson, Richard Alan (2002). Advertising localization overshadows standardization, *Journal of Advertising Research*, January/February, 79–89.

Kattleman, Terry (2003). When travel's not an option: Stock in action: Two campaigns for BMW motorcyles, *Creativity*, September, p. 54.

Kelly-Holmes, Helen (2000). Bier, Parfum, Kaas: Language fetish in European advertising, *European Journal of Cultural Studies*, 3, 67–82.

Kelly-Holmes, Helen (2005). *Advertising as Multilingual Communication*. London: Palgrave.

Kibbee, Douglas A. (1993). World French takes on world English: Competing visions of national and international languages, *World Englishes*, 12(2), 209–21.

Kibbee, Douglas A. (ed.) (1998). *Language Legislation and Linguistic Rights*. Amsterdam: John Benjamins.

Kibbee, Douglas A. (2003). Language policy and linguistic theory. In Jacques Maurais and Michael A. Morris (eds.), *Languages in a Globalising World*. Cambridge: Cambridge University Press, 47–57.

Kilbourne, Jean (1999). *Can't Buy My Love: How Advertising Changes the Way We Think and Feel*. New York: Simon & Schuster.

Klein, Naomi (2000). *No Logo*. London: Flamingo.

Koehl, Jean-Luc (2002). *Le droit de la consommation*. Paris: Editions Foucher.

Kraidy, Marwan M. (2003). Globalization *avant la lettre*? Culture hybridity and media power in Lebanon. In Patrick D. Murphy and Marwan M. Kraidy (eds). *Global Media Studies: Ethnographic Perspectives*. London: Routledge, 276–95.

Kraidy, Marwan M. and Goeddertz, Tamara (2003). Transnational advertising and international relations: US press discourses on the Benetton 'We on Death Row' campaign, *Media, Culture and Society*, 45, 147–65.

Kuisel, Richard (1993). *Seducing the French: The Dilemma of Americanization*. Berkeley: University of California Press.

Larson, Ben E. (1990). Present-Day Influence of English on Swedish as Found in Swedish Job Advertisements, *World Englishes*, 9(3), 367–9.

Lash, S. and Urry, J. (1994). *Economies of signs and space*. London: Sage.

Lasn, Kalle (2000). *Culture Jam*. New York: Harper Collins.

Lawrence, Peter (1996). *Management in the USA*. London: Sage.

Le Cornec, Jacques (1981). *Quand le français perd son latin*. Paris: Les Belles Lettres.

Le phenomène SMS ne fait que commencer (2002). *Le Figaro Magazine*, May 25, p. 127.

Lee, Jamie S. (2004). Linguistic hybridization in K-Pop: discourse of self-assertion and resistance, *World Englishes*, 23(3), 429–50.

Leeds-Hurwitz, Wendy (1993). *Semiotics and Communication*. Hillsdale, NJ: Lawrence Erlbaum.

Lemoyne, Aimé (1989). *Puissance pub: La force du temps dans la communication*. Paris: Dunod.

Leteinturier, Christine (1991). *Communication et médias: Guide des sources documentaires françaises et internationales*. Paris: Eyrolles.

Lévi-Strauss, Claude (1969). *The Raw and the Cooked* (translated by J. Weightman and D. Weightman). New York: Harper & Row.

Levitt, Theodore (1983). The globalization of markets, *Harvard Business Review*, 61, 92–102.

Lichfield, John (2003). Advertisers promise a cover-up in battle over nudity, *The Independent* (London), November 29. Retrieved February 10, 2004 from http://web.lexis-nexis.com.

Losson, Christian (2002). Les antipub s'affichent, *Libération*, March 2–3, p. 21.

Love, Tim (2003). Old ideas fail Brand America, *Advertising Age*, July 7, p. 12.

Loveday, L. (1986). *Explorations in Japanese Sociolinguistics*. Amsterdam: John Benjamins.

MacGregor, Laura (2003). The language of shop signs in Tokyo, *English Today*, 19(1), 18–23.

Machin, David and Thornborrow, Joanna (2003). Branding and discourse: The case of *Cosmopolitan*, *Discourse and Society*, 14(4), 453–71.

Malagardis, Maria (2002). Nos lectrices ont élu la française la plus sympa, *Marie Claire* , no. 595, March, pp. 88–94.

Marek, Yves (1998). The philosophy of the French language legislation: Internal and international aspects. In Douglas A. Kibbee (ed.), *Language legislation and linguistic rights*. Amsterdam: John Benjamins, 341–50.

Mariage, Sophie (2000). Les antipubs soignent leur pub, *L'Express*, May 4. Retrieved June 7, 2004 from www.lexpress.fr.

Martin, Elizabeth (1998a). *Code-Mixing and Imaging of America in France: The Genre of Advertising*. Ph.D. dissertation, University of Illinois at Urbana-Champaign.

Martin, Elizabeth (1998b). The use of English in written French advertising: A study of code-switching, code-mixing, and borrowing in a commercial context, *Studies in the Linguistic Sciences*, 28(1), 159–84.

Martin, Elizabeth (2002a). Cultural images and different varieties of English in French television commercials, *English Today*, 18(4), 8–20.

Martin, Elizabeth (2002b). Mixing English in French advertising, *World Englishes*, 21(3), 375–401.

Martin, Elizabeth (2003). Managing globally: A study of French business culture for the American executive, *The Journal of Language for International Business*, 14(2), 50–65.

Martin, Elizabeth (2005). Global advertising à la française: Designing ads that 'speak' to French consumers, *The Journal of Language for International Business*, 16(1), 76–95.

Masavisut, Nitaya, Sukwiwat, Mayuri and Wongmontha, Seti (1986). The Power of the English Language in Thai Media, *World Englishes*, 5(2/3), 197–207.

Mathy, Jean-Philippe (1993). *Extrême-Orient: French Intellectuals and America*. Chicago and London: University of Chicago Press.

Maynard, Michael (2003). Culture matters: Cultural multiplicity and local identity in Japanese advertising. In Hartmut Mokros (ed.), *Identity Matters: Communication-Based Explorations and Explanations*. Cresskill, NJ: Hampton Press, 55–75.

McDo fabrique-t-il des obèses? McDonalds France editorial ad placed in *Marie Claire*, May 2002, p. 185.

McDo vu par les nutritionnistes. McDonalds France editorial ad placed in *Santé Magazine*, May 2002, p. 197.

McMains, Andrew (2003). TBWA's True raising 'transcultural' flag, *Adweek*, December 1, p. 12.

Melillo, Wendy (2003a). U.S. again looks at ad execs for image help, *Adweek*, June 16, p. 6.

Melillo, Wendy (2003b). Ad industry doing its own public diplomacy, *Adweek*, July 21, p. 10.

Meraj, Shaheen (1993). The use of English in Urdu advertising in Pakistan. In Robert J. Baumgardner (ed.), *The English Language in Pakistan*. Karachi: Oxford University Press, 221–52.

Merle, Pierre (2000). *Argot, verlan et tchatches*. Paris: Les Essentiels de Milan.

Meurs, Frank van, Korzilius, Hubert, and Hermans, José (2004). The influence of the use of English in Dutch job advertisements: An experimental study into the effects on text evaluation, on attitudes towards the organization and the job, and on comprehension, *ESP Across Cultures*, 1(1), 93–110.

Miller, Jessica S. and Fagyal, Zsuzsanna (2003). La valeur marchande des anglicismes, *Contemporary French Civilization*, 27(1), 129–51.

Milner, L. and Collins, J.M. (2000). Sex-role portrayals and the gender of nations, *Journal of Advertising*, 29(1), 67–79.

Moody, Andrew and Matsumoto, Yuko (2003). Don't touch my moustache: language blending and code-ambiguation by two J-pop artists, *Asian Englishes*, 6(1), 4–33.

Mooij, Marieke de (1998). *Global Marketing and Advertising: Understanding Cultural Paradoxes*. London: Sage Publications.

Mueller, Barbara (1996). *International Advertising: Communicating Across Cultures*. Belmont, CA: Wadsworth Publishing Co.

Murray, N.M. and Murray, S.B. (1996). Music and lyrics in commercials: A cross-cultural comparison between commercials run in the Dominican Republic and in the United States, *Journal of Advertising*, 25(2), 51–63.

Musnik, Isabelle (2002). Change across the channel, *Campaign*. Haymarket Publishing Services Ltd, June 21. Retrieved February 10, 2004 from http://web.lexis-nexis.com.

Myers, Greg (1994). *Words in Ads*. London: Edward Arnold.

Myers, Greg (1999). *Ad Worlds: Brands, Media, Audiences*. London: Edward Arnold.

Nadeau, Jean Benoît and Barlow, Julie (2003). *Sixty Million Frenchmen Can't Be Wrong: Why We Love France but Not the French*. Chicago: Sourcebooks.

Nelms-Reyes, Loretta (1996). Deal-making on French terms: How France's legislative crusade to purge American terminology from French affects business transactions, *California Western International Law Journal*, 26, 273–311.

Nguyen, Tommy (2004). Red, white and golden arches: The star-spangled banner ad, *Washington Post*, July 4, p. D01. Retrieved July 6, 2004 from adbusters.org.

Noah, Timothy (2003). Banning French fries: You want 'freedom fries' with that? *Slate*, March 11. Retrieved July 13, 2004 from http://slate.msn.com.

Noor Al-Deen, H.S. (1991). Literacy and information content of magazine advertising: USA versus Saudi Arabia, *International Journal of Advertising*, 10, 251–7.

O'Barr, William (1994). *Culture and the Ad: Exploring Otherness in the World of Advertising*. Oxford: Westview Press.

Ogilvy, David (1985). *Ogilvy on Advertising*. New York: Random House.

Olsen, Scott Robert (1999). *Hollywood Planet: Global Media and the Competitive Advantage of Narrative Transparency*. Mahway, NY: Lawrence Erlbaum Associates.

Ovesdotter Alm, Cecilia (2003). English in the Ecuadorian commercial context, *World Englishes* 22(2), 143–58.

Pashupati, Kartik and Lee, Jeng Hoon (2003). Web banner ads in online newspapers: a cross-national comparison of India and Korea, *International Journal of Advertising*, 22, 531–64.

Pavlou, Pavlos (2002). The Use of Dialectal and Foreign Language Elements in Radio Commercials in Cyprus. Paper presented at the 13th World Congress of Applied Linguistics, Singapore, December 16–21.

Peebles, Dean, Ryans, Jr., John and Vernon, Ivan (1977). A new perspective on advertising standardization, *European Journal of Marketing*, 11(8), 569–76.

Phillipson, Robert (1992). *Linguistic Imperialism*. London: Oxford University Press.

Picone, Michael D. (1996). *Anglicisms, Neologisms and Dynamic French*. Philadelphia: John Benjamins.

Piller, Ingrid (2001). Identity constructions in multilingual advertising, *Language in Society*, 30, 153–86.

Piller, Ingrid (2003). Advertising as a site of language contact, *Annual Review of Applied Linguistics*, 23, 170–83.

Pinard, Rock (2004). Ailleurs, P.Q., *Infopresse*, September, 20(1), 37.

Platt, Polly (1998). *French or Foe?*, 2nd ed. London: Cultural Crossings, Ltd.

Prévos, André J. M. (2001). Le Business du Rap en France, *The French Review*, 74(5), 900–21.

Ramaprasad, J. and Hasegawa, K. (1992). Creative strategies in American and Japanese TV commercials: A comparison, *Journal of Advertising Research*, 32(1), 59–67.

Rapport au Parlement sur l'emploi de la langue française (2004). Annual report published by the *Ministère de la culture et de la communication* and the *Délégation générale à la langue française et aux langues de France* (www.dglf.culture.gouv.fr).

Revel, Jean-François (2002). *L'obsession anti-américaine*. Saint-Amand-Montrond: Plon.

Reynolds, Alan (2003). Why boycotting wine won't work, *The Washington Times*, March 23. Retrieved January 15, 2004 from www.cato.org.

Ricks, David (1983). *Big Business Blunders: Mistakes in Multinational Marketing*. Homewood, IL: Dow Jones-Irwin.

Ricks, David (1996). Perspectives: Translation blunders in international business, *Journal of Language for International Business*, 7, 50–5.

Rifelj, Carol (1996). False friends or true? Semantic anglicisms in France today, *The French Review*, 69(3), 409–16.

Riou, Nicolas (1999). *Pub fiction: Société postmoderne et nouvelles tendances publicitaires*. Paris: Editions d'Organisation.

Saint Robert, Philippe de (1986). *Lettre ouverte à ceux qui en perdent leur français*. Paris: Albin Michel.

Sardar, Ziauddin, and Davies, Merryl Wyn (2002). *Pourquoi le monde déteste-t-il l'Amérique*. Translated by Marie-France de Poloméra and Jean-Paul Mourlon. Paris: Fayard. Originally published as *Why Do People Hate America?* by Icon Books Ltd, Cambridge, UK, 2002.

Sartre, Jean-Paul (1965). Pourquoi je refuse d'aller aux Etats-Unis, *Nouvel Observateur*, April 1, pp. 1–3.

Saussure, Ferdinand de (1916/1974). *Course in General Linguistics*. Trans. by Wade Baskin. London: Fontana/Collins.

Schlick, Maria (2003). The English of shop signs in Europe, *English Today*, 10(1), 3–17.

Schlosser, Eric (2002). *Fast Food Nation*. New York: Houghton Mifflin.

Schmitt, Bernard H., Tavassoli, Nader T. and Millard, Robert T. (1993). Memory for print ads: Understanding relations among brand name, copy, and picture, *Journal of Consumer Psychology*, 2(1), 55–81.

Scollon, Ron and Scollon, Suzie Wong (2003). *Discourses in Place: Language in the Material World*. London: Routledge.

Séguéla, Jacques (1995). *La Publicité*. Toulouse: Editions Milan.

Sengupta, S. (1995). The influence of culture on portrayals of women in television commercials: A comparision between the United States and Japan, *International Journal of Advertising*, 14, 314–33.

Shipman, Alan (2002). *The Globalization Myth: Why the Protestors have got it wrong*. Cambridge: Icon Books.

Smet, Ria (2002). McDonald's: A strategy of cross-cultural approach? *The Journal of Language for International Business*, 13(1/2), 11–21.

Smet, Ria (2004). 'Elle' she said: Anglicisms in French lifestyle press. Paper presented at the Annual Conference of the Centers for International Business Education and Reseach (CIBER), Stamford, CT, April 1–3.

Smet, Ria and Criso, Rachael (2004). Coca-colonization? Americanization-globalization-cultural imperialism? *The Journal of Language for International Business*, 15(1), 75–89.

SOFRES (1994). *Les Français et la Défense de la Langue Française. Mars 1994*. Paris: Ministère de la Culture et de la Francophonie.

Stuever, H. (2000). Radical chic: Benetton takes on the death penalty, *Washington Post*, January 25, p. C1.

Taavitsainen, Irma, and Pahta, Päivi (2003). English in Finland: Globalisation, language awareness and questions of identity, *English Today*, 19(4), 3–15.

Takashi, Kyoko (1990). A sociolinguistic analysis of English borrowings in Japanese advertising text, *World Englishes*, 9(3), 327–41.

Tanaka, Keiko (1994). *Advertising Language: A Pragmatic Approach to Advertisements in Britain and Japan.* London: Routledge.

Taylor, Ronald E., Hoy, Mariea Grubbs and Haley, Eric (1996). How French advertising professionals develop creative strategy, *The Journal of Advertising,* 25(1), 1–14.

Tejedor de Felipe, Didier (2004). A propos de la 'folklorisation' de l'argot des jeunes. In Bertucci, Marie-Madeleine and Delas, Daniel (eds.), *Français des banlieues, français populaire?* Cergy-Pointoise: CRTH (Centre de Recherche Texte/Histoire) de l'Université de Cergy Pontoise, 19–31.

Terpestra, Vern and Sarathy, Ravi (2000). *International Marketing,* 8th ed. Orlando. FL: The Dryden Press.

Terpestra, Vern (1993). *International Dimensions of Marketing,* 3rd ed. Belmont, CA: Wadsworth Publishing Co.

Thody, Philip (1995). *Le Franglais: Forbidden English, Forbidden American: Law, Politics and Language in Contemporary France.* London: Athlone.

Thonus, Terese (1991). Englishization of business names in Brazil, *World Englishes,* 10(1), 65–74.

Tinic, S. (1997). United colors and untied meanings: Benetton and the commodification of social issues, *Journal of Communication,* 47(3), 3–25.

Tocqueville, Alexis de (1835). *De la Démocratie en Amérique,* 2 vols. Paris.

Tomlinson, John (1999). *Globalization and Culture.* Chicago: University of Chicago Press.

Toscan du Plantier, Daniel (1995). *L'Emotion Culturelle.* Paris: Flammarion.

Toscani, Oliviero (1995). *La Pub est une charogne qui nous sourit.* Paris: Hoëbeke.

Truchot, Claude (1990). *L'Anglais dans le monde contemporain.* Paris: Le Robert.

Truchot, Claude (1997). The spread of English: from France to a more general perspective, *World Englishes,* 16(1), 65–76.

Trujillo, Melissa (2003). Linguists mixed on effects of text messaging, *The Associated Press State and Local Wire,* February 10. Retrieved February 13, 2003 from http://web.lexis-nexis.com.

Tsao, James C. and Chang, Chingching (2002). Communication strategy in Taiwanese and US corporate web pages: A cross-cultural comparison, *Asian Journal of Communication,* 12(2), 1–29.

Tsuda, Yukio (1994). The diffusion of English: Its impact on culture and communication, *Keio Communication Review,* 16, 49–61.

Vaid, Jyotsna (1980). The form and function of code-mixing in Indian films, *Indian Linguistics,* 41(1), 37–44.

Valdman, Albert (2000). La langue des faubourgs et des banlieues: de l'argot au français populaire, *The French Review,* 73(6), 1179–92.

Van der Pool, Lisa (2003). U.S. marketers turn to text messaging in big way, *Adweek,* December 8, p. 9.

Van Leeuwen, Theo (2005). *Introducing Social Semiotics.* London: Routledge.

Van Son, Ludwina (2004). Loft Story ou Big Brother à la française, *Contemporary French Civilization,* 28(1), 20–32.

Vannerson, Frank L. (2004). 'Wine, Francophobia and Boycotts'. Paper presented at the Vineyard Data Quantification Society (VDQS) conference in Dijon, France, May 21–22. Retrieved September 12, 2004 from www.vdqs. fed-eco.com/2004DIJON/DOC/.

Vardar, Nükhet (1992). *Global Advertising: Rhyme or Reason?* London: Paul Chapman Publishing Ltd.

Verdaguer, Pierre (1996). La France vue par l'Amérique: Considérations sur la pérennité des stéréotypes, *Contemporary French Civilization*, 10(2), 240–77.

Vernette, Eric (ed.) (2000). *La publicité: Théories, acteurs et méthodes.* Paris: La documentation française.

Vestergaard, Torben and Schrøder, Kim (1985). *The Language of Advertising.* Oxford: Basil Blackwell.

Vesterhus, S. A. (1991). Anglicisms in German car documents, *Language International*, 3, 10–15.

Viard, Jean (2000). José Bové, pont entre le rural et l'urbain, *Libération*, June 30.

Voloshinov, Valentin (1929/1973). *Marxism and the philosophy of language.* Translated by Ladislav Matejka and I. R. Titunik (Original work published 1929). Cambridge: Harvard University Press.

Wentz, Laurel (2003). Pepsi puts interests before ethnicity, *Advertising Age*, July 7, pp. S–4, S–6.

Whitelock, Jeryl, and Chung, Djamila (1989). Cross-cultural advertising: An empirical study, *International Journal of Advertising*, 8(3), 291–310.

Wiles, C.R. and Tjernlund, A. (1991). A comparison of role portrayal of men and women in magazine advertising in the USA and Sweden, *International Journal of Advertising*, 10, 259–67.

Wilkerson, K.T. (1997). Japanese bilingual brand names, *English Today*, 13, 12–16.

Williamson, Judith (1978). *Decoding Advertisements: Ideology and Meaning in Advertising.* London: Marion Boyars.

Wray, H. (1981). Semiotics: Fad or revolutions? The study of signs is attracting students and controversy, *Humanities Report* 3, 4–9.

Yaguello, Marina (1998). *Petits Faits de Langue.* Paris: Editions du Seuil.

Zandpour, F., B. Campos, J. Catalano, C. Chang, Y. Cho, R. Hoobyar, H. Jiang, M. Lin, S. Madrid, P. Scheideler, and S. Osborn (1994). Global reach and local touch: achieving cultural fitness in TV advertising, *Journal of Advertising Research*, 34(5), 35–63.

Zandpour, Fred, Chang, Cypress, and Catalano, Joelle (1992). Stories, symbols, and straight talk: A comparative analysis of French, Taiwanese, and U.S. TV commercials, *Journal of Advertising Research*, 32(1), 25–38.

Zeff, Robbin and Aronson, Brad (1999). *Advertising on the Internet.* New York: John Wiley & Sons, Inc.

Zeldin, Theodore (1984). *The French.* New York: Random House.

Index